A Class Innings

A Class Innings

JOHN CLEARY

© John Cleary 2009

Published by John Cleary

June 2009

ISBN 978-0-9562781-0-4

Cover design by Clare Brayshaw

Prepared and printed by:

York Publishing Services Ltd
64 Hallfield Road
Layerthorpe
York YO31 7ZQ
Tel: 01904 431213

Website: www.yps-publishing.co.uk

Contents

Acknowledgements

I would like to begin by expressing my thanks to the many friends who helped to jog my memory, reminding me of various incidents, situations, and people involved in my life, during the five years I have been writing my lifestory.

There are also those who offered to read whole chapters, in which they had been a part, and their subsequent recollections helped me to edit and improve the orginal drafts. These, in more or less chronological order, include Bert Hanson, Stuart Anderson, Kenny Greaves, Arthur Pownell, Peter Greene, Maurice Lees, Barrie Coop, Damian Maloney, Don Smith, David Hindle, Philip Adshead, Danny McLaughlan, Audrey Carter, Ray Garner, Angela McCormick, John Holder and Trevor Lewis.

I am also grateful to my son Richard and daughters Lucy and Sarah for similar advice on the family chapters. Once the book was almost completed I benefited from the professional advice of Keith McHugh of the Oldham Chronicle, who had offered to read it. I also asked Bob Dearden and Arthur Gray, both of teaching and cricketing backgrounds like myself, and my friends Richard Murphy and Mike Lindley to read it. I am appreciative of their willingness to have taken the trouble to do so, and for their observations.

On a practical level my intention in attending a typing, and then computer courses – for absolute beginners! – was to try to enable me to type my book, but once realised how slow I was, and how computer illiterate I was. I was especially grateful to a tutor, Anne Hayward, who generously typed the first hundred pages during the time I attended the courses she ran. I have also benefited from the help from my computer wizard friend Paul Cooper, and Mark Preston, my tutor on sebsequent computer courses.

Preface

"I'd be honoured," was my immediate and instinctive reply to the question put to me by Howard Dronsfield, chairman of the Central Lancashire League. He had invited me to join him as we watched Royton playing one of their final matches of the 2005 season, and asked me: "What would your reaction be if I told you that you had been nominated to become president of the league?" I was stunned at hearing his question, and my reply reflected exactly how I felt at that moment, and how I have continued to do ever since. I couldn't imagine a greater honour. Howard went on to say that my many years of service to Royton Cricket Club had been recognised and appreciated, and that he and his fellow members hoped that I would accept their nomination. He outlined what my role would involve, and two months later, at the AGM, I was duly elected to the prestigious office.

It has been, and is, a wonderful experience for me, now in my fourth year as president, during I have been made very welcome by members of all the clubs in the league. I have been delighted to renew my acquaintance and friendship with many former players who are now club officials, and made many new friends throughout the league. I am pleased to have played an active role in helping to introduce the Twenty/20 competition, and to have received so many invitations to club functions. During the summer I have followed the tradition of visiting two different grounds on each match day, then, as the season ends, presenting medals and trophies to successful teams in the junior leagues, and league and cup-winning teams in the 1st, 2nd, and 3rd XIs. I have attended various meetings, and continue to appreciate the privilege of having been elected to the presidency of the Central Lancashire League, only the fourth member of Royton Cricket Club to have been so honoured.

My life has quickened somewhat during the past three years, following a rather slower one during the previous three, after my retirement. I had lived a very hectic life for over forty years in both my occupations, as a teacher for thirty years, which overlapped my business involvements totalling thirty three years, plus the many social and community service commitments I had accepted during my lifetime as a member of Royton Cricket Club, and my years in the Round Table and Rotary movements. My teaching career retirement occurred in 1990, as I approached my 54th birthday, but it was nearly twelve years later, in January 2002, before I retired from my market stall life.

I had actually begun to think seriously about my final retirement as I relaxed, sitting in my window seat on the train leaving Euston Station on Saturday July 21st 2001. I had just spent two nights in London, and a wonderful day at Lord's Cricket Ground, celebrating my 65th birthday. But for me to be enjoying a leisurely Saturday was something I had hardly ever done for the past twenty seven years, since I had I first towed my trailer to Congleton, where, as the footwear man on the local market, I was known to all and sundry as Johnny Slipper. Now I was 65, I mused, was it time to call it a day?

As I began my journey home, however, my mind was still full of the birthday treat I had just enjoyed. I had always hoped to visit Lord's, having watched many Test Matches at Old Trafford, and on four grounds in Australia, but never at the home of cricket. By happy coincidence in 2002 my good friend John Holder was one of the two umpires in the Lord's Test between England and Australia, and he generously provided me with a ticket for my 65th birthday, so on the Thursday I left Piccadilly

Station, Manchester, for the first of my two nights in London, hoping for a fine and rain-free Friday on my 65th. On that morning, even before I had finished my breakfast, I had received "Happy Birthday" calls from Richard, Lucy and Sarah, my three children, all of whom were delighted to hear me tell them that the sun was shining in London, and that soon I would be stepping into a taxi to take me to the ground, to collect my ticket at the office near the famous Grace Gates. Indeed, by 10am I was outside the ground, but was asked to wait a few moments because the complimentary tickets had not yet arrived. I rang my friend John who not only reassured me that my ticket was on its way, but that I would also receive tickets for lunch and tea in the special hospitality tents.

What a lovely day I had in prospect then and, after waiting only a few more minutes, I heard a lady's voice. " Excuse me, sir, what is your name?" I walked towards the window and replied: "John Cleary." Very formally she then asked: "And who has provided your ticket?" To which I replied: "John Holder." Again in her very officious voice she said: "And do you have any means of identification?" I was taken aback by the question, but as I stood there, quite smartly dressed for this special day, I somewhat mischievously reached into my pocket to take out a photograph, one that I treasured, taken at a sportsman's dinner I had arranged some ten years before. "That is John Holder," I said, "and this is me," as I passed her the photograph. She looked at it, and in a very surprised voice said: "Isn't that the famous commentator Brian Johnston?" "Yes." I said, as she handed it back to me. "Oh, come this way please. Let me show you which way to go, sir," in tones of warmth and friendliness. The haughtiness had melted away, and I may have had a smug look on my face as she opened the door for me to walk into the famous ground.

Before the start of play I spent a few pounds on souvenirs and presents, then made my way to my seat in the stand near the new media centre, behind which were the hospitality tents, and at 10.55 my friend walked through the Long Room and on to the field, and I watched every ball bowled. Some of them, in all fairness, I watched on the TV screens in the hospitality tent, as the tea break was not deemed long enough for those seated comfortably around the tables, sampling the generous array of food and drink. The whole day was extremely enjoyable, one for me to fondly remember, thanks to John Holder, whom I met up with at the close of play, and having spent a lovely evening, I taxied my way back to my hotel.

On Saturday mornings my alarm clock would ring at 5am, but not in my London hotel from where, after breakfast, I strolled to Euston Station for my journey home. As I relaxed in my window seat my mind relived the enjoyment of my birthday, still feeling amused by the ticket office lady's response to my photograph. I intended to make the most of this rare work-free Saturday, which I began to do with my family once the train had reached Piccadilly, where Sarah met me and drove me home, opening presents and cards from family and friends. I spent the afternoon at the cricket club meeting up with my friends, some of whom I had known since my own playing days, others whom I had worked alongside in the many years of fund raising we had spent in order to improve the club's facilities. The 1980s and 90s had been particularly busy years, but I had now stood down from all my official roles, and from organising the sportsman's dinners, of which the Brian Johnston photograph, displayed prominently above the club bar, was the most memorable one.

Saturday being Saturday, however, inevitably made me think of my market stall, and that on my next trading days, Tuesday and Saturday, I would have customers asking me why I wasn't there. And that is exactly what happened. There is a lot of good humour on an outside market, as ever so many people like shopping in a relaxed atmosphere where traders and customers can enjoy each other's company as they pass the time of day. The questions began on Tuesday morning. "Did you oversleep on Saturday?" Or: "Did your van break down?" Or just: "Where were you Saturday?" My reply to them was: "My friend was umpiring the Test Match at Lords and he got me a ticket, so I had a day off." "You're having me on," "You'll try anything you," or "You must have got up late", were just some of the smiling responses I received, until, of course, I showed them the photograph. That was the moment when they became open-mouthed at the sight of Brian Johnston and me standing together, and with me smartly dressed in a suit! For all the years I had traded at Congleton I had been dressed in dark anoraks and a flat cap – one of the scruffiest traders on the market. Now they were looking at a different Johnny Slipper, and were eager to know more, puzzled that their slipperman must have a different lifestyle than they thought.

Six months later they did indeed find out more, when the Congleton Chronicle publicised my imminent retirement. I had begun to find my market days increasingly physically demanding, leaving home at 5.45am, to begin setting up my stall an hour or so later. I would be up and down the ladder fixing the iron bars to which the plastic sheets were clipped, in order to protect the goods from any rain, so that I could begin unloading my car and trailer, carrying a ton of footwear into position for setting out on display. After a day on my feet serving customers I would begin to load up the gear, and by the time the sheets and bars had been removed and I had switched on my ignition I was covered in sweat as I began my slow rush-hour journey home. Much though I loved the atmosphere on the market, and the rapport both with my fellow traders and so many customers whom I had known for many years, I felt it was time for me to make the decision to retire before my body made it for me. So, after the traditional Christmas stampede to buy slippers, I decided to have a January clear-out sale and call it a day.

The town having been such a big part of my life for such a long time, I decided to ask the editor of the Congleton Chronicle if he would allow me to write a letter of thanks to the people of the town for their business over the past 28 years. "No problem," he said, and went on to ask me a few details about my life, where I lived, and on which other markets I had traded. When I told him that apart from Thursdays on Sandbach for the last ten years, I had only ever traded at Congleton, because my main career was that of a schoolteacher, he seemed gobsmacked. "Tell me more," he said, taking out his pen to make some notes. He soon began to realise that I was not a typical market trader and seemed fascinated by my cricketing involvements, and the many sportsman's dinners I had organised. He promised to publish my thank-you letter, and to do a feature about me the following week. In the January 18th edition they headlined my letter, "Johnny Slipper says thanks and reveals his other life," and sent a photographer to capture me making one of my last sales, which appeared the following week, headlined "Johnny Slipper leaves a footnote on his other life," which they went on to describe, and printed a second photograph, of George Best, my son Richard and I, at another of the sportsman's dinners I had arranged.

Those final three market days at Congleton were simply stunning. I couldn't believe how many people came to extend their best wishes, wishing me a happy retirement, some giving me cards and presents, and so many telling me how amazed they had been to read about "my other life." The newspaper had revealed that I had helped to raise over £100,000 from sportsman's dinners for Royton Cricket Club, where I had been president and chairman, and the local Rotary club, and that during my fourteen years as a deputy headteacher I had initiated the forming of the largest primary schools' poetry festival in the country – and much more. As the readers of the Chronicle read all this they must have wondered if this really was the same scruffy Johnny Slipper they had known, or thought they had known, for all those years, and it was on that final Saturday, as Keith was about to take over my stall, that I had a totally unexpected wonderful experience. The traders had organised a collection for me, and presented me with a lovely Acctim clock, as a memento for all my happy years at Congleton. I very much appreciated their kindness, and as I drove my empty car and trailer home that day I knew that a large and important part of my life was now over, and I was full of mixed emotions, grateful that so many people had helped to make my retirement so memorable, but sad that my days in Congleton would be no more.

In some ways this was how I had felt twelve years earlier, when I decided to take early retirement from the teaching profession. I would never have even thought of retiring so early had it not been for a change in the education system. Teachers had been able to retire more or less whenever they wished, but from Easter, 1990, Local Management of Schools would apply, and from that date it was understood that whilst teachers would still be able to retire when they wished, they would no longer be able to receive their pension until their sixtieth birthday. So for those teachers in their middle fifties there was a choice to be made – either go then on a reduced pension or wait, in my case, six more years. I had always loved my life in the classroom. Yes there had been bad days – but everybody must have those – but as teaching had been the only thing I had wanted to do, I was still gaining as much satisfaction from inspiring my pupils in 1990, as I had when I began teaching in 1959. However, things were changing in the education world, and, in my opinion, not for the better.

I had enjoyed a fairly wide ranging career, beginning in an all-age school, then moving on, specialising in English and games in a secondary school, before becoming a head of department, teaching English to both 'O' and 'A' levels for five years, before ending my career as a deputy headteacher. Throughout those thirty years I had always been innovative, both in and out of the classroom, probably having arranged more school visits than 99% of other teachers, and, especially during my fourteen years in a council estate primary school, believe that I succeeded in motivating my pupils to achieve exceptionally high standards of descriptive writing. I had gradually developed my own ways of teaching my pupils to write well, and was perhaps fortunate in that I always felt that I had the support of my head teachers when I tried my own methods, such as taking my class outside, to get the best out of my pupils. Later in the book I have included many examples of these, of which the following give the flavour of what my style of teaching produced. I sent copies to Mr Chris Woodhead, a former Chief Inspector of Schools, who described them as 'fine, precise and imaginative', and that as an ex English teacher himself, he had very much enjoyed reading them, adding that 'These are passages which confirm what I have always believed is that a child's background is irrelevant given a talented teacher with high expectations'. Whilst I was flattered by his final remarks I very much appreciated his willingness to read the pages I had sent him, and was thrilled that he so highly praised them, as I was when Gervase Phinn, a celebrated writer himself, and a schools inspector for ten years, wrote "I very much enjoyed reading the splendid creative writing of your former pupils. There is real quality here and I am sure that the descriptions will add a great deal to your autobiography".

The Snowflakes

The dizzy snowflakes twist and twirl as they tumble down to earth. They slip silently down, some alighting on bare twigs or branches, and others landing on windowsills to form drifts. The heavens seem full of it, and so do the trees, their bows weighed down with crisp, soft snow. Suddenly the fall quickens its pace, blown on by an icy wind, as many more billowy, feathery flakes come, drifting slowly down to a white snowy grave on the ground, now totally disguised by a white eiderdown. The exquisite flakes fall, veiling the snow capped hills in a grey mist, over which an eerie silence remains, only to be broken by the noise of a traveller returning to his warm home.

Frances Turner

A Bright November Day

On this bright November day the sky is summer blue and cloudless. The sun blazes down, but it is still cold with frost. Minute jets leave their long forgotten trails to stray high above, while we look at the little aircraft as it glides across the sky to its destiny. Birds sing high in the treetops, their shrill notes like nightingales in top form. Gulls swerve in circles and swoop down like bullets to peck thrivingly into the soil at the worms, giving them no chance of freedom. They screech noisily like motor-bikes slamming their brakes, scaring off all the other timid birds. The long grass is frozen to the tip of the blades with the powdered frost. They stand out like knives pointing out of the ground ready for battle. It has been so cold that the insects have evacuated the place. The distant hills are covered with a sheet of mist like a graveyard, and the buildings on the hills look like silhouettes. Trees are trembling without protection. Now they have to survive the gale force blizzard in winter. Young saplings worry as winter draws near, and the helpless roots have difficulty supporting the tree at war, the furious winter blast.

Gavin Haslam

Both the pieces are exactly how Frances Turner and Gavin Haslam wrote them, when they were ten or eleven years old, at Limehurst Primrary School, and it gave me immense satisfaction to re-read these and other excellent descriptive writings that many of my pupils produced during my career. Later in the book I describe the ways I tried to inspire my pupils to do well in all subjects, but in order to do that a teacher needs to be able to work in a disciplined environment. Sadly, that was becoming increasingly difficult to do in some schools in the 1980s, when unruly pupils and many parents had begun to take advantage of the changes in the law. Teachers were being suspended for allegedly physically punishing pupils, and I found myself pondering my position as the deputy head in a council estate school where, although the general behaviour was excellent, there would be occasional indisciplined outbursts, usually by pupils of families who had moved into the area from another council estate, and whose behaviour was out of control. School discipline was my responsibility, and in enforcing it I was likely to be in the firing line from pupils and parents if I had been deemed to have acted illegally.

Would I be wise to make the decision to commit myself to six more years in the classroom, despite the increasing risks I would be running, or go in 1990 with a reduced pension? Fortunately I was probably one of very few teachers who already had a sideline, my market stall at Congleton, so if I did take retirement I could work an extra day or two to top up my pension and keep myself active. It seemed the right decision to make, and with all doubts about the wisdom of so doing having disappeared, I applied for, and was offered, retirement.

Becoming a teacher in 1959 not only fulfilled my ambitions, but those of my parents', who had worked so hard to give my sister and I a better start in life than they had experienced in the 1920s and 30s. For them to have children who became teachers meant that we would never have to suffer the indignities of the 'dole', as so many of their generation had had to do. My dad, Richard, born in 1907, was the second of four children of William, 'Billy', and Annie (nee Hyland) Cleary. On leaving school he became an apprentice at Platt's, Oldham's largest textile engineering company, but immediately on completing his apprenticeship he was made redundant, as were virtually all apprentices in those years of the 'slump', following the First World War. He hated being unemployed, and decided to find work by going to London, where he stayed for four years, working on the construction of Wembley Stadium, and at a Heinz factory, before coming back to Royton where he set up his own window-cleaning round, going on to have two men working for him.

My mum, Noreen, born in 1911 in Wigan, was the second of two children of John and Eleanor (nee Stapleton) Devine. John worked down the coalmines and Eleanor, whose family came from St. Helens, was a dressmaker. Tragically, when my mum was only two years old, her mother died in childbirth, and six months later her father died, said to have been 'of a broken heart'. My mum and her brother Frank were then brought up by her father's sister and husband, living close to other relatives, for the next eight years. That changed suddenly when they moved to Royton, and it must have been difficult for my mum and her brother Frank to adjust to, being so far away from their roots. They both did so, however, and some years later, in September 1935, my mum and dad married, and when I was three years old, in 1939, we moved into Queen Street, Royton, where my life, as I recall it, began.

1 Life in Queen Street

My dad picked me up, sat me on his shoulders, and took me into our back yard one dark winter's night – my earliest memory; that of the vivid red sky over Manchester. It was the night of the bombings, and even watching from where we lived in Royton, seven miles away, the whole sky was ablaze. I was four years old and life with the 'black-outs', air raid shelters, and the sound of German bombers droning across the sky at night, was just normal. Every night, as darkness fell, my dad would put the boards up at all the windows, before we switched a light on. Not a chink of light must shine into the street. Air raid shelters were on or near virtually every street; ours, on Queen Street, was a brick one. Some small groups of houses had the Anderson metal shelters, and in some open areas there were groups of separate ones, mostly below ground, with their roofs grassed over. Some nights we would hear the air raid warnings, get well covered up, hurry down to the freezing and pitch black shelter, then stand nervously until the all-clear siren sounded to tell us that the bombers had flown by. For all those of my age, never having known life in peacetime, this was our everyday existence. We lived in a dark world. No street lamps were lit, the buses drove without headlights, and even our torches – and no one went out at night without one – had to be dimmed. The best light in the house, though, was from the coal fire, especially in winter, when life revolved around the fireplace.

There was an art in making and maintaining a good fire, and that was my dad's job. The coal bucket was always at his side of the fireplace, as was the long iron poker, which he used to adjust the pieces of coal as they burned.

Coal was not plentiful, especially in winter, when every house was limited to one bag each week – hardly enough to keep the house warm all day. The coalmen would come round every week. They would stop at the bottom of our 'back', which we called the back alley, then they would carry the hundredweight sacks of coal to everyone's back yard, and tip the contents into the 'coal holes'. They had to be strong men to spend each and every day delivering their heavy sacks. In our back yard we had two 'coal holes', and during the summer my dad would order an extra ten or twelve sacks so that it would be there when it was most needed on cold winter nights. He would separate the different sized pieces into different corners, shovel the slack into one large pile, then chop the biggest clumps into more manageable sizes for our fireplace. We also had a lock on the 'coal hole' doors – just in case!

Making and maintaining a fire to burn through the night, so that the house was warm when we got up, was an art form, and my dad was a sublime artist. It was his last job before going to bed, carefully positioning the large chunks of coal like a wall at the front, with other pieces delicately placed behind them, followed by a shovelful of slack, thus sealing off the tiny gaps in order to suffocate any flames, to make sure the fire did not blaze away, and be burned out by the middle of the night. Finally, he put the fireguard in position, just in case sparks flew. There was something special about sitting round the fire on winter evenings. It was more than just keeping warm. Somehow the fire created a comforting atmosphere in the fearful times and, with all the shortages, restrictions and rationing, the home fire was a treat. It wasn't much of a treat on Mondays, though, if it had been a wet day. My mum did washing on Mondays, as did every other mother in Royton. On fine days the washing would be pegged out to dry, but on wet ones it was draped over the clothes maiden which was right in front of the fire. As we sat behind it we had to breathe in all the steam. It was horrible – thank goodness she only did the washing once a week! One of the delights, when sitting in front of the fire, was making toast. A long metal fork with fine sharp prongs was needed. The idea was to place the slice of bread carefully on the end of the prongs, keep it as close as possible to the flames, but avoid getting it overdone and burned black, turn it over, toast the other side, and make sure it did not drop off and fall on the burning coal! It made your hands very warm too!

As Mondays were washing days, Fridays were bath days. Everyone had a bath – but only on Fridays! In virtually every back yard would be a tin bath hanging on a nail on the wall, and it would be brought in, gradually filled up with pans full of hot water, and everyone in the family would take it in turn to have a bath; but not our family, because we were lucky, in that we had one of only two houses in the row with an upstairs bathroom. It certainly was a luxury in those days to have an inside toilet and bath – but we still only ever had a bath on a Friday! Every back yard had its own toilet, and we often used ours even though we had the inside one. No such thing as toilet rolls in those days, either. Behind the toilet door was a nail, with sheets of newspaper, cut to size, hanging from it. The biggest problems came during the winter months when the water pipes froze. We used to have a special thick candle in a container positioned just below the pipe to try to prevent the water from freezing, but on the coldest of winter days the pipes froze. All the houses in Queen Street had their own outside toilets in the back yards, but there were many houses, especially the back to back ones, those with only a front door, which did not have their own individual toilets. There would be a passageway at the end of the terrace, and a toilet block would be round the back, with perhaps three families sharing one toilet. Today the idea seems gruesome, but in those days it was everyday life. So was the existence of a chamber pot under every bed. How times have changed!

Most houses in Royton had four rooms; two bedrooms upstairs, and a living room and a 'front room' downstairs. Only posh people claimed to have a 'lounge'. All four rooms had a fireplace, but most people could only afford to light a fire in one of them. At Christmas we lit the front room fire, and sat round our best table for our Christmas dinner. That was the only day of the year when we enjoyed the luxury of eating chicken.

In those days it was a rarity – very different today. Only in the front room did we have a carpet. Every other room had oilcloth covering the flag floors in the living room and kitchen. We never had slippers, so we always wore our shoes until we climbed into bed, where the hot water bottle had been warming the sheets. The worst moment of the day for me was just before I went up to bed, because my mum and dad insisted that I had a spoonful of Scott's Emulsion. It tasted horrible, but they said it was essential for all young children in those days. Thankfully I was allowed a toffee afterwards to take the taste away – as long as there were any left from the meagre weekly amount we could have because of rationing.

Everyone had a ration book, each with its own number, without which people would have starved. Families had to sign up at the shop of their choice, thus enabling the shopkeeper to obtain sufficient food supplies for his registered customers. Ours was the Maypole, and when my mum saw a queue there she would join it, assuming that the shop had received a supply of something special. It was the only way. Word soon 'got round' but supplies were limited, and it was first-come, first-served, even though the amount you could buy was limited by the number of coupons the customer had.

It was the same at our local green fruit shop – Mrs Wright's. If word had it that she had got some oranges, everybody quickly made a dash for it. I can remember my mum sending me down to join the queue, and after about half an hour, when it was my turn, I was sold exactly four oranges, because that was the size of our family – one each! Fresh fruit was rare, of course, and so was tinned fruit. In our kitchen cupboard my mum and dad had stacked away some tinned pineapple chunks at the start of the war, but by the time I was seven or eight there were not many tins left, and, like the chicken, became a 'Christmas Day only' treat. Just after the war, with everything still on ration, of course, I saw my first banana, and, after another long queue at Mrs Wright's, I sat on the flags at the top of Queen Street with the other lads in our gang, all of us tasting a banana for the first time. Everyone had said how lovely bananas were, but that day as we learned to peel the skin back and take our first bite, it tasted awful. Nobody had told us we had to wait until the fruit had ripened. Our bananas were still green, and as hard as iron!

4

One of our favourite shops was Mrs Jewhurst's, across from The Jubilee Gardens, where we could buy lovely sticks of liquorice for a penny each. They were about as long as a pencil, but three times thicker, looking just like a twig that had been chopped off a tree. You could chew them for hours, and they tasted lovely. That was where we bought our big Sarsparilla bottles – our hot water bottles! At the end of Church Street was Cocker's Grocer's shop, where we bought our broken biscuits. All biscuits then were sold by weight, from the large tins on his counter. There were inevitable breakages but Mr Cocker used to put all his broken biscuits into a sack behind the counter, and sell them for a penny a bag, or two pence if you could afford a bigger one. They tasted lovely, especially if our bags had some of the creamy biscuits amongst them.

Our favourite shop was Billy Cardiff's, on John Street. To enter you had to walk down the back alley and go through the back door. When you stepped inside the picture was always the same. Billy and his brother, Tommy, would be seated on either side of the fire, which was in the middle of the room, a large cylindrical contraption based on four strong legs, with a front door which would usually be swung open, warming the room nicely. Billy and Tommy always had their caps on, wearing suits, too, smoking their clay pipes, happily puffing the time away. Billy sold us our cigarettes, not in full packets of ten, but loose, as many as you wanted. At the time 'Woodies' i.e. Woodbines, were 10½d a packet, so the first cigarette cost 1½d, but any more went for a penny each. We would then go across the street, into St Paul's School yard, climb on to the low sloping roof of the toilets and enjoy our 'fags', unseen by anyone. Whenever we were sitting there and caught sight of anyone walking along Church Street, we would lie back out of their view, then sit up again as the sound of their footsteps faded away, carrying on with our illicit smoking. Illicit for seven and eight year olds, anyway!

At the time there were five of us in our 'gang'. Alan Wild was the 'cock'. He was a year older than Peter Ainsworth, Brian Sangster and me, so he quietly took charge. Kenny Greaves was one year younger than us, and although there were others who would come to join up with us from time to time we five always did and played everything together

– football, cricket, tabcards, kickoutaball, hide and seek. Whether it was on the street, in the school yard, on the 'tip', down by the brook, or in the 'backs', we were all part of one gang. It grew in size as Norman Kenyon, who lived back to back with us on Church Street, and who was three years younger, along with Stuart Anderson, Jack Wrigley, Norman Starkey and Trevor Turner, began to join in. Stuart and I became good pals in later years when we played cricket for Royton, and Norman and I became step-brothers some thirty years later! Other lads also joined us in the following few years when we played all our football and cricket on what we knew as the 'top field', including Brian Green, who went on to have a career in football, both playing and managing; and a future England goalkeeper, Eddie Hopkinson, who played briefly for the 'Latics' before joining Bolton Wanderers.

We all got on fine, and I can only ever remember being in one fight. It was in our 'back' after I had walked into our yard looking miserable, or perhaps crying, and my dad wanted to know what it was all about. Whether he had overheard us I do not know, but I must have bottled out of a fight with Brian Sangster. Immediately my dad took me out again, up to the gang who were still there, and he insisted that I had a proper and fair fight with Brian – no kicking. We did, and I landed a punch on Brian's nose, which began to bleed, and then he screamed and ran off home – so I had won. My dad went back home, quietly happy, as indeed I was, and the gang thought I had done well. But I was never a tough lad, never went looking for a fight; very different, I am sure, from my dad when he was young.

Thankfully that was a one-off incident and as a crowd of pals growing up we all got on well. When we were not playing football or cricket we would be competing with one another at tab-cards. These were cigarette cards, one in each packet, with a photograph of a well-known sportsman. Everybody saved them, swapped them and played 'skimming-on' and 'bottle' with them to win, or lose, more from each other. We sometimes went down to the River Irk, the brook which ran near the cricket field, and generally messed about, and then usually went under the bridge where no-one could see us enjoying a smoke. I got caught one day, though. It was on a Sunday when we always had to wear our best clothes.

I asked my mum if I could go out playing and she said as long as I got changed, then yes I could. I was grumbling about having to get changed when my dad reached into one of the drawers and threw my trousers to me, and out of one of the pockets dropped a cigarette. Needless to say I did not go out to play!

Most children had two sets of clothes; Sunday best, and every day ones, and the switch took place on Whit Sundays. First we would go to Mass, then begin our tour to show off our new clothes to relatives and friends. Most people would pop a 'threepenny bit' into our pockets but my grandma always gave us sixpence. The meanest of them all though, was my dad's Aunt Mary who lived on the far side of Royton – we had to go all that way for a penny! We thought she was miserable. The following week was Trinity Sunday, Royton's procession day. Every church in Royton took part in walking through the streets, each having its traditional route, and its own starting time. The streets were closed to traffic – not that there were many cars on them anyway – whilst parishioners walked. Bands would play, people sang hymns, and everyone walked gracefully and proudly in long lines, all wearing their smartest attire.

So now our new clothes were our best ones, last year's became the every day ones, and the old ones, now two years old, were mostly thrown out, but not into the dustbin. The man who collected the old clothes was Joe Baty. He was the rag-and-bone man, and must have been the laziest bloke in Royton. He had a pony and cart which clomped its way round all the streets. Joe sat on the flat cart, his legs dangling down the side, smoking all the time, while his wife did all the work. Mrs Baty walked alongside the pony and collected all the old rubbish people were giving away, for which she handed over some donkey stones. These were what people used to clean their front and back doorsteps, and it was a matter of pride for every housewife that her front and back doorsteps were smartly cleaned, and yellow donkey stoned for the weekend. Every day, late in the afternoon, Joe's pony and cart would trot along Middleton Road towards their house, isolated on Holden Fold Lane, surrounded by piles of junk. While they obviously made a living out of it, their house was regarded, by those who walked by it, as a veritable pigsty.

All the milkmen had a horse and cart, and delivered their milk every day, except Sundays. Ours was Tom Buckley who would arrive in Queen Street about 11 o'clock every day. From the four huge urns at the back of his cart he would fill his can with a gallon or more of milk, then walk up the backs, into his customers' yards. He would politely knock on our door, push it open, pour the pint measure into his own pint jug, from which he poured it into the empty jug on the table. The he would add a touch more for good measure, bid you 'good morning' and be on his way. For those not at home a jug would be left on the window bottom, covered by a saucer, so he would fill it, cover it, and go. He would go back to his cart, climb up two steps, cling on to the urns, while Mrs Buckley, sitting at the front, would crack the reins and the horse would trot to the next street.

Maybe pulling a milk cart was easy for a horse, but pulling the coal carts could not have been. These always had two horses, but there must have been nearly a hundred bags of coal on each cart as it left Royton Railway yard. It must have been hard enough to pull such a heavy load in good weather, but it had to be sheer agony when there was snow and ice on the ground, as they struggled to keep their footing. Tarmac roads would have made their task an impossibility, especially on sloping streets. The setts, bumpy perhaps for cars and bicycles, were essential for the horses to get a grip. Not that there were many cars in those days. The only ones I can remember belonged to the doctors, visiting their patients. On the main road there were buses. People caught the bus, train, rode their 'bikes', or walked.

The best wheels for us, though, were those on bogeys. The difficulty was acquiring the wheels, which were scarce then, but if someone could get hold of an old pram, there always seemed to be ways of converting them into a bogey. We had a lot of fun racing each other down Charles Street, with its steep slope, flying straight across Middleton Road, totally oblivious to the No. 11 and 12 buses which passed by, to see who was first to the Vine Mill railings. Charles Street was also our favourite for sledging down, and every lad had his own makeshift sledge. The more it snowed the more we sledged, the shinier the iced snow became, and the faster we went. And the noisier we became, too, until the householders had seen and heard enough, and scattered their hot ashes across our tracks, thus making sure we moved to another street.

Whether it was winter or summer there was just one form of entertainment in Royton – the 'Bug-Hut,' which is what everyone called the Pavilion Cinema. With two 'houses' every night, at 6.30 and 8.30, and new films every Monday and Thursday, the bug hut was very popular, many people going twice weekly. It was 7d for a seat near the screen, 9d for the better ones further back, but if you were well off you paid a shilling to sit in the upper circle. On Saturday nights the queues seemed to stretch for miles. It must have made a fortune for Mr Cheetham, but it did not prevent him from walking round, inside and outside, shining his torch on the floor looking for cigarette ends, 'dimps,' picking them up and putting them into his pocket to make his own 'fags.' He certainly was different, but he provided the people of Royton with plenty of good films every night – and on Saturday afternoons too, when it was completely full of youngsters, hardly an adult in sight, to see the weekly episode of Buck Rogers.

After the war the most exciting time of the year was Royton 'Wakes.' Every cotton town had its own holiday week when all the mills shut down, and virtually all the shops did too. Royton's was the first week of August and anyone who took a holiday went that week. But the entertainment began on the previous Thursday when the fairground switched on its loud music and provided fun for everybody. We never described it as a fair, or fairground – it was 'The Wakes'. The travellers' caravans would begin to arrive, park up in nearby streets, on Monday and Tuesday, and then on the market square behind the Town Hall the rides, stalls and shows would be erected, with the travellers probably working through Wednesday night ready for the Thursday afternoon opening. For those of us only eight or nine years old, never having seen anything like this before, it was magical. My favourite ride was the Waltzer, and I enjoyed throwing mops at the tin cans, playing roll-a-penny, or trying to win a goldfish on the coconut shy; like all my pals, I would walk home with my pockets empty, looking forward to a repeat performance on Friday.

Then on Saturday we were out of bed early, suitcases filled, and soon on our way by train to Oldham Mumps station, which was always packed tight with families all waiting for the big train – to Blackpool. We would scramble to find seats, and then all the way to the seaside every girl and boy would be looking through the windows to see who could be the first to catch sight of Blackpool Tower. The excitement increased as it came into view, and soon we were walking off the platform towards our boarding house. Blackpool had thousands of boarding houses. We were given our own places at the table, six or eight on each table, for breakfast, dinner and tea, and we ate whatever was served up. There were no such things as menus. During the summer Blackpool must have had more people per square yard than any other place in the world. Everywhere wasn't just crowded, it was log jammed. It was even difficult to find enough space to fit four deckchairs next to each other on the beach – even when the tide was out! All down the promenade were various kinds of shows and entertainments, and of course, the Pleasure Beach, with the most exciting rides in the country.

On our Blackpool holiday 1947.

We would go on each of the three piers, enjoy donkey rides, chew the Blackpool red and white rock, and the week would fly past – just like the trams scuttling up and down the promenade. We always enjoyed a tram-ride, too. A week in the sun was a rare experience for those of us who lived in the cotton towns. As we made our way home the sky would darken, and we would soon be back under the dull smoky haze that forever hung over us. We grew up thinking this was normal and natural, and that only at the seaside did the sun really shine all day.

I never realised that the constantly gloomy sky was caused by the vast amount of smoke being spewed from the hundreds of mill chimneys, and from every house chimney too. Only on windy days did we ever see a blue sky.

Royton would return to normal for the next 51 weeks after we had arrived back home, and I would have another three weeks to spend playing cricket and football before the school term began. I attended St Aidan and Oswald's School, and in Junior 1 and 2 I finished near the top of the class, so both my parents were eager for me to do well and to go on to pass the scholarship. My dad was always conscious of the days of his youth when jobs were virtually impossible to get, and he dreaded that there might be another slump, as there had been following the First World War. It had been mainly the manual workers who had suffered, so he was anxious for me to go into a more secure clerical job, being less vulnerable to redundancy – the 'dole' – in his day. Junior 3 was Miss Hickey's class, a teacher who always seemed to have the cane or a ruler in her hand, and she was forever giving somebody a smack with it. She terrified everyone, and in later years, on a rare school trip to the 'bug-hut,' she took her cane with her, according to a story told by the famous Oldham Tinkers.

Luckily for me I was not in her class for long, because she fell ill, and while she was off school her class was divided up, some moving down to Junior 2, others, including me, into the examination year class, Junior 4. By this time the new headmaster, Mr Critchley, had been at the school three or four years and was having a strong influence, especially in preparing the scholarship year pupils for their examinations, which an increasing number were passing. The school's reputation was growing, as was Mr Critchley's, who had been a total stranger to everyone in Royton before his appointment – except my mum and my uncle Frank. They had all attended the same junior school in Wigan and Frank and Eric [Critchley] had been good pals before my mum and Frank came to live in Royton with their aunt and uncle, having been adopted by them following their parents' early deaths. Mr Critchley was pleased to meet up again with Frank and my mum, and I think, maybe for old times' sake, he kept an eye on my progress.

He kept an eye on those who attended Sunday Mass, too, and those who didn't. At Monday morning assembly he made every pupil indicate which Mass they had attended, with questions about communion confession and benediction. Most pupils came from practising Catholic families, but some did not, and these would often have to remain in the assembly hall while the rest of us went to our classrooms, as they then received a caning for their sins. The Cleary family had a fine Catholic reputation. My grandma, Aunt Agnes and Uncle John would not only attend Sunday Mass, but daily masses too. There were three priests in the parish, and they would make visits to the homes of all the parishioners from time to time. They may have made slightly more frequent visits to those houses where a drink of whisky was on offer, but that would not have applied to our house, because my dad never touched alcohol, and he would never have dreamed of offering anyone a drink, except on Christmas Day when even he had a sip of sherry.

During one priestly visit by Father Birch, I had been invited to become an altar boy, quite an honour for me and my family, and by the time I had reached Miss Hickey's class I was serving a morning mass every day, and the 9am Sunday mass. It was quite a privilege to be wearing the cassock and cotta. At that time I had no idea, nor, I am sure, had my parents, that becoming an altar boy was often the first step a boy would take towards the priesthood. Being a successful altar boy involved many things. He had to be reliable in attendance, be on time, always clean and well behaved. He had to be able to recite the Latin responses to the priest's proclamations, and to conduct himself formally during the whole of the mass, kneeling upright behind the priest and in full view of all the congregation.

The parish priest, Fr Wainwright, had talked to my parents one day, and had complimented them on how well they were bringing me up, and had also said that I was doing very well as an altar boy. He said that I was a well-behaved good boy from a good Catholic family. Such good boys should want to become priests, and it would be a great honour to the Cleary family if I became a priest. He suggested that they had a talk with me about my ambitions, which is what they did one night. They did not put any pressure on me directly, but I can remember having the feeling that if I said that I did not want to become a priest I would really be saying that I was not a good boy. Fr Wainwright had assured my parents that such discussions always remained discreet and confidential. No-one at school would know that I wished to become a priest, so there would be no sarcastic comments made. Nothing would change, but I was actually stepping on the first rung of the priestly ladder when I said "yes". A few years later I would jump off, but the memory of that initial experience would come back many years later.

I was continuing to enjoy my school life both in and out of the classroom. For a while I seemed to be following in my Uncle Frank's footsteps – he was still playing in one of the amateur leagues every Saturday – by being selected as the goalkeeper for the school team. This was quite an achievement for me when most of the

Junior 4 in 1946.
I am third left on back row.

team were from the senior classes, mostly three years older than me. Alas, I let six or seven goals past me in one match, and was dropped. But it was cricket I enjoyed best of all and my ambitions soared after I had top scored in one school match which my dad had come to see me play. He could tell that I loved the game, and always gave me plenty of encouragement from then on. My parents had already bought me my membership of Royton Cricket Club and I had been watching virtually all their matches for the past three or four years.

In the classroom, in those days of tip-up wooden desks and inkwells, long before the words 'biro' and 'ball pen' had been invented, I was doing well, and despite being a year younger than the Junior 4 pupils, I was seventh in the class at Easter. Being only nine years old I was not entitled to sit the scholarship examination, but then a strange thing happened. Mr Critchley approached my parents to ask if they would like me to sit the St Bede's College entrance examination. No doubt the secret priestly ambition information had passed between priest and headmaster, for in June 1946 I was taken down to St Bede's. I was unaware of it at the time – perhaps my parents were too – but St Bede's was regarded as a junior seminary, the school to which boys with priestly ambitions were encouraged to attend, many of whom were boarders, especially those who lived too far away to travel daily.

All the time I was doing my studies in the classroom, both my parents were busy too. My mum was good at sewing and dressmaking, and during and after the war an increasing number of ladies would buy their material, bring it to our house, where my mum would measure them, make the dress, skirt, or whatever clothing they wanted; they would come back a week later for a try-on, and collect the finished article a few days later. She spent hours at the table in the front room, as her reputation grew. She was so busy that it was usually after 9 o'clock before she joined us in the living room, which was the moment for me to go the other way. It was my job to pick up all the pins that had fallen on to the floor. On my hands and knees I would move around the room, holding the large iron magnet which sucked them all up in no time.

Meanwhile my dad was walking up and down ladders all day. Following the war, when as an engineer he had to work at A.V.Roe's rather than be allowed to go into the Army, he had gone back to his window cleaning round, the business he had set up in the 1930s, and with Frank and Bert, whom he had employed before the war, also re-joining him, it was a successful venture. The first signs of this success were evident when I came home one day to find we had a carpet in the living room, and not long afterwards we had a brand new piano. That was when I began to have piano lessons, taught by Mr Dunkerley in the room over his wife's baker's shop in Market Street. My mum insisted that I practised half an hour every day and at first I enjoyed it, but gradually the novelty was wearing off. I wanted to stop having music lessons, but she was adamant that I carried on, and started to buy copies of popular songs for me to play. Soon I never practised any of the music Mr Dunkerley set me every Sunday; instead I spent the half hour each night playing music we all liked, including my mum's favourite 'Galway Bay' which we all sang out loud together, as well as lots more well-liked tunes. It was a good thing she had been adamant, after all.

We still had our lovely warm fire, and still had the miserable steamy Monday evenings, but now Thursday was best day – rag-puddings! My mum would make them during the morning, wrap each one in a large thick handkerchief, secured with a safety pin, then put them into our largest cooking pan where they would boil away all afternoon. The steam rose to the ceiling, then drip its way down the kitchen walls. The puddings were 'done' when we arrived home, and soon with roast potatoes, mushy peas, and lots of gravy, our plates were crammed full. Her rag-puddings were delicious.Our other favourite meal was one my mum did not cook, it was from the 'chippy.' There may have been a dozen chip shops in Royton, but Mrs Broadbent's on Middleton Road was the best – so we all said – and if the queues that formed before she opened every night were not proof of that, then who cares? Her husband Joe did the labouring, carrying the buckets full of potatoes to the machine on which he placed each potato one by one to chop them into chips, and then she took over. Her chips were always tasty and we always ordered a mixture, chips and peas in well wrapped newspaper, and a meat or a meat-and-'tater' pie. It was always a lovely supper. Another good thing about a 'chippy' meal was there was no washing up to do, but there was after our other meals, and I would wash up and Winifred did the drying. Not that I minded washing up, except in the cricket season.

The Central Lancashire League clubs did not employ professionals during the war years, but in 1945 everything returned to normal. Royton's pro was the Surrey and England fast bowler Alf Gover, and big crowds watched every match. During the week we would go down to see them practise in the nets and enjoy fielding the ball when it was hit across the field. Royton had some well known good amateurs too, such as Geoff Bispham, Harry Broadbent and Alf Etchells, who had played during some of the war years. One who did not, however, was Dr

Donald Longbottom, an outstanding cricketer and sportsman, serving in the Army, and for three years he had been a prisoner of war in Japan. All the lads of my age were eager to see Donald play following his return home. He was the player everyone who had seen him bat and bowl said he was good enough to play for Lancashire. How shocked I was when I first saw him walk on to the field. He looked like a skeleton. One glimpse of him – even to a ten year old – confirmed the stories of cruelty the prisoners of war must have suffered in Japan. Wonderfully, he would gain in strength, reproduce his outstanding cricketing form, and play until 1961. Later, as I grew up and caught the Royton first team, I was thrilled to have played in a team he captained, and to have become one of his friends.

The cricket we played as ten year olds, though, was on the tip or the dirt track, play areas that no longer exist. Any 'batter' who hit a house wall or fence without a bounce, scored a six. If he hit a window or knocked the ball into someone's garden he was out – and had to climb over the fence to get the ball back. They were simple rules. As we only used soft tennis balls, there were not, luckily, any windows broken. Likewise, when we played football, usually in St Paul's School yard, we used a tennis ball, because no-one had a real football then. The 'Latics' had, though – Oldham Athletic, our team! We had watched them playing during the end of the war years, and then when the Third Division began again in 1945/6 season. Their style of play was simple – boot it up field as far as possible. The farther it went the louder the crowd cheered, and it was up to the forwards to dribble it around to try to score. Not surprisingly, with their kick and rush tactics, they did not get promoted.

At ten years old my whole life had been spent in Royton. There had been visits to Oldham of course, and the exciting Blackpool holiday weeks, but I more or less walked everywhere. Some things were changing, some were not. There were no black-outs now. Lamplighters walked round the streets every day carrying their long poles, switching off the gas lamps, switching them back on as it went dark. Even earlier in the morning Mrs Higgins, Royton's 'Knocker-upper' was carrying her long pole too, which she tapped on people's bedroom windows to wake them up, so they were not late for work. As the men walked to the mills in their clogs the sound their irons made must have wakened all Royton up before 7 o'clock. They certainly did in Queen Street. Nearly everyone wore clogs, ladies usually with rubbers, men with irons. Lads did, too. I loved it once I had got a shine on the irons, being able to skate and skim on the smooth flags. We were clog-skaters when going down Charles Street.

But I would not be wearing clogs when the new school year started in September. With only a week or so before the summer term ended I realised that it would be my final week at St Aidan's. Everyone was delighted that I had passed the examination. My parents were ecstatic, and Mr Critchley was as pleased as anyone, with one more success for him and the school, as seven of the Junior 4 class members leaving go to one of the convents or colleges in September. So during the holidays I would be having new clothes, a school cap, schoolbag and leather shoes, ready for my first day at St Bede's College on September 16th 1946.

By 1946, life had more or less returned to what it must have been like before the war except for the rationing, of course. New films were being shown at all the six or seven cinemas in Oldham every week, and on Saturday nights the queues seemed to stretch for miles. We did not see any films on Saturdays, though, because my mum and dad had queued for hours themselves to become members of Oldham Repertory Theatre, a somewhat privileged status as membership was limited. For three or four years we saw a different play every Saturday night, always in our reserved seats on the back row, centre circle. It was a great night out, and quite a few of the actors and actresses went on to become famous, such as Dora Bryan and Bernard Cribbins. Then we travelled home at about 10 o'clock on the bus, and usually called at Mrs Broadbent's for some chips for supper.

2 St Bede's College

Going 'up town' from Royton to the large town centre which Oldham had, was popular for both shopping and entertainment, and it seemed a huge place to lads of my age brought up in the war years. But in September I travelled to Manchester for my first day at St Bede's College, and I remember thinking that by comparison Oldham was like a village. I am sure my parents must have been concerned about my safety knowing I had to change buses and walk across Piccadilly through traffic the like of which we had never seen in Royton. The only uniform we had was our school cap, and as I reached the No. 80 bus stop in Piccadilly that first morning there were quite a few new caps on display. There was not a single adult in the queue. Everyone was wearing a cap like mine, so I suppose my school day began there at the bus stop, standing quietly with others, all waiting for our first ride on the No. 80. I managed to get a window seat upstairs, and just stared in amazement at what I saw. There were huge buildings everywhere, crossroads, traffic lights, cinemas, shops, The Palace Theatre, buses galore, churches, pubs, cafés, derelict bomb sites, office blocks – it was mesmerising. My No. 2 bus had taken half an hour to reach Stevenson Square, and from Failsworth I had not seen a blade of grass as the bus went down Oldham Road, but now the 80 bus was weaving its way left and right through a brick built jungle. Eventually we went through more residential areas, and on to Alexandra Road, where we all stepped on to the pavement.

Suddenly I was out of the concrete jungle but now looking at a forest! Alexandra Park was the length of three bus stops. Royton Park, by comparison, would have fitted in our back yard. The bus moved on, we crossed the road, and I saw the huge three-storey building. I had just left a school with only five classrooms and a hall, and was joining one with five massive buildings, all linked up, with a playground larger than a football field. The sheer size of the complex was awesome. The bus journey had opened my eyes to the enormity of the city, and now as one of more than 500 pupils in the playground, I would remember that morning's experiences for ever. I had now entered a new world.

Coming from Royton, with my broad Lancashire accent, meant that I stood out from virtually all the other lads, many of whom lived in south Manchester, and with posh accents. Looking back on those early days, remembering how similar situations affected other lads differently, having my broad Royton accent made me feel superior, even when they mocked and mimicked it. I had always regarded people who spoke with posh accents as 'toffs', and I just assumed they were jealous, and took it as a compliment. It was around that time that I can recall my mum suggesting that I might go for elocution lessons. Piano lesson, yes, but definitely no fancy accents for me! My dad must have thought the same, because it was never mentioned again. It was during my first few weeks at St Bede's that my dad told me that he hoped I would not feel ashamed of inviting any of my new school friends to our house. I couldn't understand what he meant. Ours was a nice house; we had a carpet, a piano – what was there to be ashamed of? My dad would have been aware, of course, that many of my classmates would live in detached or semi-detached houses, with their driveways, garage and gardens, not a back yard like ours. He was understandably concerned that it could have worried me, but as far as I was concerned I was proud to come from Royton, proud of my accent, and all the lads just accepted me for what I was.

If my accent was better than theirs my academic level was not. All the class were a year older than me anyway, and I struggled somewhat, which was difficult to come to terms with when at St Aidan's I had been in the top two or three in my own age group. I did not finish at the bottom of the class, and I did have one great day when in a maths test I scored 100%, and the genius Gus Dearman could only manage 97%. My mum remembered that one all her life. I was enjoying myself, having settled into the new environment, and adjusting to my new school life.

Out of the classroom I was enjoying myself too, discovering the huge city bit by bit. Having caught the 80 bus to Piccadilly a group of us might walk down to Deansgate, Albert Square or Market Street, wander through Woolworths, Lewis's or various book shops, St Anne's Square – wherever we fancied, for half an hour or so, then split up and catch our various buses home. We didn't do that on the foggy days, though, and there were many of them on winter days over the next three or four years. I remember more than once when the bus conductor walked about two yards in front of the bus, guiding the driver, all the way from school to Piccadilly. On the worst days we would be allowed to leave school at 2 o'clock. Buses leaving Manchester sometimes went no further than Hollinwood, and we had to walk it home from there once or twice. On one of those occasions my dad had been out looking for me, worried to death, and we met up with each other as I came along Church Street at 7.30 pm, over five hours since I had left school. I doubt if my mum made me have my piano lesson that night!

If the fog was thick in both Royton and Manchester I soon realised that in winter the two places could be remarkably different – when it snowed! Over the 1946 Christmas holiday we had some very heavy snowfalls, and in Royton the snow was still deep until March. But not in Manchester. The new term opened and as I travelled into the city, going slightly downhill all the way, of course, the snow gradually disappeared. There was not a speck of it in Whalley Range. That was the winter which persuaded my dad to go back into engineering. He had his successful window cleaning business, but when temperatures are below zero there are no windows to clean, and therefore no income. He got a temporary job during the freezing weeks, and then with Harold Lawson, another engineer, they started up their own business, repairing flyers for the cotton mills.

Meanwhile at St Bede's we sometimes finished at 2 o'clock when there was no fog, but because of a football match. Monseignor Cook, the Rector, very kindly allowed the home-time bell to be rung early if there was a soccer match at Maine Road. Both City and United played at the ground because Old Trafford had suffered bomb damage, so a number of games were played on Wednesday afternoons – before floodlight days, of course. It was great to walk across Alexandra Park and then watch a first division football match. Soon the Rector would retire, but his successor, Fr Duggan, did not ring the bell early, but it had been good while it lasted. I was a Latics supporter, of course, but enjoyed it if one of the Manchester clubs won.

Fr O'Keeffe was the form master of the upper 3A class I was in, and he must have recommended that I remained in his class for another year, so that I was in a class with others of the same age. One of these was Sandy Busby, son of United's manager, who had been in the Lower Third class, and another was Terry Greenwood from Shaw, who travelled on the same No. 2 bus as me. He had an accent as broad as mine, enjoyed football and cricket, and for the next two or three years we were good pals, travelling to and from school together every day. Academically I was about average now, and the decision Fr O'Keeffe made had been the right one. It was a year in which I enjoyed sport, too. In the football season I often played in some Saturday morning inter-school matches, and afterwards we often walked to Maine Road to see United or City – unless, of course, the Latics were playing at home. It was in the summer, though, when I enjoyed my sport most of all, playing cricket. The first-year teams at all the grammar schools were called the 'Juniors', and I was selected and did well in the first two matches, under the captaincy of John McMahon. He and I were rivals on and off the field. It was a total surprise, however, when for the next match I was named as captain, and for the rest of the season, too! What a thrill it was. I enjoyed every minute of it, especially as earlier in the term Fr McLernon made a comment during one of his lessons to the effect that no-one with a broad Lancashire accent could expect to captain a team, looking at me as he said it. I simply lived cricket that summer, and my parents were delighted too and proud that their son had been bestowed the captaincy role. They perhaps were less delighted when my exam results took a tumble during the summer term and it would not be the last time for that to happen!

St. Bede's Junior Team 1948.

Back Row: (L to R) Hurst, Sandy Busby, Mike Lawler, Arthur Pownell, McIlroy, Paddy Quirk

Front Row: John McMahon, Ben Mooney, Peter Murphy, Me, Terry Greenwood, John McDonell

We were asked to state our preferences for which subjects we wished to study from the following year until the Upper Fifth. In my case, and Terry Greenwood's too, and all the boarders', it was the classics course we would take, because we were potential church students. So Latin and Greek were added to our syllabus, but no science. I never attended a single science lesson in all my days at school. There had to be something wrong there. However, at the time, it did not mean anything at all, and it was in the Lower 4th class that I was seated next to Arthur Pownell, with whom I would become best pals, also playing in the same house and school football and cricket teams, and we remain good friends to this day.

It was through my friendship with Arthur that my dad's comment that I should not be ashamed of inviting anyone to our house came back into my mind, maybe two years later. Arthur lived in Audenshaw, and he invited me over to his house for a day during the holidays. As I got off the bus, Arthur was waiting there, and we began to walk towards his home. All the houses we passed were semi-detached, all with driveways and front and rear gardens. In Royton in those days there were only three or four streets like that, but here they were everywhere. We played cricket in his driveway, and kicked a football around on his lawn. It was certainly different from our back yard. Arthur would come over to our house in Queen Street, and while no comparisons were ever made, I could understand how my dad had anticipated the possibility that I could have felt somewhat inferior. I'm glad that I never did, but looking back on it I rather think my cousin, Anthony, three years younger than me, seemed to feel embarrassed by his working class background. I'm glad it never troubled me. Perhaps I was an inverted snob. I simply never felt a trace of inferiority or jealousy. We lived in Royton and, just like virtually everyone else in Royton, we lived in a terraced house. End of story.

I was still serving on the altar, but only at Sunday masses now that I had to leave home too early to be able to serve on weekdays, so along with Terry Bradbury I moved slightly upwards in seniority by the subtly understood progress to the 8.00 am and then to the 10.10 am Sunday masses. I continued to receive the occasional word of church student encouragement from the priests, but by now I had ceased to have any such aspirations, although I had never mentioned it at home. At St Bede's there was never the slightest pressure. Never since I arrived at the school was there ever a reference made, but my automatic place on the classics stream meant that my church student status was recognised.

At home, though, I began to feel uncomfortable about my situation. The idea that "good boys would want to become priests, and your family will feel very proud" made it difficult for me to say I no longer wished to be a priest, because it was synonymous with admitting I wasn't a 'good boy'. I also felt uncomfortable when, on many occasions, my grandma would quietly make a knowing comment, and then slip a ten shilling note in my pocket. In the end I made the decision and waited until my dad and I were on our own and told him that I no longer wanted to be a priest. I need never have worried a jot. His reply was instant and full of understanding. He did not make the slightest attempt to ask me to think about it a bit more, or to change my mind, or even to ask me why. It lifted a load off my mind, and I have always appreciated his instant and genuine acceptance of my decision.

That moment passed, and life moved on, but many years later the significance of that day came back to me in stark contrast to what I assume had happened in Terry Greenwood's life. Having travelled to and from school together every day for three years I could not believe the change that occurred in him as he suddenly became a boarder when he was 14 or 15. He was simply not the same person. No charging about; no playing football in the school yard; no running; always speaking slowly and correctly; Terry became style, dignity, posture and pretence – or so I believed. With carefully measured steps he walked formally, as if on parade, never a hand in a pocket. Whenever we said prayers in the classroom his eyes were locked shut and his hands, tightly joined, his voice the loudest in the room. I simply could not believe what I was seeing. He was holiness personified. It was obviously linked to his having become a boarder, and therefore now an official church student, but who had done the brainwashing? At that time in my life there was no way that I could have suspected or concluded that he had been under pressure from an outside source to behave so differently. I just assumed it was his decision and from then on our friendship just ebbed away; but on looking back, relating to the experiences I had had, it must have been the result of very strong priestly pressure, using the family honour and pride, which changed Terry into a totally different individual, now striving to live up to the highest standards, which he continued to do for many years into his priesthood days, before taking a disastrously sad turn.

In my case the priesthood was never mentioned again, and I was going along enjoying life. I used to watch the Latics and Oldham Rugby virtually every home game, and Royton Cricket in the summer. I played for the Under-14s team, and continued to enjoy my cricket best of all. My school work was not improving, though. Doing homework was not easy, sharing the table with Winifred, whilst my dad listened to the radio ('wireless' in those days) and talked to my mum's Uncle Frank, a retired miner who had now come from his 'digs' in Wigan to live his elderly life with us, smoking his clay pipe. The front room was where my mum was still doing her sewing every night, so there was nowhere quiet for me to sit in order to concentrate. We did not have a single book in the house, not even a dictionary, and I began to regard homework as a chore, but that all changed, thanks to Fr Reynolds, our English teacher in the Lower Fifth. He knew how to make Shakespeare and poetry enjoyable and was a good motivator. Acting on his advice I began to read the Manchester Guardian, paying for it out of my spending money, and loved reading Neville Cardus, H D Davies' 'The Old International', Alistair Cooke, and the leading articles by C P Scott. Fr Reynolds also recommended the Central Library and its facilities with so many reference books which would help us to develop our understanding of our set texts, so quite a few of our class began to go there after school. It was to totally change my outlook on studying.

It was a culture shock for me when I stepped into that magnificent hall for the first time. I was surrounded by thousands of books all the way round the large circular room, rows of long tables with comfortable seats, and a totally silent atmosphere. People of all ages were seated reading, writing, and studying. Soon I was spending more time in that room than I did at home. My parents realised that it was much better for me to use the library's facilities, and soon I would be walking up the steps to my library seat at 4.30 pm, and apart from a quick break for a sandwich at Lyon's café, would stay until its doors closed at 9.00 pm. So I was arriving home at about 10.00 pm, five days a week and more or less straight to bed.

My homework was improving now. Firstly, it was the right environment to study without any distractions. Even more so were the books on the shelves. Now I began to read eminent scholars' comments and interpretations of Shakespeare's plays we studied, and I became absorbed by the theories and opinions they expressed. I had begun to enjoy the fact that my school work was improving and with each complimentary remark made by Fr Reynolds I gained in enthusiasm to do even better, not simply in Literature, which had started me off, but in other subjects too. My termly report at Easter said it all. Whereas at Christmas I had been placed 30th in Literature, at Easter I was top of the class. My parents were both full of encouragement for me to progress, but as they had never had any advanced schooling themselves, I think they felt powerless to help me. Now they could see what a difference using the Central Library had made.

Now I rarely ever had a book out of my hand, always reading on the bus, learning poems by heart and improving, and enjoying my other subjects too. I was constantly reciting my poems, and the two most memorable lines from John Keats' 'Ode on a Grecian Urn' seemed to sum up my philosophy, one that I had obviously inherited from my dad.

> *"Beauty is truth, truth beauty, – that is all*
>
> *Ye know on earth, and all ye need to know."*

These lines still reflect my attitude and personality, even though being blunt with the truth may have got me into hot water on occasions. I would never have made a diplomat!

Whilst I enjoyed my increasing number of hours studying in the Lower and especially Upper Fifth, my social life was widening too. I kept in touch with my pals in the 'gang' mainly in the school holidays, and on Saturday nights, following the years of family Oldham Repertory Theatre treats, I was palling out with Terry Langan and Geoff O'Brien, also my St Aidan's classmates. I was travelling to school by train now, with a free pass so my parents didn't have to find any bus fares for me, and Terry occasionally opened the carriage door for me as I was dashing on to the station with the train setting off before I had got on. Luckily there were no accidents! On Saturday nights it would be the best film we fancied at one of the 'pictures houses', before the compulsory pie and chips on the way home. Soon it would be a pint of beer (or two) before going to Tommy Smith's Savoy ballroom, but not just yet.

Cricket at Royton was thriving in the years after the war with lots of famous professionals in the league. In seasons 1948 and 49 we had the Australian Jock Livingston, a great batsman, who on one magnificent day shared a stand of 259 with Geoff Bispham, a famous Royton amateur, against Radcliffe who had the West Indies' future captain Frank Worrell as their professional. For the next two seasons Vijay Hazare, the Indian captain, was our pro. These were great years to watch league cricket, and I always had the hope and ambition to play for the team one day. That would still be a decade away though, as I played in the Under-14s and Under-15s school matches, and scoring my first ever 50 at Stoneyhurst College. Such moments kindle one's dreams, of course, and provide thrills and excitement. My Stoneyhurst 50 certainly did.

School and sport, watching and playing, were the two main preoccupations during my early teenage years. Working for a living seemed over the horizon but it wasn't. A summer holiday job was an attraction because of the spending money bonuses. I had earned my first ever wages at my dad's engineering business which he had started up with Harold Lawson following that 1947 winter, but these were only on a few days here and there. Now I was going to spend nearly two months at Heyside Co-op as the 'flour' boy. Mondays I spent in the back room filling blue bags of various sizes with sugar from a large heavy sack, weighing every bag with absolute accuracy so that not a grain was wasted – on the manager's orders. Then it was stacking shelves, unloading delivery vans, and countless other labouring jobs, but not serving customers. I was just a labourer. Then came the best part – delivering the weekly orders to customers' houses. The store bicycle had a large box, like a frame, above the front wheel, into which a basket was placed, filled with whatever the customer had ordered. I would slowly pedal my way to a house, deliver the order, gratefully accept the usual three pence tip, and cycle back to the store to collect my next order. I made sure I didn't hurry, so Thursdays and Fridays were the best days of the week. Saturday mornings were good too, especially in those days of rationing, when the manager allowed his staff to buy things like butter without coupons. My mum was delighted when I came home with a pound of butter on most Saturdays. By now she was running a shop herself. My parents had bought a wool shop in the centre of Royton, so she was doing less sewing but working all day in the shop. It was the following Christmas when I went abroad for the first time, on a school skiing holiday. I had never imagined that I could have ever had the chance to enjoy such a luxury but my dad's business was thriving, and he was thrilled himself to be able to pay for my holiday. Having endured life in the 'slump' between the two World Wars when it was a luxury to actually get a job, he was enjoying his business success. The holiday itself was an exciting experience for all of us who went to St Anton, Austria, but there could have been one or two unexpected cock-ups. Fortunately there were not. There must have been some last minute changes made to the schedule, and we realised later that the company the holiday had been booked with must have gone bust. Then on the holiday itself it must have been difficult for Fr Lindon, because he was the only adult in the party of thirty or more. And it would have been even more difficult, for him and some of us, if our train had not remained stationary for half an hour at a platform in France on our journey from Paris to Austria.

The whole group of us were spread across two railway compartments, and at about midnight we were all tired, sitting, falling asleep in our seats waiting for the train to set off again, when we were suddenly awakened and told to get off immediately. Apparently all those in the other compartment where Fr Lindon was sitting, had got off the train, gone into the station café to await our next train, and it wasn't for half an hour or so before Fr Lindon realised that nearly half the party were missing. Had the train moved on, who knows where we would have ended up – not skiing, that's for sure. Luckily we survived, reached St Anton, and had to make some moves from one boarding house to another until we were all accommodated under one roof. The skiing was brilliant, and we thoroughly enjoyed the holiday, enjoyed a few mischievous moments, which my good friend Arthur recalls, and we all returned better for the experience. Even better was one of the best decisions I ever made in my life – I stopped smoking. On our return journey, travelling through France, I bought a packet of French cigarettes, which tasted and smelled awful. I suppose that it was in my lofty and arrogant manner that I threw them away and announced that I would never smoke again. I was giving up. What a good move!

Back at school in 1952 we were six months or so from our 'O' Levels, and from now on it would be heads down and studying all the way, well most of the way. I still watched the Latics, who were improving now,

The Upper 5th Class 1952.
I am on the back row fourth from the left.

and Oldham Rugby who were also a team to be reckoned with, now with some outstanding players. I also played in the 2nd XI cricket team at school. My enthusiasm had slightly waned in the previous summer because there were very few matches, unless, like Arthur, you had been good enough to catch the 1st XI. The Stoneyhurst 50 had played its part for me, of course, and I had a good season in the 2nd XI.

Everyone focussed on the 'O' Levels, especially as in the previous summer, the first time that 'O' Levels had replaced the old School Certificate, we all realised that this new examination was at a higher standard than the old one, and the 1951 results had left very many entrants disappointed. Even the teachers were shocked by the lower success rates in most schools, so the pressure was on everywhere. Four subjects were regarded as sufficient to obtain a 6th Form place. That was most people's target. To my parents this was a totally different world than they had lived in, and they just hoped and prayed that I would do well. The exams came, went, and the school year ended. I worked at the Co-op again, and then the big day came. I went down for what might have been the final time to St Bede's to collect my exam results. Unbelievable! Five passes! English Language, English Literature, Maths, History and Greek. I couldn't get home fast enough. My mum and dad were ecstatic at my success. It was the first time in my life that

I had experienced the feeling that I had achieved something special. I certainly had worked hard since my Central Library studying began, but I appreciated the support I had received from my parents, given their own poorer childhood and disadvantaged earlier life experiences, which had enabled me, as they perceived it, to have climbed the social ladder, and have job security for life.

What job though? Did I want to work or study? For the past two years I had been an avid reader of books from Royton Library about lawyers winning court cases for their clients, and I dreamed of becoming a lawyer. I also dreamed of following Neville Cardus reporting cricket for the Guardian. However, reality clicked in. My dad took me to see his solicitor, George Cheetham, whom I recognised as a former Royton Cricket Club captain. He outlined the work a solicitor did, becoming articled at 16, learning to draw up wills, arrange the buying and selling of houses, with any court work on minor cases only. I never gave it a second thought. I was on cloud nine on having obtained my five 'O' levels, was basking in praise everyone had expressed on hearing of my success, and all I wanted to do was to enter the 6th form and continue studying.

Indeed from the day I learned of my 'O' level success I looked forward to continuing my studies. At the same time I was thoroughly enjoying my summer holidays. My Co-op wages were very handy, too. I was no longer spending them on cigarettes, but I had started to spend them on a pint or two of beer on a Friday and Saturday night in Oldham. We had begun to go to the Savoy ballroom, and it was always well crowded, with many attractive young ladies! So life was opening up gradually as the new term started, but in many ways it was something of an anti-climax. We were not being pushed to any high standards. Perhaps the staff philosophy was that sixth form pupils should motivate themselves and thus mature, but I'm afraid that with there being no serious exams for two more years, there always seemed plenty of excuses to leave the hard work until the following week. I invariably completed all the homework, of course, but never got into overdrive. The timetable included some study periods where we were unsupervised, and these soon became rest periods, or time when I could study something else – the racing paper!

I was a gambler now. How I started I cannot remember but one day I had a 35/2 winner, much to the envy of some of my school pals. Soon many of the lads were asking me for tips, and I was not just buying the Guardian every morning but a racing paper, too, studying form as I travelled on the train. Then at lunch time after we had walked down Alexandra Road to one of our sandwich shops, I would go a little further, into Moss Side, down a back alley, open a gate and step into a bookie's back yard. It was all illegal, of course, in those days. The yard had covered areas where the pencils hung down on string, enabling the punters to write out their bets. They had to write a *nom-de-plume* on their bets; mine was 'Sleeping Beauty', my favourite piece of classical music, which I was beginning to enjoy. Having made out my bet I would then tap on the door, a small flap would open, and I would hand over my money. It was much more exciting, of course, when my horse had won and I was tapping to collect my winnings!

Walk back to school, then at 4 o'clock, catch the 80 bus back to Peter's Square, and buy an Evening News to see if I'd backed a winner. I still studied in the Central Library every night until 9 o'clock, but the tea time break began to grow longer. There were one or two entertainment arcades on Oxford Road, and the temptation was difficult to resist. One of the lads who also enjoyed this was Frank Manning, younger brother of the soon to be famous Bernard. Life back at school was certainly enjoyable, but not for the reason I had imagined in my summer holidays.

Soon I became a bookie. I was putting bets on for some of the other lads, mainly the boarders who were not allowed to go off the school premises. They did not know the odds, because the only newspaper in the school was The Times, which in those days did not publish anything about horse racing, so I laid some of the bets off at the bookies, others I accepted myself. This was far more exciting than studying history or French, but I did complete all the schoolwork that the teachers set, but not with the same zeal that I had the year before. The freefall was gradual. I no longer raced to catch the 7.50 am train; it was easier to go on the 8.30 am, which Norman Bodell had always used, on his way to Xavarian College. We got on well, strolled from Victoria Station to Albert

Square, caught our separate buses and took life easy. I began to join him at weekends along with his pal Mike Beresford, and then with Eric Parker from Shaw who had palled up with us. We became a foursome for two or three years, and well beyond that too. We were all football fanatics, and Norman went on to become a professional footballer with Rochdale, and later went into management, coaching and scouting.

We were all Latics supporters, of course, and the 1952/3 season was fantastic, thanks to the great contribution of George Hardwick, the former England captain. He transformed the team, and it was at Bradford City when a no score draw ensured that we topped the Third Division. The crowd was so big it was difficult to find anywhere to see the game, so I climbed up the drainpipe on to the turnstile roof, along with many others. It was like being in an executive suite! When the final whistle blew everyone was ecstatic with Latics' supporters well out-numbering the Bradford ones. Champions! Alas there would only be one season in the Second Division, but thankfully we were not to know that as we celebrated.

Cricket also played a big part in my lower sixth year. I began in the 2nd XI in which I had played the year before, but was doing well and was selected for the 1st XI, batting at five or six. Playing in the 1st XI, be it at school or club level, is everyone's ambition, and now I had achieved it. My best pal Arthur Pownell, who had first caught the team while still in the lower fifth, was still opening the bowling, but an injury forced him to stop playing in mid-season. Mike Child was captain, and two others with whom I was very friendly, Mike Sedgewick and Len Whelan, were two of the outstanding members of the team. I adjusted to the higher level of play, but reserved my best innings of the season for the game at Xavarian College. The game was memorable for two other reasons than my match-saving innings, as a good friend of mine Paul Rocca, one of their team then, and later of amateur fame in the CLL, and of professional in other leagues, readily testifies. Xavarian batted first and made 122. Then we batted, and our wickets began to fall. I came to the crease, and played defensively, particularly against Joe May's round-arm swing bowling. Joe and I travelled on the same train to Manchester.

He caught it at Mumps station and always came in to our carriage. He was a real character, and he could drink too! On that day, though, friendship mattered not; runs and wickets did, and Joe kept appealing for LBW when he hit my pads.

Fr Coulthard, our team manager, was umpiring at Joe's end, and he explained to Joe that it was impossible for a bowler pitching the ball outside leg stump, to successfully claim an LBW decision. Joe was bowling round the wicket, so every one of his appeals was turned down. Joe was fuming, and at the start of the following over he threw his cap on to the grass at the end of his run instead of handing it to the umpire, who had infuriated him. Fr Coulthard turned round, and reminded him that if a batsman struck the ball which went on to touch his cap, it would count as five runs. Joe ignored him and bowled to me. Two balls later, I played a straight drive along the ground, hit Joe's cap, then on to the boundary. Fr Coulthard immediately signalled to the scorers "Nine runs. Five for hitting the cap. Four for the boundary". Never in my life, before or since, have I ever seen that happen. Certainly it cannot happen now because the ball is declared dead after hitting a cap. If Joe had been angry before he seemed suicidal now! Then came the second memorable incident. Our score was 54 for 9, with me 31 not out. Suddenly Fr Coulthard took off the bails, announced to the Rev Brother Cyril, who was umpiring at the other end, that we would have to end the game at that moment because, "Our students are to attend Benediction." So the match was drawn. We had not been beaten. The Xavarian team were not happy chappies. Nothing has provided more banter between Paul Rocca and me than the recollections of that game, adding to the inter-school rivalry.

The same day was a memorable one at Lord's too, when Trevor Bailey and Willie Watson battled defensively to save the Test Match, which later in the summer would end with Dennis Compton hitting the winning run to celebrate the Ashes Victory at The Oval. That stroke I saw on television, just as I had watched the Matthews' Cup Final and the Queen's Coronation, in the first year we ever had a TV. All those events were memorable that year – but not nearly as memorable as our Benediction day. Even Paul would confirm that, albeit reluctantly!

Within a few weeks the term had ended and another summer holiday began, but this time I couldn't be bothered to get a job. I spent much of the time studying the racing paper and was betting every day. Suddenly, however, just as it had happened when I gave up smoking, I kicked my betting habit. I had run out of money, embarrassingly so. It was even more embarrassing for my mum, whose wool shop in Royton centre was next to Barclay's Bank. One day the manager came in to tell her that I had overdrawn my account by £2. Obviously this was not much by today's standards, but all accounts then had to be in credit – certainly mine had, and I was saving up to buy a drop-handlebar bicycle, and at one stage I had about £40 saved. I had wanted about £10 more and I could have joined another of my pals from St Aidan's, Edward Taylor, who was enjoying going on long cycle rides at weekends. Once my betting increased so did my withdrawals from the bank, and now I was overdrawn. My mum was not happy. She obviously knew much more about my betting than I had realised, and seemed very worried. I must have done some hard thinking about my way of life and decided not to have another bet. I stuck to my word for some thirty years, when there was another memorable moment, after I had placed £100 on a double, at Aintree, on Grand National day – and won!

Meanwhile, in 1953, I was soon back for what should have been my last year at St Bede's, promising myself to put all my bad habits behind me, to work hard, apply for a University place, and try to pass my 'A' levels in Literature, History and French. By and large I worked conscientiously during the year, but there was one big distraction – cricket! It began fairly soon after we had returned in September when it became known that Fr Hanlon would be taking over from Fr Coulthard as the 1st XI coach/manager. The first thing he did was to appoint me as the team captain, more than six months before the start of the season. Once again I was on cloud nine, thrilled by the honour, yearning for the season to begin. I began to read one cricket book after another. Neville Cardus, Jack Fingleton, and countless others became my travelling companions, at least they seemed to be, as I analysed their writings on the art of captaincy, and the many great players and Test Matches they described.

During the autumn and spring terms I perhaps balanced my school work and cricket reading fairly well, but things would be different during the final, and crucial, summer term, when the exams took place.

I had been offered places at two or three universities, conditional upon my 'A' level results, and during the year I studied in the Central Library until 9 o'clock virtually every night. I needed to, of course, because I had quite a lot of catching up to do following my wasted lower sixth year. Alas, when the summer term started my focus was on one thing – cricket. During the Easter holidays I had practised in the nets at Royton, and had been offered the captaincy of the under 18s team, another honour, but one I knew it was impossible for me to accept. All the under 18 games were played on Monday evenings, which was our net practice night at school. There was no way I could have been back to Royton in time, so I had to decline the offer. There was a similar clash on Saturdays. I was now eager to catch the Royton 2nd XI, but all our school matches were played in the afternoon, so it was not until the end of the school year that I could become available for Royton, by which time they had a settled team, so I only managed to play the occasional game.

At school I loved my season as captain, strongly supported by Fr Hanlon who had been the 2nd XI coach during the previous two years, and who had described me as 'already a good batsman' in Baeda, the school magazine. Field placing, bowling changes, general motivational tactics, and other captaincy responsibilities – all these I found absorbing, and I enjoyed helping to organise, and be influential, at net practices. I spotted Dave McGarry, then only a lower fifth pupil, bowling his leg-breaks in the school yard, and persuaded Fr Hanlon to give him a place in the team. He did. It worked. Dave became an outstanding bowler, and batsman, and a good friend too! By the end of the season I had thoroughly enjoyed the captaincy experience, but not having scored enough runs myself I felt my batting should have been better.

So should my 'A' level results. During that final term when every minute of the day should have been spent revising, it wasn't, and I failed in all three subjects. The contrast between the 'O' level celebratory feelings two years before, and now that of utter failure, was immense. I knew that I had let my parents down, and felt embarrassed and ashamed. Two years previously I had been walking around Royton hoping that people would ask me if I had done well in my exams. Now I didn't want to meet anyone. The sooner my call up for National Service came, the better, was what went through my mind.

I had already got a summer holiday job, this time working as an electrician's labourer, for Maurice Lees, at the Roy Mill. The wages were good, and again useful at weekends spent with Norman, Mike and Eric, in the same routine, drinking, dancing and hoping for an enjoyable last waltz. St Bede's swiftly went out of my mind, but it came back just before the new school year started, when my dad sat me down to have a word. He suggested that it would be better for me to go back for a third year in the sixth form, and to try to pass some 'A' levels, rather than leave with none at all. He persuaded me that I would have a better chance of being successful, and, after all, I had only just turned eighteen. I was totally surprised at his suggestion, but what he said made sense the more I thought about it, and the school agreed to accept me for a further year. My subjects would be Literature, History, and instead of French I would take Scripture, and be taught on a tutorial basis by one of the priests.

The term began well. I was full of determination to pass my exams, but once again life at school was different. Those in the 3rd year sixth didn't form part of the upper sixth group, but were based in an upstairs library, used as our study room, from which we moved to the classroom for, in my case, just two subjects. There was no register, no one checked if we were late, or even in school at all, and any discipline involved had to be self-imposed. I did not drift back into my lower sixth mode when gambling had taken over, but the repetition of the syllabus in History and Literature somehow failed to ignite my initial eagerness to achieve success. Maybe I never really had the academic ability to go much higher, and I think the total freedom we had slowly ebbed away at my determination to do well. And then, of course, cricket! As soon as I had returned in September our new coach/manager Fr Pessagnio, re-appointed me as captain for the following season, so once again as

Easter approached, at the height of the swotting period, my mind was back between the wickets. I had the full support of all the team, and my sheer love of the game took over. It would not be the first nor the last summer that cricket dominated my life, but in doing so that year there was one unexpected bonus.

During my time as the 1st XI captain I had responsibility for various matters delegated by Fr Pessagnio, and often I would be in charge of the net practices on Mondays. Nearby were the 2nd XI and under 14 team nets, and on some occasions I would offer them advice, acting as a coach to those coming through the system. Advice on bowling actions, batting stances and other techniques helps players to develop and I enjoyed helping them. And it was after one such session

First XI 1955.

Back Row: (L to R) 'Fat' Carter, Graham Ryan, Tom Rabbit, Ian Galleymore, John Fitzpatrick, Vinny Needham, John Glennon, John Brandreth

Front Row: Denis Wright, Len Whelan, Me, Fr Pessagno, John McMahon, Dave McGarry, Ken Redfern

that I came home with a feeling of satisfaction that I had helped some of the younger players to improve, and felt, too, that they had appreciated it – and this led me to wonder if helping other people would be a good career for me. Should I become a teacher?

The feeling stayed with me, and as I never had any financial motivations career-wise, I warmed to the idea, sought my parents' thoughts on it, and long before I had received my National Service call-up papers I had settled on my future career, at least in my own mind. My decision to apply to go to a teacher training college pleased my parents. They saw it as a step up from our working-class way of life, where people had been vulnerable to redundancy and, through their eyes, brought up in the 1920s, their son would become a respected member of society. Things were changing, of course, and would change more rapidly later, but at the time I wanted to teach, having absolutely genuine vocational ambitions. Some sixth formers who wanted to keep on studying but were unable to get a university place regarded going to a teacher training college as a second best option. I did not. It was my career choice, and throughout my thirty years I never lost the feeling of achievement and satisfaction in having helped, explained and motivated pupils to improve, understand and enjoy their studies.

Perhaps I needed someone like that during my final year at St Bede's, because in so many ways I was becoming something of a rebel. Most teenagers go through such a phase, and it is better to get it out of one's system earlier rather than later, but I think there were times when my dad despaired about my anti-this, anti-that attitude, and on one occasion told me I sounded like a communist. Certainly I had become very critical of some of the Catholic Church's strict authoritarianism. Eating meat on a Friday a mortal sin? Attending any service in a non-Catholic church another mortal sin? Those were trivial matters, and have since been abandoned, but fifty years ago the church insisted it was unchangeable. By this time, too, I had ceased to be an altar server. For a year or two I had been the senior one, thus the one to carry the cross and lead the church procession round Royton on Trinity Sunday, and while everyone's time on the altar comes to a close, mine reflected the increasing unease I felt about the church generally.

Not only was I rebellious, I was rude. Maybe I still am, but I can still recall one incident when I was lucky to get away with it. It was early in my final year in a History lesson, taught by Fr Burke, the senior priest of the college. I had written the required piece of homework on a topic he had set, and it was my turn to read it aloud. In my essay I included a statement made by an American historian (one that I had completely invented, implying that I had researched well to complete my work), and when I mentioned the historian's name, Fr Burke interjected, "I've never heard of him!" To which I instantly replied, "I don't suppose he's ever heard of you, Father." I got away with it, but if looks could have killed I would not be writing this now. Perhaps it was a good thing that I would soon be joining the RAF.

As senior altar boy, carrying the cross on Trinity Sunday

It was during those final weeks at St Bede's, eagerly anticipating life after school that I also looked back upon the years I had spent there, and begun to appreciate what it had done for me. I knew I owed a great deal to the college, staff and also fellow pupils, who had helped to provide the foundation upon which I could build my future. No doubt I had taken things for granted, but when as an 18 year old I looked back, I was just a lad from Royton, from a two-up and two-down terraced house, striding confidently and arrogantly through my days at a college dating back to 1876, rich in tradition, highly respected in the religious and academic world. It had accepted me for what I was, and offered me encouragement and opportunities, some of which I had eagerly grasped, especially in the 'O' level period, and the cricketing honours most of all; but others I had let slip through my fingers, ceasing to study conscientiously enough as the outside world offered some of the temptations to which I had succumbed. But even allowing for the moments of my rebelliousness, my strangest feeling was one of pride in having attended St Bede's. There was an understandable rivalry between ourselves and the De La Salle and Xavarian pupils, but we knew they all envied the senior status that St Bede's had – demonstrated on the sporting field by the top schools we played against at cricket, football and rugby, whereas they could never aspire to the prestige fixture list which included Bolton School, King's College Macclesfield, Stoneyhurst, and MGS. Ours did! I think I also appreciated the freedom, tolerance and trust that was part of the philosophy of the school, enabling maturing minds wrestle with adolescent doubts but stay within the flexible disciplinary system. Certainly at the point when I was preparing to leave I was a very different person from the 10 year old who had turned up for my first day in 1946, but it was only after I had left that I fully appreciated what I owed to St Bede's.

Perhaps it was appropriate, then, that the last full day I would spend there was one of the best, the annual Past v Present cricket match, usually played on the Sunday of the final week of the school year. There was something of a re-union atmosphere as the 'Old Boys' arrived, meeting up again, and the game attracted quite a few spectators including many of the priests. The game was always played in a good spirit, and the umpires usually gave their 'Old Boy' friends the benefit of the doubt in LBW, stumping or run out appeals! The game commenced in the late morning, but we stopped for our lunch break at 1.00 pm, and this was what made the day the best in the year for every one of the boarders, whether they liked cricket or not. It was their biggest feast in the school calendar. The boarders always grumbled and complained that they never had enough to eat all the year round, but on Past v Present day everyone was served fresh salmon, and plenty of it! The 'Old Boys' and the 1st XI were seated at the top table, headed by the college Rector Monseignor Duggan, where the first large tray was served on which the huge salmon sat. We all helped ourselves to as much as we wanted, and passed the tray down the table. It was sheer luxury. At home we felt it must be Christmas if we had a tin of salmon. I'd never seen a fresh salmon before my first Past v Present match.

Unsurprisingly it was usually a lengthy lunch break, and members of the Old Boys joined the staff behind closed doors for a quiet drink, after which we strolled back to the field to complete the match. The result was often a draw, with honours even. Always an enjoyable day, and in that my final one, it led to a very enjoyable week too. The Old Boys went on an annual tour, and they were having difficulties in getting a full squad, and they enquired if any of our team wished to join them. I jumped at the chance, and looked forward to meeting up with them in five or six weeks' time, along with Len Whelan, Dave McGarry and John Glennon.

It was on this exciting note that my last full day was completed, and other than the morning some weeks later when I went to discover my examination results.

My links with Old Bedians generally were strong, mainly through the cricket tours and other Sunday matches I would play for the next few years, but as someone who lived in Royton, and no other Old Bedians living nearby, leading a busy life myself, my links with others gradually faded into the memory, an accident of location, not intent. No such excuse for my examination results, though. This time I passed one subject at 'A' level, Literature. Enough said!

Meanwhile I was now an electrician's labourer at the Roy Mill. Stepping into a cotton mill for the first time must have shocked everyone, with the noise simply deafening, machines clanging away all day. People had to lip read, they simply could not talk or shout loud enough to be heard. I had been first introduced to mill life the previous Christmas when I worked at The Spinning Company as a labourer for Ronnie Dewhirst. There the biggest challenge was to avoid breathing in the cotton itself as we walked through the blowing room in order to reach the mill canteen. Cotton was everywhere. No wonder the workers wore masks over their mouths and noses.

Now I was working for Maurice Lees, and I enjoyed the experience and the wages too. The days were long, 7.30 am start until 5.30 pm, but I was glad I wasn't one of those having to spend all day glued to their machines. Maurice had two other labourers, and he was re-wiring the frames which involved drilling and various other engineering skills. My overalls soon became full of oil and grease, and like everyone else I had two sets so that one could be cleaned each week. Well, not everyone had two sets – Billy, who brewed up for Maurice's men, just wore the same one every day. It was filthy, covered in grease, and the way he brewed up was gruesome. He collected the four pint pots, took them to the 'brew' room, attempted to clean his greasy right hand by wiping it underneath his left armpit, and then dipped his whole hand into the tin full of tea leaves. He shook some into each pint pot, then dipped his hand into the tin of sugar, again shaking it into each pot. He filled them up with water from the boiler and then took out his screwdriver, wiped that under his armpit, and stirred each pot. Gruesome or not, though, his pots of tea tasted great.

I worked at the Roy Mill every week between leaving school and beginning my National Service, except for the week of the Old Bedian's cricket tour. We all travelled by coach from Manchester on the Sunday morning, and played our first game at Shrewsbury on the way down to Leominster, which was our base for the week. Everyone played three or maybe four of the five games, and helped out with umpiring and scoring. It was a fine week, no rain, plenty of cricket and cricket chat, and that was usually in the hotel bar, until quite late. So late that on some nights the owner went to bed and one of the trusted senior players was left in charge of the bar. Apparently it happened every year.

There was a special friendly atmosphere during each game between the two teams, and we were made very welcome, both on the field and in their club bar afterwards. Very different from the great rivalry that I had just begun to experience in the Central Lancashire League, where players rarely spoke to their opponents on or off the field, the rivalry being so fierce. It was something of a new experience playing in countryside cricket grounds, seemingly in the middle of nowhere; with fields all around by contrast with the League grounds surrounded by seats and boundary rails. I enjoyed the whole week, but best of all the game at Ross-on-Wye, where I scored a 50. Scoring a 50 is always special, particularly when you don't score many, and I never did. The following day we played at Leominster, the only ground I ever played on where a large tree stood thirty yards in from the boundary. Finally we played the last match of the tour on our way home, at Shifnal, and that Friday evening I was bidding a long farewell to Len, Dave, John and the rest of the Old Boys, before making my way home.

Just over a month later I was saying farewell to my Mum and Dad too, for on Tuesday October 6th 1955, I caught the train to Cardington. I was no longer a student, or an electrician's labourer, but Airman "2772895, Sir."

3 National Service

I was one of countless eighteen year-olds who had been granted deferment from National Service, but once I had left school I went to complete the formalities, preparing for the next two years. The man behind the desk asked me which one of Her Majesty's Services I would like to apply for. I said "Which is the easiest?" To which he replied, "The RAF". Instantly, I said "RAF please." Then he said, "Do you wish to fly?" "Don't I have to?" I asked. "No," he said. "No, it is then," I said, and a few weeks later I received my call-up papers.

There were tears in my mum's eyes as I kissed her goodbye, setting off for the train to Cardington. I was moving into unknown territory that day, and even though I knew many lads who had completed their two years, and had given me advice, I felt understandably apprehensive that morning. I was confident about what I was going to do first, though, before I would catch my train – go for a haircut! My mum would not let me have a crew-cut, which had become trendy then. I had to keep my wavy hair with its parting. But I knew that if I reached Cardington like that the RAF barber would shave it off and leave me with an extremely 'short-back-and-sides'. So once I arrived in Manchester I went to a popular barber's for a decent crew-cut, and then smiled my way to the station.

Relaxing in our week at Cardington.
I am 2nd left, back row.
Peter Greene to my left

Many of the carriages were more or less full of lads of my age, all on their call-up day too, and one of them was Peter Greene, a lad from Rochdale whom I had known when we had played against each other at cricket, he being a De La Salle student. We got on very well, and our future lives would run on fairly parallel lines, and we would become and remain good friends. When we reached Cardington, however, there was not much time for being friendly with anyone – it was do what you are told time. The week was full of medicals, checks, tests, trying on the uniform, and generally making sure everyone in the barracks was prepared for the training to come.

That, for me, and Peter Greene, was to be at West Kirby, and for the next eight weeks, he and I slept in the next bed to each other with about twenty in our billet. This was 'square-bashing' time. Orders were barked at us, all day, and every day. We were marched everywhere and hardly had a moment to ourselves as we cleaned, polished, tidied, everything we wore, bed clothes, the lot! The corporals were the worst, out and out bullies, just having got their two stripes on their shoulders. They seemed to be trying to out-shout each other, especially on the parade ground, when there would be five or six billets full of recruits being frogmarched, learning how to march, left turn, right turn, halt, eyes right, eyes left, whatever. We even got marched to the toilets – but only to the door, thankfully.

There were some moments though, amid the intense disciplinary atmosphere, when we could not stop laughing. There would be the occasional "Left, Right" order when one recruit would get his timing wrong, and being on the wrong foot, caused a pile up as the one behind caught his foot and overbalanced. Corporals went mad at the mayhem, and we would be desperately trying to keep our faces straight. On one occasion the recruit on the front right hand line failed to hear the corporal call out "Left Wheel," and as everyone wheeled to the left, the front lad continued marching on his straight ahead, eyes forward, totally unaware for about twenty yards that he was by himself. We were all watching him as he suddenly realised what he had done. We were all delirious. Even the corporal seemed to think it was funny. There must have been something human under his helmet after all! Moments such as those relieved the tension.

So, too, did the way we were paid, when we had to stand smartly and salute the officer, reciting the last three digits of our number, followed by 'Sir.' No-one who has served in the armed forces can have forgotten his number. 2772895 was mine, so it was '895, Sir' every pay day – not that there was much money in the packet. There was enough, though, to pay my train fare home after four weeks at West Kirby when we had been given the token 48-hour pass, and a momentous week-end it was too. I went with my dad to watch Oldham Rugby play the almost invincible Wigan, the team my Uncle Frank supported. Oldham gave Wigan the biggest drubbing at home in their history. We won 48-23. What a wonderful 48-hour pass that had been! I never let my uncle Frank forget it, either.

The next four weeks soon slipped by, and it ended with our Passing Out Parade, to which all our parents were invited. Soon we were being applauded by the large crowd of spectators as we made our final marches, demonstrating that we were fully trained airmen. My parents enjoyed it, having driven to West Kirby, and soon the car was full of my RAF kit ready for the drive home. Before that, though, it was handshakes all round, as everyone in our billet would be going to a different RAF camp after the ten-day Christmas leave period. My posting was to Wellesbourne Mountford, near Stratford-upon-Avon, for twelve weeks on a photography course. I had been fortunate to be allocated a place, for they were usually only given to airmen who had signed up for four years, so I looked forward eagerly to my first day at the attractive sounding camp.

What a rude awakening I had! It was a bleak winter, and the camp was covered in snow. Its facilities were primitive. Each billet contained thirty beds, and even though I managed to grab one near to one of the two fires, my washing bag had a film of ice on it all day. Our wash-house and toilets were fifty yards away, and we froze as we made our way to them at 6.30 every morning. Then the photography started – but not the way I had imagined it would. We never came near to a camera. All we were being trained to do was process films, those taken from aircrafts. All the glamorous ideas of my becoming a photographer vanished. And soon we began to realise that once the course was over we would be posted to Cyprus, not the holiday resort it is today, but the battleground of the Greek and Turkish armies. So many British troops were being sent out that there was insufficient accommodation for them, and it would be a camping site for us. However, it turned out not to be so. As luck had it I failed the photographic examination test at the end of the course – not a new experience for me, in failing examinations! So I was posted to Halton, one of hundreds of airmen, some of whom would be part of the RAF PE Display Team, televised at the Royal Albert Hall memorial service.

There were already too many airmen sent to Halton for this display team, but we were all given a chance to be selected. I never had a chance with my low level of PE skills, but I had a chance of getting 'jankers' for a week when I spoke to a sergeant in the gym. He had us all lined up in our shorts and said something to me about muscles. I said, "I haven't got a muscle in my body, Sergeant." He looked at me, walked towards me without saying a word, while I waited for the imminent blast. He looked at me, then said, "Yes, I see what you mean." Thankfully, he had a sense of humour. I would not have got away with that at West Kirby. There was another unusual encounter when I was on guard duty one night after I had saluted an officer who was passing by. He spoke to me, and when I replied he recognised my Lancashire accent, so he went on to ask where I came from. "Oldham, Sir," said I. "Which part of Oldham?" "Royton, Sir." Then he told me that he too was from Royton, and it turned out that he was from the Jinks family from our parish, and he had known my dad many years before. It did not take me long, two or three days later, to enquire of him if I might be granted a 48 hour pass. He even gave me a 72 hour pass. What a good chance meeting!

Soon I was on my way to Nuneham Park, Oxfordshire, signing in on my first day there, when one officer asked me "Do you row?" in a very posh accent. Remembering our enjoyable Sunday afternoons having fun in the rowing boats, splashing at each other, flirting with girls we fancied, on the shallow Alexandra Park lake in Oldham, I replied, "Yes, Sir." "Jolly good, jolly good," he said, and walked off. What a strange question, I thought. I had not realised that this was indeed rowing territory, near Henley, and near the River Thames, University boat race country. Luckily I did not have to prove my rowing skills, and was soon signing out, this time to be seconded to Benson, the camp where the Queen's Flight was based.

There would be no royal duties for me at Benson, however, where I would remain for the rest of my National Service. My duties would be confined to the bomb bay site, half a mile or so outside the main camp. There were no bombs there now, but it was where they had been stored during the war. It was now used as a storage base for every RAF film. I spent my first two or three days absolutely bored to death. Vans would come to a bay, and a line of eight or ten of us would pass cans left to right from the van into the bay and on to the shelves. Then we would reverse the process, this time right to left, from the bay to the van, until off it would go for whatever they wanted the films for. The thought of spending the next eighteen months doing that even made me wish I had passed the photographic exam.

"A C Cleary." said the Sergeant as we were rearranging the tins of films the following day. "Yes Sergeant." I said. "Come with me," he ordered, so I followed him to the small office building where the officer wished to speak to me. Apparently my records had now been delivered to the camp, and the officer had seen my education results, noting that I had an 'A' level in English. The section had recently lost the services of a qualified clerk, could not replace him, and the officer wondered if I would like to do his duties. When being offered the choice of standing in lines all day passing and stacking tins of films, no doubt in freezing cold during winter, or sitting in a warm office, completing paperwork, answering the telephone, doing errands for the officer and sergeant, who spoke politely, not barked – I was obviously only too delighted to accept.

It must have been during those early days at Benson that I wrote an apologetic letter to my mum for my behaviour at home. I have not the slightest recollection of ever having written it, or of knowing that it had been in my possession since my mum's death in 1990. I had been looking through the contents of a large envelope containing various family documents and certificates when I came across a small sealed envelope addressed to me.

TO BE OPENED ONLY BY JOHN
KEEP SAFE. PRIVATE LETTERS

On opening it, in 2004, I discovered two letters, both written by me during my National Service years, now almost fifty years ago. I was stunned when reading my own words from so long ago, looking, as it were, at myself through an historical mirror.

2772895 A.C.2 Cleary J
C.N.L
R.A.F. Benson
Oxon.
Monday Night
14.5.56

Dear Mum

Because of the constant moving about that I have had to do recently it has not been possible for me to answer that part of the letter which you wrote to me whilst I was at Halton appertaining to my speech, conduct and manners in general. I have not the letter in front of me now, for I am on duty here at the section, and as with most of my kit it is back at the billet. But I can, I think, remember quite plainly what you wrote and how you feel. It is not easy to attempt to answer it properly either, no doubt it did not come to your head quite so easily as the usual everyday conversation does.

What I want to say is that for all the things I have said, for the things that I have done, the things that I have omitted to do when I should have done them, or anything else that has hurt you – I am sorry. It is easy to feel sorry, but it not easy to face up to things and I say it; that, I am afraid, is where I slip up. Usually when I say something I shouldn't I do not realise it until it is too late, and then the damage is done. You, maybe, don't say anything because I am not at home all the time and the mistake is let pass – but your feelings and my conduct are no better for it.

Believe me, Mum, I don't try to say or do things that you don't like – and I am now more determined than ever to put things right. Since I came into the RAF and have been meeting people and weighed up what they are and what kind of families they have I have had my eyes opened. Only lately have I fully realised how well done to I have been.

All the hard work and struggling that you and dad have put in to give me and Winifred a better chance than you had has always, since I was in my early teens, say, been apparent. But never has it been more obvious than it is now. And yet by the way that I have reacted to your love, generosity and kindness one would have hardly thought it possible. It seems, when I have thought (and there is plenty time for thought for everyone in the Forces), or talked about home amongst the lads with whom I have made close friends, obvious that I have not been the son I should have been. To come to this conclusion is not pleasant either – and it makes me feel very small, especially when I get a parcel from you like the one I opened not many minutes ago. It really is a smasher. Thanks a million!

However, it is better to face up to it now, and resolve, which I do, to do better. It is not possible, I know, for me to make up to you all that I owe you – no child could do this. But I will do my best to show how much I really appreciate all you have done for me in future. This is a promise.

My coarse manners and poor speech go hand in hand with this, and I shall strive, without adopting swank (and there is swank) to put myself in order. What I have just written may be in parts "wordy", or lacking, in appearance, in sincerity. But I am sincere. What I am trying to do is convey to you my thoughts, and words do not come easily at times.

And though sentimentality does not play a big part in my life I would like you to know that I know that I have the best Mum and Dad in the world. When I think, too, of the chances that you have given me, that I have failed to take, I am more and more determined to alter.

Just have a bit of confidence, and slowly but surely, I shall make you proud of me.

It will be better, perhaps, if you do not show Winifred this: and, anyway, what does she want for her Birthday?

Good Night, God Bless,
& All the Best,
from your loving son

John

The fact that in my letter I accepted her criticisms of my attitude and manner of speaking may have given my mum a glimmer of hope that I would improve. I hope it did, and the fact that she kept the letter all her life must have meant she treasured it. Almost fifty years later, so do I, especially if it did indicate a turning point in my life, and fewer worries for my mum.

That week at Benson was certainly the start of better things RAF-wise. Not only did I have my cushy office job, but I had the section's bicycle too. Instead of having to line up with the other lads to be marched to and from the bomb bays every morning and afternoon, I used the section bicycle. And it went better. It was my job to collect the post for all the section members, which gave me an extra half an hour in the billet to read my morning newspaper before the post had been sorted. I still bought the Manchester Guardian, but the local newsagent who delivered them did not receive delivery of the Guardian until 11 o'clock, but I ordered it nevertheless, each day reading the previous day's edition. I had time to read the paper on some afternoons too. There were items to be collected for everyone in the billet, such as clean sheets, and this was another of my jobs, leaving the section at least an hour before the others. It was also my cycle in the evening and at weekends, and more than once I cycled to Oxford to enjoy a day there. National Service was becoming very enjoyable. It was especially enjoyable for me in that I had been posted there in early May, at the beginning of the cricket season, and I was offered a place in the section team, and played a good innings in my first match, against another section, which must have attracted the attention of one of the officers involved in the Station Cricket Team.

Soon I was playing cricket three days each week. Wednesdays were the inter-section match days; the Station Teams would play on a Tuesday or Thursday, and if we were playing away we would travel by coach – and I may have had to leave the office at 11 o'clock to do so. Then on Saturdays I began to play for a local village team two or three miles away. What an unexpectedly pleasant summer I had. At Benson, where our section was not formally part of the station, everything felt more civilised, if not civilianised. We never had to do general duty, or go on the parade ground, except on The Queen's Birthday, when, after the formalities, everyone was given the day off. We more or less stuck together as a group, using the Naafi, competing against each other at snooker and darts, but there was none of the West Kirby atmosphere.

It was during the summer when playing for the Station Team that I noticed how friendly and civil the officers were. After one game when I had failed to score the captain sat next to me on the coach journey back to the camp and not only reassured me that I would keep my place on the team throughout the season, but he talked to me, not down to me, and called me John, just as a friend would. It was the same when we had a drink after a game, the atmosphere in the bar was just as in one's local pub, all equals. I noticed, though, how corporals and sergeants were always very polite to the officers. Understandably, maybe, when it was their career, and currying favour might assist their promotion. For me as a National Serviceman with no such ambitions, it did not apply, and I could joke and enjoy the fun on equal terms.

I was not treated on equal terms in one match though, when a sergeant was umpiring. I was having a good innings when the officer batting at the other end called for a run when there was definitely not a run on. I did not step out of my crease, having called "No" instantly. The officer continued to run to my end, and the bails were taken off at the striker's end. By the rules of cricket I was not out, never having left my crease. The umpire looked at me, raised his finger, and off I went to the pavilion. I think he knew what I was thinking, but I never commented on the decision.

If there was a Wednesday or Saturday when there was no match arranged I would often go to Oxford. I just loved the atmosphere in such an historic city. The University buildings I had never seen the like of before, and walking into one of the quadrangles was just like stepping back in time. There were many bookshops, and just as I had done in Manchester in my Central Library days, I loved spending time in the second hand bookshops in Oxford. Perhaps there was a feeling of nostalgia, too, walking around such an educational environment, bringing back the better memories of my student days. Whatever it was I simply loved to spend hours absorbing the atmosphere, and discovering more of its long history.

I travelled further than Oxford, too, on some weekends, whenever I had a 48 hour pass. It was tricky to get the timing right, and in order to arrive home on Friday night I needed to be given to leave Benson early in the afternoon. The best way was to keep my uniform on, and thumb a lift towards Birmingham, then catch the train from there. Thumbing a lift is not easy if dressed in 'civvies', but in uniform I could more or less pick and choose which vehicle I wanted. I would enjoy a full Saturday at home, well perhaps not quite a full Saturday. The evenings were spent with my pals in Oldham, of course, having a typical teenage night out. I always enjoyed them, but the best one of all was when Oldham Rugby played Hull at Odsal Stadium in the League Championship Final. I had made sure I got my 48-hour pass that weekend, and Saturday May 18, 1957, is still one of the best days in the club's history – but it nearly wasn't. Oldham had dominated most of the game, and seemed to be cruising to victory, when they conceded two late tries. Then in the final minute Hull were just one point behind with a conversion to come. My dad and I were standing behind the goals along with thousands of other Oldham supporters and we watched in nervous silence as their full back placed the ball. He kicked, and it was followed by the loudest roar of the day, as we could see that the ball was going wide. The great escape!

We came back to Oldham, stood outside the Town Hall, watched our great team step off their coach to loud cheers, then I joined my pals for a good night out. The following day would have been a normal Sunday for me, beginning with the 11 o'clock Mass, Sunday lunch, get changed into my uniform, when, in the early afternoon, my mum and dad would drive me to the south of Manchester, from where I would thumb my way back to Benson. We used to get a 48-hour pass once a month, so I was able to keep in touch with my parents, friends, aunts and uncles reasonably often, far more than those who had been posted abroad, and might not be home for over a year. I would write a letter every week to tell my parents how I was doing, and my mum would write each week too, and also send me a parcel every week – with some of her home made cake. It was always delicious.

Playing cricket for the local team meant that I saw quite a lot of the many small country hamlets and villages in that part of the world, and very attractive they were too – and with none of the smoke-filled skies I had grown up under! The nearest town to our camp was Wallingford, and we would often visit the cinema there, enjoy a drink or two in their friendly pubs, and sometimes on Saturdays watch the large number of people rowing on the River Thames. To someone brought up on cricket and football, the popularity of rowing in Oxfordshire seemed amazing.

In the billet there were about twenty beds, and as one airman was demobbed his bed was soon taken by another. There was a good atmosphere, and virtually all the lads got on well, with Cockneys, Brummies, Scots, northerners, all with our different accents. All with our different backgrounds, too; more of which later. Two of the lads I was most friendly with were Mike Holland, known as 'Dutch', and Malcolm Scholar, a Yorkshireman. There was plenty of rivalry in the billet, too, mainly on sporting matters, especially football. We all had our favourite teams, and 'Haggis', the Scotsman in the next bed to me, was a Rangers fanatic. He was an 'F' word fanatic too, and it got him into a scrape once. There had been an incident during the working hours when the sergeant had criticised him, whereupon 'Haggis' swore at him. He was put on a charge, which took place at the main camp headquarters, and I was given the role of being his escort. There was a new, younger, officer hearing the charge, and, rather surprisingly, instead of accepting the sergeant's word against Haggis's, a mere AC1, he deferred the case for a week. All the odds were still stacked against him of course, and seven or fourteen days jankers was everyone's best guess. Then the film at Wallingford cinema the following week was '12 Angry Men', involving the court case where one member of the jury, on his own initially, votes 'not guilty,' and in the next two hours persuades every other juror to do the same. I escorted Haggis once again and the officer finally let him off. We thought the officer must have also been to the same film, and perhaps as an inexperienced officer he felt he did not have enough proof. Haggis was a very lucky lad.

I do not recall any of the others in our billet to be placed on a charge. In my own case I was obviously better behaved at Benson than in Royton, at least in my mum's opinion. Time moved by and I had been accepted at Hopwood Hall Teacher Training College in Middleton, near to our home, so I applied for an early release from the Air Force to enable me to attend the course when it was to begin in early September. My request was granted, so after another summer of successful cricket, I prepared firstly to celebrate my 21st birthday, then have my two weeks' leave, shortly after which I would be taking off my uniform.

The second letter which my mum kept, again of which I had not the slightest recollection of having written, was obviously not in response to any comments either of my parents had made, but must have been based on the thoughts in my head as my 21st approached. Sitting on one's bed in a billet for hours on end, as we all did, and had to, gave everyone plenty of time to think, and this letter certainly reveals, long-windedly perhaps, how I felt at the time.

2772895 AC Cleary J
CNL
RAF Benson
Oxon
16.7.1957

Dear Mum & Dad

In a few days I shall be twenty one years old. The event is regarded as significant in everyone's life, just as, only to a greater degree, a wedding is. And yet no change takes place with the marking of a birthday – it is just another day which starts nothing and ends nothing. Yet according to law, customs and tradition the coming of age marks the entrance to adult life – after this stage one can do all sorts of things at will and get away with it.

Life, of course, is changing all the time, and whereas my life is marked by the date I first went to St Bede's, the time I scored my first fifty at Stonyhurst, the day I left school, and, more significantly, the day I went to Cardington – October 6 1955, these dates didn't alter anything, they simply marked another stage in my life. And so it will be on Saturday – but as it is the day on which I touch manhood for the first time it might be wise to put together some thoughts which have been in my mind – especially since I have been in the RAF.

In the Forces people of all sorts are thrown together, from all kinds of homes, good ones, broken ones, happy ones, tragic ones. And the lads from this large collection of homes provide an even more varied assortment. But character and background are always visible, especially when one is revolted by a sudden action, or – less often –

highly pleased by an act of kindness and friendship. In all these things one can read the kind of homes people come from – and it is impossible not to draw comparisons with one's own home.

I have never been one to lavish praises – indeed however easy it has often been to find fault or to be sarcastic it has been difficult for me to give a real and wholehearted tribute. This is part of me which is not yet complete. Why it is so or why it should be so is hard to tell – for in my life the things for which I should have been grateful have been so many that to say "thank you" properly should have been as easy as it is has been easy to say "can I?" – and I have said this often enough.

Probably the root of the matter is that I have never known what it meant to do without the pleasant things. One does not value a thing fully until one loses it, and familiarity breeds contempt. But by being in the Forces I have learned a lot. One of the things everyone learns is to appreciate, for the first time, home. And in nearly two years I have never, never met anyone who could possibly have come from a better home than mine. Some think they have a good home, and mention arguments and fights to prove (they think) the liveliness of it all, others who have been spoonfed and spoiled think they have had the same – but they cannot stand on their own feet.

I would just like you to know that all the things you have sacrificed, all the tireless effort and long hours you have put in to see Winifred and I better off than you were I really appreciate. But not only that – which in itself is a giant's task, but the general upbringing and outlook on life which you have given me is second to no other. And when you see me do something or hear me say something which hurts you you must stop and wonder if it has been all worthwhile. Well I stop and wonder too – not if it has all been worthwhile, but why on earth I should so often be such a fool. In my time I have "put my foot in it" many times, sometimes grievously, but the humiliations I feel when I think about it puts me lower than the ground. Believe me, for all the things I have done and said, or not done when I should have, I'm sorry.

I know, and I want you to know that I know, from experience and common sense, that there are not in the world a finer Mum and Dad. I want you to know that all the things you have done for me, and are still doing, are so good and so many that I can never hope to be able to repay them – that I appreciate them in my heart. And I want you to know, too, that I think the world of you. You have tried to mould me in the same way I would try to mould a son of mine, and your marriage is the kind I would like mine to be – even half as good as yours would be great. Probably I shall go on just as before, and you will not notice any evidence of what I have written in my ways – but always underneath, when I really think to myself, I will be trying, trying to be worthy to be your son, as you want me to be.

Finally, I pray that God gives me the grace, and the health and strength, when the time comes, for me to look after you, and make you as comfortable as you have made me. Never does a day go by but I think of you countless times, and when we are talking I mention you often. You see, you mean everything to me.

Your loving son

John

On reading my letter for the first time I felt very emotional, happy with my adolescent self for having written it, and once again glad that my mum had kept it. Little did I know, however, when I wrote those words in that final paragraph, that less than five years later, 'that time' would indeed come, and that I would be as good as my word.

In July 1957, though, my main thoughts were about the imminence of my demob. First of all I got a 72 hour pass for the week-end of my 21st, then I had two weeks' leave, one of which was spent in the Isle of Man,

Mum and Dad.

with Eric Parker, Mike Beresford and his cousin Brian. The holiday started on Friday night when we caught the train to Fleetwood, where we caught the midnight boat to Douglas, always filled with people of our age, where we were wondering around the empty streets from 6.00am. There were no 30 minute flights in the 1950s. I'm sure we all behaved ourselves, no doubt enjoying a drink or two. Those were the days when pubs in England opened only in the evenings, but in the Isle of Man they were open virtually all day.

Having returned to Benson during August I was totally at ease, knowing that my National Service was virtually over. My demob party was arranged for the last week of the month at one of our favourite pubs in Wallingford, and we were joined by Mike and Brian. There were one or two spare beds in the billet, so they both stayed overnight, and joined us for breakfast before setting off home.

I was soon making my way home from Benson too. On August 30th I said a fond farewell to the many friends I had made over the previous fifteen months. I valued not only their friendship, but also the maturing influence that life during my National Service had provided. It was a good preparation for my return to an academic way of life, and my future career in the teaching profession, which had been triggered by those afternoons when I was coaching at net practices at St Bede's.

4 Cricket and College

There were only two Catholic Teacher Training Colleges for men in the country, one in London, the other, De La Salle, at Hopwood Hall, Middleton, just a short bus ride from Royton, so having spent the last two years away from home there was no way I would want to spend the next two years away as well.

Soon after my demob, then, I was walking into Hopwood Hall. And who should I meet on my first day at college, as I had done on my first day in the RAF? Yes, Peter Greene, my square-bashing companion. It was good to meet up again, as it was to meet a number of other former school friends who had also completed their National Service. I had intended to study English and History as my two main subjects, having acquired 'A' levels in them, English at St Bede's, and History whilst at Benson, but my friend Jim Murphy, who had just spent two years at Hopwood, persuaded me to make life easier, studying-wise, by taking only one academic subject, English, and one practical subject, thus having a wider range of qualifications. He also assured me that woodwork at Hopwood Hall was an 'absolute doddle.' As I was, and still am, the worst DIY man for many miles, I perhaps should have ignored his advice, but I took it, only to discover that the college had just appointed a new woodwork lecturer, so the doddle Jim had just enjoyed would not be repeated for me. I had known Jim from the days when we travelled by train to Manchester, and by the time I was demobbed Norman Bodell had started his army days, Mike Beresford was courting, and Eric Parker was married, so I started going out for a pint with Jim, soon to be joined by two more lads who lived near to Jim, Richard, also called Murphy, but no relation, and Alan Colton. We all got on well, became very good friends, Richard and I having been best mates all our lives.

By comparison with the RAF disciplines, college life was very relaxing. The most rigorous times would be the weeks we spent on teaching practice, three separate spells of four weeks at different schools. Otherwise, apart form the build up to the final examinations, we enjoyed a leisurely life, arriving and departing at times of the day to suit our lectures. Some days I would not start until 11 o'clock and others I would attend for just the morning. The biggest challenge we had was in the common room where we attempted to complete the Guardian crossword. It felt good, though, to be once again in an educational environment, and both my main subject lecturers were excellent – Brother Hillary in English, and the newly appointed Mr Sergeant, whose individual assistance enabled me to acquire woodworking skills. I was less impressed, however, by some of the lecturers expounding their theories about how we should teach – when they themselves were known to have hardly ever been in a classroom themselves. I thought then, and I still believe now, that college lecturers should have spent a significant number of years as teachers before they are ever considered for a lecturer's post.

One experience, that occurred whilst I was at Hopwood, explains my total lack of respect for the teacher training system. There was a student who had obtained his university degree, and was then completing his one-year course at Hopwood to obtain his teaching certificate. At the end of my first year Brother Hillary was promoted to a senior post, and the one-year student, academically well-qualified, became an English lecturer. During my second year, at my final teaching practice, he was my tutor, the man who had to assess my performance in the classroom – never having spent one day in one himself! He was modest when he discussed with me on how I had performed in the lessons he had observed, and never pretended to be an expert in the way he gave me his advice. He knew, of course, that I was aware of his circumstances. But how would he be over the next few years when the students would not be aware of his lack of classroom experience?

These thoughts on teacher training which had run through my mind whilst at college, were strengthened during my first few years as a teacher. I became aware that some recently qualified teachers who were struggling to maintain discipline in their classrooms, or who were perceived to not be doing very well, were applying for assistant lecturers posts involving research, etc. in order to get out of a job they could not do very successfully. Those who obtained such posts would gradually work their way on to the lecturer's ladder, again with virtually no teaching experience. Throughout my career I spent evenings, weekends, and holiday weeks, on various education courses to extend my experience, only to be far too often frustrated by the nonsense the speakers talked. The fancy theories they expounded were being imposed on their college students, who were being brainwashed by the new ideas as they entered the profession. Some of these lecturers seemed to be competing to think up the latest classroom craze, and were dismissive of teachers who believed in traditional values. I noticed that on a number of occasions on the courses I attended, any teacher who questioned a theory or a teaching style that the lecturer had promulgated would be shot down haughtily. They all believed that they knew best. Teachers were just lackeys who had to take orders. They were in control, and would not tolerate being questioned.

None of this, of course, was within my awareness during my two years at Hopwood preparing for my own first classroom experience. That took place at South Chadderton Secondary Modern School, where I looked forward to teaching my specialist subject, English, to various classes. I was in for a surprise, however, as the head teacher had other ideas, a tactic he apparently always employed on college students. I had visited the school a fortnight or so before my teaching practice began, to meet and be interviewed by the head teacher, who gave me relevant information about the school, and the role he expected me to play. He also asked me about my specialist subjects. When I turned up for my first day and collected my timetable I thought I had been mistakenly given another student's. But no, the head's policy was to widen a student's experience, and I was not allocated a single English lesson. I spent every hour, every evening and weekend, for four weeks, preparing lessons in every other subject about which I knew very little. It was a tough month. I survived, felt that I had learned a lot from it, but never expected the shock of it all. My college tutor assessed me as having done well in the lessons he saw – but I was glad when the month came to an end.

Challenging though the four weeks had been, they had in no way diminished my ambition to become a teacher, and during the summer term I looked forward eagerly to fulfilling my other big ambition – to play cricket for Royton's first team. I was now nearly 22, and had never yet had the chance to fight for a regular place in the second team because of the St Bede's Saturday fixtures and my National Service, so the summer of 1958 was one eagerly awaited. From the start of the season I played in the second team, batted quite well, and scored two or three innings of over 50, including a 73 against Middleton. On that same day our first team had been bowled out for 49, with Roy Gilchrist, the West Indian, then the fastest bowler in the world, taking 8 for 27. I have never met anyone who professed to having been pleased to face "Gilly's" bowling, and I was lucky in that I benefited from our team selectors' decision to make changes following the batting collapse, so I was promoted to the first team for my debut on July 8th.

It was the day I had dreamed of since I became a club member as a seven-year-old. From the moment I saw my name on the team sheet in the chip shop window on the Thursday morning, until I arrived at the ground on the Saturday before the start of the game, I was filled with a mixture of emotions; thrilled and delighted, but apprehensive and nervous. Would I make the big stride from second to first team or would I mess it up? Everyone must go through the same process, but I wasn't thinking of anyone else as I walked out of our house, having been wished 'good luck' by my parents, carrying my whitened boots, clean flannels, shirt and sweater in my bag. Second team matches were watched by a few spectators dotted around the ground, but there were hundreds at first team matches. Going out onto the field would be like walking on the stage. Anyway, it was now or never.

I went in to the dressing room, and that felt different, too. It was full of players I usually only saw on practice nights – the first teamers who all claimed their own pegs to hang their clothes on, and their spaces on the bench to sit and put their bags. As a newcomer I had to wait to find a space not occupied – all part of the tension I felt that Saturday afternoon, welcomed warmly as I was by all my new team-mates. These included one of my pals Stuart Anderson, another, Derek Stuart, and Johnny Taylor, a good left arm spinner who also played on the Top Field as part of another gang from down the 'Scotch'. They were of my age group, but the senior players were led by my boyhood hero, Dr Donald Longbottom, along with Alf Etchells and Kenny Lees, who had played for Royton for many years.

We went out on to the field for fifteen minutes of practice, then returned to the dressing room where our professional Eric Dennison, and Kenny Lees were padding up, ready to open the innings. I was to bat at number 7, so I began to go for a stroll around the ground with Stuart, who batted at 10 or 11, being a very quick opening bowler. I did not stroll around for long, though, as the Littleborough bowlers were giving our top order batsmen a rough time. We were 10 for 3, and I had to go quickly back to the dressing room to put my pads on. Before long, with the score on 21 for 5, it was my turn to walk down the pavilion steps, the moment I had dreamed of all my life. As I did so my dad had his fingers crossed as he stood watching by the fence at the bottom of Queen Street, and so too had my uncle Frank seated on his usual bench near the gates.

What a time to make my debut! All the top batsmen were back in the pavilion, and the Littleborough bowlers had an attacking field set to complete the rout. Somehow, though, it went well for me, and I scored an early boundary. The large crowd cheered as I scored four or five more, and with another two or three wickets having fallen, I was 33 not out, partnered now by Stuart. Unluckily I was given out stumped when I knew that my right foot was clearly partly behind the crease. Lots of those seated in the pavilion could see that too, and shouted their objections to the umpire. I did not wait when I saw his finger raised, and walked up the pavilion steps to rapturous applause. Never in my life had I experienced anything like it. Such moments are few and far between for those of us who never became star players, and that was a treasured one for me.

Soon we were all out for 98, with Stuart 27 not out, and I had top scored! My head was in a whirl. The fact that we lost by seven wickets did not have much impact on me, trying as I was, to adjust to my memorable debut. The Oldham Chronicle reporter interviewed me after the game, and in the Monday evening's edition the match report headline referred to me as 'New boy John'. Fame at last! My mum kept that newspaper too.

Having achieved my lifetime ambition to play for Royton, and to have done so with a good innings, could have gone to my head, but while I enjoyed the acclaim from the other players and my friends, I also knew that things could easily go the other way, finding myself back in the second team, so I didn't do any bragging. The Central Lancashire League has always been one of the best in the country, and with professionals such as Frank Worrell, Sonny Ramadhin, Vinoo Mankad, George Tribe, the standard was high, so every amateur is proud to have played with and against such great players. Little did I realise at the time, though, that only one week later I would play against a cricketer whose fame would be greater than those I have just referred to – Gary Sobers.

Royton's first fixture against Radcliffe had been rained off earlier in the season, so none of our team had played against their professional who was already famous for having scored the world record Test innings of 365 not out during the 1957/58 series against Pakistan, and was now enjoying a successful first season with Radcliffe. He played a majestic innings against us, driving the ball all over the field, scoring 102 not out. It was obvious to all our team that he was going to be one of the greats, but of course we did not know just how great he would become. Radcliffe declared, and we went in to bat, and when we were 34 for 4, I went to face the music. All we were trying to do was avoid getting out, trying to draw the game. We ended the game on 66 for 8, of which I scored 17, one of only three to make double figures.

Sobers had opened the bowling but by the time I batted he had begun to bowl his spinners, and I managed to survive for quite a while, and even scored a five off him, thanks to an overthrow. I also cut him past gully for another boundary, and his response was to bowl me a really fast delivery which I hardly saw, even off his short run. Luckily it missed the stumps. I kept him out for another two or three overs but then he bowled me, and as I turned to walk off the field he said, "Well played son," a remark I appreciated very much, praise indeed from the player who is ranked along with Don Bradman as one of the greatest cricketers of all time.

After my promising debut games I came down to earth in my next two innings, scoring eight in one, and a duck in the other, so reality was inevitably setting in. It was doing so off the field, too, by the end of July, during the long College holidays. Jim Murphy had gone over to Douglas Holiday Camp in the Isle of Man to work as a waiter, so I decided to join him. For the next three weeks I was pushing a trolley round the dining room collecting all the dirty plates, then taking them into the kitchen and helping to wash them. It was non-stop. I got an hour's break between breakfast and dinner time, and two hours in the afternoon, then not finishing until 7.00 pm, when I stank of food and the kitchen cleaning materials. The wages were poor, there were no tips, except for the waiters – so Jim was OK – but I would have been better to have stayed in my job at the cigarette factory in Middleton where I had worked the previous two weeks. It was a seven-day working week with no days off, so I decided to pack it in, and craftily carried on sharing the free accommodation with Jim, and walked into the dining room as if I was a guest on holiday, sat at Jim's table, where I kept my head down if any of the managers were around. So I was able to enjoy a free week in Douglas before Jim and I began our return journey on the Friday night. Midnight boats were routine, of course, so we enjoyed a long farewell drinking session with the many others about to return to England.

I certainly drank more than my fair share that evening, and as soon as I stepped on to the boat swaying ever so gently – the boat, that is – I felt sea-sick and made a dash for the toilet. Without going into any gory details I merely recall that I spent the whole night in the toilet, until we reached Liverpool, to catch the early train to Manchester, and then caught the bus to Royton. It was about 7.00 am as I walked slowly towards Queen Street when I spotted the team sheet in the chip shop window, and saw that I had been selected for the first team away to Rochdale that afternoon. It was a nightmare afternoon, trying to field at cover point when I could hardly stand up. I didn't want the ball to come anywhere near me. There was one ball a batsman hit, though, that did come towards me, and just as I bent down to field it I could hear the sound it made as it smacked into the wall some twenty five yards behind me. Alan Howarth, the bowler, was not very happy as he stood there, hands on his hips, staring at me. He did not know what sort of night I had had – nor did I, really, but I felt relieved when the rain washed out the match before it was my turn to bat. One match later the season was over, just a year following my demob, and a lively year it had been too.

With Jim, Richard and Alan, I had enjoyed my social life. On Saturdays we drank and enjoyed the sing-songs at the Friendship pub before ending up at Frogatt's, the dance hall where we always hoped to 'trap' with an attractive young lady for the long slow last waltz. Similarly at the Savoy on Sundays, and later at the Jazz Club in Greenfield. We enjoyed all kinds of music, often going to the Hallé concerts in Manchester. We spent many Saturday afternoons in the city too, at Old Trafford, watching the Busby Babes, one of whom was the best I ever saw on a football field, Duncan Edwards. Sadly, on that fateful day February 6th 1958, was the Munich disaster, and the world mourned.

One game I especially remember following Munich was the FA cup 6th round replay against West Brom. Jim, Kenny Greaves and I set off very early because a very big crowd was expected, and a good job we did too. We were in the ground by 5 o'clock, and less than half an hour later it was full, the gates locked, with thousands outside the ground and even more still on their way, two hours before the kick-off. I recently discovered the match programme, which I must have stowed away in the loft, on which I had written, "This was the most exciting and dramatic game I have ever seen". Indeed it was, and with the new players taking the place of those killed or injured United battled away, then, near the end, following Bobby Charlton's superb run down the right wing, Colin Webster scored the winning goal. United went on to reach Wembley where they met Bolton Wanderers, but the post-Munch success came to an end, and while I was sad to see them lose I was pleased for our friend in the Bolton goals, Eddie Hopkinson, whose goalkeeping talent had been obvious to all our gang, when we played on the Top Field a decade earlier. Eddie was also a superb cricketer, and although he was somewhat restricted in his availability to play for Royton because of his football commitments, he could walk to the wicket, not having practised or played since the season before, and score a 50, and, on one occasion, a century.

That was something I could never do, but I did look back on the 1958 season with more satisfaction than disappointment, as I prepared for my second and final year at College. Before the term began, however, following my return from the Isle of Man, I started my third job of the summer – for my dad. He had been two years out of the engineering business after the break up of the Cleary and Lawson partnership, but then he started up a new business, 'Junction Flyer Repairs', on Shaw Road, Oldham. He built it up successfully in what was the time when the cotton industry was declining, and very soon he had two of his previous employees working for him, Fred Colman and Jack Heatherington. It was a small workshop, the size of a house, with every inch cluttered with machines, benches, drills and skips full of flyers. The back room was known as the 'Buffing room' with a long noisy machine with leather belts rotating fast, buffing i.e. polishing, the flyers, carefully handled by Jack or Fred, who wore goggles to protect themselves from the many sparks that flew. The noise was deafening, and the only way to attract the buffer's attention was to switch the light off.

Repairing, polishing and finally balancing a flyer took almost thirty different operations. I spent most of my time at the drill, using emery cloth to clean and polish the awkwardly shaped part of the flyers that the buffing could not contact. As the skipfuls of flyers were brought in from the mills each flyer would be coated in oil, grease, dirt and rust, many as black as the ace of spades, and it took a lot of physical effort to do everything necessary so that they were returned to the mills, a week or two later, looking brand new, shining silver. As I did my menial jobs there, hour after hour, conscious of the incessant demanding work being done all day and every day by my dad, Fred and Jack, it made me determined never to work full time in a job like that if I could possibly help it, and I was glad to be going back to college, with a classroom career to look forward to.

What I did not know or suspect, though was that my dad's health was beginning to cause him some concern. He was suffering from angina, and the two or three weeks I spent working for him that summer would not be the last, and during the next ten years Junction Flyer Repairs would have a big impact on my life. Meanwhile he continued to drive his van to work each day, but he had bought a car too, so at week-ends, and especially on Sundays, he and my mum would enjoy a drive out somewhere. Soon it would mean that, having passed my driving test, I could drive whichever of his vehicles he wasn't using. My world was becoming even bigger! It was just the same size at Hopwood, though, as our final year began, and the leisurely approach we had adopted in the first year began to diminish. As we started to focus more seriously on our studies, knowing that in order to be appointed to a teaching post we had to pass the examinations and do well in our two remaining teaching practice months. So I got my head down, worked hard at my main subjects, and completed the special projects that had been set.

In order to avoid a repeat of my unexpected experience at the South Chadderton School, I decided to ask if I might have a Primary School teaching practice session, and was duly assigned to Werneth Junior School, one which had a good reputation in the town. It was an experience I enjoyed, especially when, after my first week, I was asked if I would be willing to take over a class on my own, to cover for a teacher who was ill. Until then I had taught all my lessons under the scrutiny of Eric Taylor, the deputy head, who was very helpful. But to have the opportunity to go into another classroom and teach most of my lessons without being observed by a teacher at the back of the room, was great, and I jumped at the chance. I felt that I did well at Werneth. A number of my lessons were observed by the Head, Miss Baker, and by my college tutor, but I relished the overall experience of having my own classroom for three weeks. Interestingly, some fourteen years later, I would have my own classroom there again, with Miss Baker and Eric Taylor still there.

But first it was back to the college routine, and the first thoughts about the following academic year – where would we be teaching? One or two students were suddenly announcing that they had applied for this or that advertised post, then coming in smiling having had a successful interview, so the ball had begun to roll. I completed my third and final teaching practice at St Patrick's Junior School, Oldham, with my totally inexperienced tutor complimenting me on my ability, and I shortly afterwards applied for a post at St John's, Rochdale, an all age school, which had advertised two posts, one senior, one junior. The head teacher Mr Devlin interviewed me, and I was delighted to accept his offer for me to become the teacher of the senior 2 class, in September. And who was the person appointed to the junior post – non other than Peter Greene! Peter was a member of the St John's Parish, and had attended the school as a young lad, so he was able to give me useful details about the school, thus helping me to prepare for the start of my career. That was still a few months away though, as we prepared for our examinations. My woodworking skills had turned out to be better than any bookmaker would have laid odds on, and I used my dad's van to collect the near perfect dressing table I had made, following the coffee table I had completed earlier in the year. My parents were delighted, but totally surprised – and so was I. Maybe I had a little help from Mr Sergeant!

It was also during the final term that I made the first of what would be quite a number of visits to the Royal Shakespeare Theatre, at Stratford-upon-Avon. Brother Hillary was organising it, and after he had booked the coach he realised that it was not big enough to accommodate the whole party. As he was explaining his dilemma to us I told him that I had a good friend who could provide us with a car and drive to Stratford if he was part of the group. Brother Hillary was relieved, but first enquired if my friend was a Catholic. "Of course he is, Brother," I said, and when I told him that his name was Richard Murphy, Brother Hillary accepted the offer gratefully. Anyone called Murphy must be a Catholic – well, so he assumed, but Richard was and still is a devout Anglican. Not only had I told a lie about Richard, but about the car, too, for it was my dad's we went in, with me driving it, Richard and two other college pals as passengers. It was a splendid three-day visit, seeing three different plays, the highlight being Othello, starring John Osborne, Mary Ure and Sam Wanamaker. I have always loved the Shakespearean atmosphere of the town, with the River Avon flowing by the famous theatre.

Perhaps the deep impression made by my visit in 1959 was what prompted me, about ten years later, to organise the first of a number of school party visits to Stratford, which some two hundred pupils have enjoyed and appreciated. But on the first occasion it was even more enjoyable for Richard and me, for whereas the coach party set off back to Middleton early on Friday morning, we enjoyed a leisurely day strolling round the town, and being rowed up the River Avon by two attractive young ladies we had met, finally arriving home late evening. Brother Hillary, by the way, having closely observed that Richard did not quite make the sign of the cross very convincingly, let it be known that my friend was not a Catholic after all. It did not matter a jot once we were at Stratford!

This being the summer term it was also the cricket season, which I had been looking forward to eagerly since the end of the previous season. Our professional Eric Dennison had completed four years at the club, and our new pro was the most charismatic sportsman I have ever met, Cec Pepper, then aged 39, who had played in the Victory Tests in 1945. As a result of a number of altercations with Don Bradman during the 1945–46 season in Australia, he came over to England to begin a lengthy career as a club professional, beginning at Rochdale. He had altercations with virtually everyone he played with or against; he was fierce, combative and unforgiving as soon as his feet stepped on to the grass – but with a brilliantly sarcastic wit, as well. In the dressing room he was very likeable, humorous and relaxed. Cec was the first Aussie I got to know well, and it was through him that I grew to understand their aggressive but generous nature. Late in his career though it was, he was very successful with both bat and ball for Royton, there was always a buzz in the dressing room or on the field when he was there, and he was usually the first to buy a round of drinks.

He did not buy me very many though, in the 1959 season, because after a run of low scores I spent most of the remainder of the season in the second team, but I did play in two games that I remember vividly for different reasons. The first of these was at Middleton when the ferocious Roy Gilchrist was still their pro. Our whole team was apprehensive about him, of course, after his performance the previous season, so when Donald Longbottom, having won the toss, asked Middleton to bat first, all our team understood why – despite it being a good batting wicket – and felt relieved. During Middleton's innings, 'Gilly' came out to bat at number 6 or 7, and as he played a defensive shot we could hear Donald saying 'Well played Roy,' or 'Good shot, Roy,' from his position in the slips. None of our bowlers bowled him a bouncer – we didn't want to wind him up, did we? Then, despite our efforts to keep him calm and friendly, 'Gilly' was out, and their innings continued, when, during one change of overs, Donald, with his arms outstretched, said, "Jimmy, (Wood) it's raining," with a smile on his face. Soon their innings were over and the rain became heavier. In the dressing room Cec was muttering about having strained his knee – his less than subtle excuse for not wanting to bat high up the order – and as we sat looking out across the field Donald said, "John, I've put you down for number 3 today." "Right," I said, not letting on that I knew I was the sacrificial lamb, but mightily relieved when the umpires abandoned the match when the heavens opened.

The other game I remember is the Wood Cup Final later in the season, played on our ground, against Werneth. Still a second 'teamer' I turned up to watch the big game hoping that Royton would win the cup for the first time, and discovered during the evening (Wood cup matches were always played on mid-week evenings) that I was named in the programme as 12th man. It was a big surprise because no-one had told me, so I had not brought my kit. As we were batting first I did not need it anyway, but I brought it the following night, and a good job too. Cec had gone for a duck, Stan Boyes had made 29, and Eddie Hopkinson, on the verge of a glorious 50 and a whopping collection to go with it, was stumped on 49. Eventually we were all out for 168, and with Stan having twisted his knee during his innings, I walked out as the 'sub' with the other ten fielders.

My moment to remember was when Werneth were on 100 for 4, and their pro Jack Ingham had come to the wicket, and had soon hit Cec for two boundaries. I was fielding at mid off to Cec's bowling and spotted Ingham moving aggressively forward to drive Cec's delivery. I quickly turned, and as the ball soared high over the umpire's head I was racing back towards the boundary, looking up to my left, watching the ball as it began to drop, then clutching it as it came down over my shoulder, spinning in my hands, but safely held – the best catch I ever made. Spectators around the ground stood up and cheered, and I could see the delight on the faces of those near the sightscreen where I ended up after racing to catch it. Now at 100 for 5, their pro out, the game was tilting our way. I walked back towards the wickets surrounded and congratulated by all the team, except that is, by one member – yes – Cec! As I walked towards him to give him the ball, expecting a 'Well done,' or 'Good catch,' he simply said, "He never could f***ing well bat!" That was it. Typical of Cec. He never praised anyone. Never.

Not that it bothered me in the slightest. I felt so thrilled at having taken the catch, which would simply go into the scorebook as "Ingham, caught sub, bowled Pepper 8." Alas, Werneth fought back and eventually won the game by four wickets, and to this day, fifty years later, Royton's name is still not on the Wood Cup. As for me I was back in the second team, and no wonder. According to the scorebook I played in eleven first team matches that season, batted seven times, and averaged 2.86. I must have been lucky to have even been in the second team!

Immediately after the Wood Cup Final I was off to London with Jim Murphy, in his car, not my dad's van, making our first ever journey on a motorway, the recently opened M1. We had decided to surprise Richard Murphy who had been seconded to a London office for a few weeks. The following night the three of us went to the London Palladium to see 'My Fair Lady,' from the luxury of a box. Not that we were throwing our money round by so doing, more that the cashier took pity on us when we told him we had travelled all the way from Oldham to see the musical, to find that all the seats had been sold, and as it was just about to start and with one box empty, the cashier offered it to us at ordinary ticket prices. We thoroughly enjoyed the performance, and the impeccable service of the theatre staff who assumed we were wealthy celebrities and it helped to erase the disappointment of losing in the previous night's Wood Cup Final.

I was back home by the weekend to open a letter awaiting me to find that my Teaching Certificate had arrived. Soon I would be starting my teaching career at St John's, Rochdale, but for the next two or three weeks I would be once again working for some well earned spending money on Shaw Road, in the noisy engineering shop. I actually enjoyed it, too, because I seemed to spend more time on the road than at the drill. During the previous summer as I worked there my dad would occasionally ask me to go with him as he was delivering or collecting flyers from the mills. This summer, however, he said he was busy in the workshop and often asked me to go to various mills, especially where he knew that I had met the carder or manager, and where I knew my way around the mill. Often I was coming back home at tea time having spent half the day on the road to mills in Stockport, Middleton, Rochdale, Heywood and West Yorkshire.

What I did not realise was that he may have been making sure that I knew everyone I needed to know, and be known by them, at all the mills for which he repaired flyers – just in case! And whilst he was delighted I had qualified as a teacher, and with a secure and respected career lying ahead, he knew that his business was providing a good income for my mum and him, and must have been secretly worried about what would happen if his health worsened. His health was not something he ever referred to in my presence, so I was hardly aware of it, but by having ensured that I could step in if needed would prove to have been a wise move in the not too distant future.

What lay ahead for me just then, though, was my first day in the classroom as a teacher. I had had my ups and downs at St Bede's, enjoyed my break from the education world whilst in the RAF, then I had spent an enjoyable and not too demanding two years at Hopwood. But now I was to step over the Maginot Line, from a role where one could be rebellious, lazy, carefree and indifferent to authority, into one which imposed discipline, correct behaviour, and good standards. I was the poacher about to turn gamekeeper. Would I make it?

5 St John's and More Cricket

St John's, Rochdale, here I come! As Peter Greene and I waltzed into the staff room on that September Monday, perhaps the two long serving spinsters might have felt uneasy about our arrogant confidence, particularly Miss Holden, who had taught the Senior Two class for nearly twenty years, and who now found herself having to move to another class in order to accommodate me, following my interview with Mr Devlin when I had persuaded him to give me that class; and Miss Randle, who conducted herself in a rather convent mode, insisting on the strictest of Catholic rituals. We were made very welcome, nonetheless, and in the classroom itself I could not have had an easier start. Mr Devlin told me on my first morning that he was preparing my timetable – but it took him three weeks to do so. In other words, "teach them what you want", was his message, as he sat in his room, with the door locked, all day. It was then that it dawned on me that my school days at St Bede's were not going to have much practical value. There I had studied Latin, Greek and French, but never a single lesson in Geography or Science. So I began by concentrating on English, Maths, History and, of course, Religion. Learning the catechism was a must in Catholic schools, and the first hour each morning was a compulsory religious lesson – and the parish priest, Cannon Kelly, would walk into our classrooms from time to time, making sure the rules were being obeyed.

One thing I quickly learned, and which really surprised me at the time, was how satisfying it was to teach Maths. Whereas in English pupils have to grind away, being set back by poor spelling, grammatical or punctuation mistakes, which attract the red ink, in Maths, when a teacher has explained how to do the multiplication, division, or whatever, on the blackboard, and ensured that the pupils understand how to do it, then to find a few minutes later that most of the class have got their sums right, the delight on their faces says it all. In English improvement comes slowly, but in Maths it can be instant. I have often seen the look of disbelief when a pupil who had lost all confidence in him or herself, suddenly realising that he or she is not so 'dense' after all, and looks forward eagerly to the next challenge. That very often has a beneficial knock-on effect to their other subjects, too, and coming to school in a morning ceases to be such a miserable prospect. Throughout my career, that was what I strove to achieve, starting at St John's.

Another thing I realised early in my career was that children are very reluctant to ask questions, thereby announcing to the whole class that they do not understand something that a teacher is trying to explain. It is so easy for a teacher to stand at the blackboard having explained how to do a type of sum, and then say, "Do you all understand?" followed by a murmur of "Yes Sir," but then as they get their heads down quite a few of them are staring at the desks, obviously not having understood. Having recognised the problem I tackled it head-on, and did so for the whole of my career. I made it clear to every class I taught that if ever they were unable to understand what I was trying to teach or explain to them, they must – absolutely must – ask me to explain it again. I gave them my total assurance that I would never be angry or impatient with them for not understanding something, nor would I humiliate them or make them feel uncomfortable. They would never be in trouble, in other words, for not understanding something. They would be in trouble, though, if they did not ask, or raise their hand, whenever they could not understand something. At first I could see the suspicion in their eyes as I said this, but as they became used to my style they began to trust me, and soon realised that I was as good as my word.

It was not at St John's, of course, that I fully developed my theories and philosophies, but that is where they began, and I am sure I speak for every teacher when I say what a delight it is to see the sudden happiness in a child's face when he or she has done something really well for virtually the first time. It requires a mixture of dedication, motivation and essentially a background or basis of discipline to enable the teaching process to have its effect. When I began my career the current disciplinary chaos did not exist, and teachers were able to establish the necessary authority, untrammelled by the law as it is today. I must have made millions of mistakes, of course, as eager and enthusiastic teachers do, but teaching is a learning process in itself, and I feel that I began to mature, maybe slowly, and began to anticipate situations better, and thus avoid a problem. Whereas I had probably assumed that discipline was established by being strictly enforced, I slowly realised that subtlety, humour and diplomacy works too, and making shrewd assessments of various pupils' characters results in a stronger classroom atmosphere.

The playground and playing field are important too. At lunch time the lads played football, and very often Pete and I would join in, which brought us into contact with those in the top class, taught by Paddy Carew. The lads enjoyed our participation, and as I took them once a

St John's 3rd and 4th Year Boys 1960.

week to Lennybarn playing fields for their games lessons, and took the school football team, which played other schools on Saturday mornings, I was accepted and respected – and liked too, I think – by all the senior pupils. By the end of the first football season, I had got to know where all the Rochdale Secondary Schools were – because we played them at football – and I began to feel part of the Rochdale scene socially, too, as I attended various meetings and lectures, along with other teachers, followed sometimes by a convivial drink. A good friend of mine was also working in the town, Norman Bodell, now playing professional football for Rochdale FC and he was one of the players undertaking coaching duties in the local schools, and he was assigned to St John's for a few weekly sessions. The lads were thrilled to be receiving tuition from one of their star players and on the final assignment day Norman brought four of his Rochdale first team players, and, joined by Peter Greene and myself, our team of seven played against the St John's team, and we craftily ensured that the lads won. They loved it. Another moment I remember with amusement was when he had given me some complimentary tickets for a Rochdale game, and, as I had a spare one, I stood outside the ground, before the kick off, to offer it to anyone I knew. Just then Freddie Thompson, one of my St John's class, came by, so I said, "Hi Freddy, I've got a free ticket. Would you like it?" "No thanks, sir," he said. " We always climb over the wall!"

Having been at St John's for just two terms, I was to have a change of classrooms after Easter, because Paddy Carew had left to become head of a new school. I was now in charge of the Senior 3 and 4 boys' class, in a prefab building. Half the boys were now entering their final school term, and my walking into their classroom must have seemed an opportunity for mischief, but all went well and I enjoyed the unexpected challenge of teaching the top class. There was one thing I learned during that term which would stay with me throughout my career, when teaching children to write essays. The standard way I had inherited from my own school days was to set an essay title, discuss it with the class, and they would then complete it and hand it in for me to mark. The problem was, I felt, that such a system offers pupils no awareness of how others in the class are writing, and how they can all learn from each other. This is what happens in art and various practical subjects, where they benefit from working along side each other. In essay writing, however they are blinkered, going from page to page in total isolation.

That had been the system at St. Bede's until the day in the Lower Fifth when Fr. Reynolds read out two or three of the essays he had enjoyed reading, and as I listened to them I felt as if my eyes had been opened, never having been remotely aware of such imaginative ways of writing. My own writing began to improve after that day, and now that I was back in the classroom myself I tried to look for my ways of opening up my pupils' eyes. The first time I really succeeded was when, instead of collecting their books, I asked them to read their essays aloud. One of the first benefits is that there is no awareness of any spelling or punctuation errors when pupils read their essays out loud, it is simply the story that counts, as it did when Barry Jones read his. The subject was 'My most unhappy memory' and as Barry read out his story about how his dog had suffered an accident and had died, expressing very movingly his feelings of grief, the whole class applauded him, and he sat down with tears in his eyes.

From that day Barry Jones was held in much greater respect and esteem by his classmates, and he himself grew in self-confidence, and he approached all his other work with increasing enthusiasm. I am in no way advocating that punctuation, spelling or grammatical errors should never be pointed out or marked, but if the red ink is used on every single error every time a pupil writes the task will seem so onerous that he or she will lose heart, feel despondent, and give up trying. I believe that a teacher must look for the good aspects of a pupil's work, acknowledge it, and try to build on it. I think that the freedom I enjoyed during my first year at St John's was one of the factors that enabled me to begin to develop my own teaching techniques. I was, and remained, enthusiastic, always hoping to inspire and motivate my pupils to enjoy learning. Throughout my career I developed and believed in my own way of teaching, for better or worse, but always with the conviction that it was in the best interests of my pupils. And it was in that first twelve months when I started my career ball rolling.

Outside the classroom, though, during the 1959-60 season, the ball I saw most weeks was at Boundary Park. The good times were returning, following Jack Rowley's appointment as manager, and especially when he signed Bobby Johnstone. Bobby may have been in the twilight of his fantastic career, but he had lost none of his superb skills, and soon the ground was nearly full to capacity every home game, everyone enthralled by his brilliance. The Latics were playing good, attractive football, and growing in stature. Sadly, at Watersheddings, the great 1950s team had virtually disbanded, so we rarely watched any rugby now, and spent most alternate Saturdays at Old Trafford, where United were rebuilding after Munich, or we would go to Bolton or Burnley if they had an attractive fixture, as Burnley often did around that time.

If our Saturday afternoons were invariably spent on football grounds, our Saturday evenings often began at a rugby club – Oldham's RUFC on Keb Lane, where Richard Murphy played. Not many people can claim to have a better reputation for downing a few – or more than a few – pints, than rugby union players, so Jim and I often collected Richard there, and we would make our way in to the town, ending up at Frogatt's before the tantalising last waltz. They each had their own car, as did Alan Colton, while I continued to drive my dad's van or car. In the summer our night out often started at the cricket club, going to wherever we fancied, even, once or twice, to Blackpool, before arriving back home around 2 o'clock on Sunday morning, with only the driver, usually Jim, awake.

Jim Murphy, Me, Alan Colton and Richard Murphy on a night out in Blackpool.

It was Jim, too, who had heard about a Treasure Hunt Charity Car Rally being organised by the newly formed High Moor Motor Club, all of which led to a very enjoyable Motor Club social life for the next five years. Jim was very keen, so I went along too, and soon Jim volunteered that "we" would write a monthly newsletter. "We" soon became "I", and I thoroughly enjoyed my involvement in the development of the club, and the many friends I made as the membership grew, offering me many opportunities to write humorous reports about the various characters and personalities who met up so regularly. The newsletter came out virtually every month, and after it had started as a one page letter it soon grew into an eight page booklet. Jim and I were, as editors, elected to the club committee, and it formed a regular Monday night out at the Roebuck. There we became friends with another Murphy – again, no relation! This was Francis Patrick Murphy, another long time good friend. Another I met and very much respected was Ken Whatmough, whose wisdom and shrewdness in committee meetings I admired. More than once he would sit silently listening to all the rubbish ideas some of us would be putting forward, and then with great subtlety and tact, without any criticism or argumentative expressions, would gradually point out the difficulties and snags in our proposals, and we would always be persuaded to follow his recommendations. I learned a lot from Ken.

Jim and I had started to produce the newsletters in November 1959, but our best edition was a magazine entitled "SPOTLIGHT", described as the 'High Moor Motor Club Year Book', in 1961. It was full of articles, photographs and advertisements, with 54 pages, and it sold well, adding to our membership numbers, too, as people became aware of our existence. Gradually the Club became more rally orientated than 'treasure hunted' and all-night rallies became the big events. I had no ambitions to drive or be a navigator in these rallies, but did contribute by being a marshal at one or more check points on the route. The Club was an enjoyable part of my life for the five years I edited the newsletters and served on the committee.

Everything took second place to cricket in summer, of course, and by the 1960 season I was part of the scene at Royton, feeling assured of my place in either first or second teams. Standards were high in the Central Lancashire League, and it was something to feel proud of simply to be a regular first or second team player. I never thought I would ever be good enough to be an automatic first teamer, even though I would love to have been. But I was never one of those who are happy to play in the second team every week, scoring runs or taking wickets, or both, fairly easily, against lesser players. During the 1960 season I played in the first team for a few games later in the summer, but played more for the second team. I also enjoyed playing the occasional Sunday game for Old Bedians, and that summer I went on their tour to Shropshire, once again scoring one of my rare 'fifties' there.

I was also playing some Sunday matches for Prescott Cricket Club, along with one or two other Royton players, mainly at the invitation of 'Doc' Longbottom, who had strengthened their Sunday team for a number of years. That led to my going on tour with their team, known as 'The Merseysiders', to Devon in 1961, along with Jack Scholes. We enjoyed playing on some lovely grounds, especially the very attractive Sidmouth, nestling by the sea, surrounded by picturesque rolling hills. The most memorable part of the tour for Jack and me, though, was before we arrived in Devon. We were to travel by car, and their captain, Bobby Mawdsley, had arranged to pick us up at Mere Corner, near Knutsford. Having set off south in his Jaguar we suddenly stopped. Bobby and his fellow 'Merseysider' were quickly out of the car, their heads under the bonnet. It transpired that the accelerator had snapped, so they fixed a piece of string to some part of the engine, and then Bobby drove us down to Devon, pulling on the string, albeit with the window slightly open, all the way from Cheshire. Not many can have had that experience of being driven from Cheshire to Devon thanks to a piece of string. The story is still talked about at Prescott Cricket Club. I heard Barry Rishton, one of their veteran players, talking about the incident in a footwear wholesalers in Rawtenstall in 2000, almost forty years later, and I immediately told him that I was one of the passengers in the car. He was dumbfounded!

Again, in 1961 I spent more time in the second team, but in one of my first team games I was impressed by the brilliant batting of Basil D'Oliviera, who was soon to become an England Test Player of some renown, especially with the South African controversy. He came in to bat on 28 for 2, and out of the remaining Middleton 154 runs he made 128. It was he who caught me out too, but not before I had shared a good ninth wicket stand with Jack Rowley, who, unluckily, was 29 not out as our last wicket fell just nine runs short of the Middleton score, after recovering from being 90 for 6. Two weeks later Gary Sobers hit another century against us, but when he had me LBW for a duck later on, this time he did not bother to say "Well batted, son," as I walked off.

That day was one I remember for very different reasons. It was Dr Donald Longbottom's final game for Royton. But for the war, as I have referred to earlier, Donald would probably have been a Lancashire player, and he had an outstanding career in the CLL following his return form the war. More than once he topped the league bowling averages, and with his lovely smooth action he was a model fast bowler who was respected by all the great professional batsmen, such as Frank Worrell, whose wicket he took a number of times. He also scored many runs for Royton, just a naturally gifted all rounder. Add that to his talent for Water Polo, where he was one of the stars in Royton's post war success, and he represented Lancashire in the water too. He was liked and respected by everyone, and never played selfishly, but for the team. Some first team players, when turning up for the Tuesday night net practices, would have a spell of batting and then vanish. Donald always carried on, offering coaching advice to the younger players until it went dark, as would Alf Etchells. For Donald, though, it was a long night, living, as he did, in Knutsford where he was Medical Officer of Health, for after net practice he would always stay to enjoy a friendly drink in the bar, always jovial. Everyone referred to him as 'Doc', but he never exuded the slightest snobbishness or seniority. Cricket is a game which brings people of all ages together, where teenagers and those in their forties share a love of the game, everyone delighted at his team-mate's success, and often leads to lifelong friendships.

Donald was 23 years older than me, but we got on as if we were mates, despite the age gap, and I valued his wit, modesty and wisdom. It was after the Radcliffe game as we called for a drink on our way home, when we all felt apprehensive, knowing that it would be his last game in that season, as he was to go into hospital during the following week for treatment for what, very tragically, was cancer of the pancreas. It was incurable, and a consequence of the suffering he had endured when a Japanese prisoner of war, where he was beaten and starved for refusing to order his soldiers to undertake tasks that the Japanese were instructing officers like Donald to authorise them to do. Sadly he passed away in the autumn. His widow, Hannah, asked me to be one of the pallbearers, and I felt honoured to be asked. Even though Catholics were then not allowed to take part in a church service of any other denomination, I never hesitated for a moment, and was proud to have been one of the six members of the Club to carry his coffin. He was one of the finest cricketers and gentlemen I have had the honour to know.

One of the many cricketers to attend the funeral was Cec Pepper, who had just completed his three years as our professional, and was nearing the end of his outstanding career. It might have been even greater but for his confrontation with the great and powerful Don Bradman. Cec had been a member of the Australian Services XI which toured England in 1945, and he was hoping to be selected for the full Australian Test Team as cricket resumed following the war. He was playing in a State match where he and Bradman were on opposing sides. Cec, frustrated at being denied LBW appeals for Bradman's wicket, began swearing at the umpire, accusing him of bias, and of being scared of offending the great Don by giving him out. Cec's subsequent verbal assault went on ferociously, and he went on to make offensive remarks about Bradman himself, in his frustration at the umpire's temerity to raise his finger. What Cec told me he had forgotten, though, was that Bradman had taken a single, and was standing just behind him as he made his remarks. Bradman was a very dominant character, and he made it clear that there was now no way forward for Cec in Australian Test cricket, which is precisely why he came over here in 1946 to begin his CLL years, at Rochdale. He was generally regarded as the best Australian never to have been capped for his country, and in his sixteen years as a professional at Rochdale, Burnley, Radcliffe, Oldham and finally Royton, his startlingly good performances with both bat and ball exceed virtually every other professional's since the war. He might have become one of Australia's most famous all-rounders, as did his friend and teammate in the Victory Tests, Keith Miller, had he not upset Bradman. He would have commanded a place in the team simply as a bowler, and with his leg spin, googly, and cleverly disguised 'flipper,' he might have made as big an impact as Shane Warne did fifty years later.

Everyone who knew Cec liked him – off the field, but not everyone did once he had stepped on to the grass, which was when his aggressive nature took over, and whether you were an opponent, umpire or teammate, you got both barrels if he thought you had in any way slipped up.I thoroughly enjoyed his company. Maybe because I am an aggressive person myself I was never overawed by him, and just spoke to him as I would to anyone else, and as I was to discover many years later when I followed our Test team to Australia, Aussies love aggressive people, and even buy them a pint! Cec bought me plenty, and all the players at Royton liked him, even though there were one or two rather nervous of making a missfield, knowing the insults they would receive if they dropped a catch off his bowling. Not that he ever said "Well done," even if you did take a catch, of course!

There was one occasion, though, when his foul tempered comments were thrown back at him by the calmest member of the team, Dennis Hasty, one of the club's most stylish and elegant batsmen. He normally fielded in the slips, but during one game he was at cover point, and the batsmen set off for a quick single as the ball was pushed towards him. The keeper shouted for a quick throw and as Dennis was about to release the ball Cec, at the bowler's end, screamed for him to throw it to him. Perhaps totally confused by the screams from both ends, as he tried to change direction, the ball went straight across to mid wicket. Cec then unleashed his f*****g this and f*****g that. Dennis, the quietest and calmest person on the field, simply walked up to Cec, and in just as fiery a way as Cec had spoken, said, "If you ever talk like that to me again you'll get it right between your f*****g eyes!!!" Cec, and the rest of us were dumbstruck. "Beware the wrath of the patient man," goes the proverb, and it shut Cec up, who went quietly back to the end of his run.

Cec had the last word, however, in another game, following a provocative action by a Crompton Pakistani player, Shoib, who was batting against Cec's bowling. I was fielding at leg slip, and Shoib and Cec were in a straight line view from my position. Shoib waited until Cec was about to turn and begin his run to the wicket, then slowly strolled up the wicket, gardening, very slowly indeed. He came back to his crease, again slowly, looked round to take note of all the fielding positions, and as he put his head down ready to take guard, shouted out, "I'm ready now, Pepper." Cec, meanwhile, had just stood there, motionless. He now bowled a massive leg spin, which Shoib played and missed. Then he bowled him a massive googly, again totally beating the batsman. Finally, next ball, he bowled his flipper. Clean bowled! "You weren't ready for that f****r were you?" screamed Cec, as Shoib made his way to the pavilion. Just as Shoib was about to leave the field, Cec shouted, "And get back up your f*****g tree before it gets dark!" Whereupon Shoib started to walk back, towards the bowler's end, holding his bat as if he was going to hammer Cec with it. Cec stood silently, close to the umpire. We all watched, uneasily, as the umpire and mid off, Kenny Boss, tried to stand between them, before Shoib stopped, turned and finally walked up the steps. We breathed again. Incidents of this kind occurred throughout Cec's fifteen years as a professional, as those who played with or against him at Rochdale, Oldham, Radcliffe and finally Royton will testify. I am grateful for having had the chance to know him and have played with him, and to have enjoyed his genuinely good company in the dressing room and the bar. He was certainly one of cricket's outstanding characters. Unfortunately for Cec it was only in England that his talent was realised, but the same fate very nearly befell his good friend and cricket legend Keith Miller. It was only in 2006, When I was in the Rawtenstall Cricket Club committee room, and read the copious correspondence between Miller and George Whittaker, the club president, that I realised the significance of a story Cec Pepper had once told me.

Miller had served for three years in the RAAF, having been a fighter pilot, and the way he played his cricket after that was, as Michael Parkinson wrote, "as much a celebration of surviving the war as it was the product of an impulsive nature." One man who did not approve of his cavalier approach to the game was Bradman, and perhaps Miller believed he too might be sidelined. At that time many Australians were signing to play as professionals in England, New Zealand and India, desperate to find employment after the war. It is probable that a combination of both these factors led to Miller signing a three-year contract with Rawtenstall in July 1946, to begin in 1947.

By that time Cec Pepper was playing for Rochdale, and quickly learning how to make extra money from benefit matches, acting as a deputy professional in other parts of the country on Sundays or during the week, and claiming lower wages and higher expenses, hence paying less tax. All of this experience he passed on to his friend, whose letters to Rawtenstall began to be responded to derisively by George Whittaker, and who actually names Pepper as the malign influence behind Miller's requests for changes in his contract. Although Miller would have been looking forward to coming to England, his main ambition was to play for Australia, and in one of his first letters to Rawtenstall after he had signed, he asked the club not to go public, "lest it leads to my not being selected for Australia." However, once the Daily Mirror published the story in December, the Australian press began to speculate as to whether Miller would be dropped, "despite his outstanding success in the recent Test." When interviewed, Miller said, "I cannot say one way or another," as to whether he would fulfil his contract, and as the pressure he came under from Rawtenstall became immense. But for Miller to break his contract would have cost him £100, said to have been six months' wages in Australia at that time, and Miller did not have a job!

The correspondence clearly shows that Miller would not formally agree to break his contract, but he made it obvious that he would not be coming, pleading with the club to look sympathetically on his changed circumstances. He says that it would not be fair for his "new bride" for them to be living in a hotel for three years, and that his mother had become seriously ill and she wanted him to be near her. By February 11th Rawtenstall had signed Ken Grieves, but continued to demand £100, and more. By that time, of course, Cec Pepper would have been in regular contact with Miller, having travelled back to Australia at the end of his first season at Rochdale. Then, as the Australian 1946-7 season ended, with Miller still out of work and uncertain of Bradman's attitude towards him, he did, I believe, decide to come to England after all, in order to play as deputy professional for any number of clubs, and generally benefiting from Pepper's increasing number of contacts. Miller had already played in England, of course, during the Victory

Tests in 1945, a summer in which he also played some club matches as a deputy professional, under an assumed name. He played three matches for Heywood under the name of Nigel Stocks.

My conviction that Miller might never have continued his Test playing career is based on what Cec told me while he was at Royton. He said that he and Miller had both travelled to Freemantle to catch the boat to England, and had boarded it during the evening before it was due to set sail the following morning. That was when Miller received a telephone call from Bradman, who asked him not to travel to England, and guaranteed him a place in the Australian team to tour England in 1948. That was all Miller must have wanted to hear, and he stepped off the boat. At that time a promise of a place in the team for a tour still more than a year ahead could not possibly have been made public. Whether Bradman had made the call with the knowledge and approval of the selectors, or on his own initiative, would be pure speculation, but in any event it confirmed that while Bradman may still not have liked Miller's way of playing, he knew that if he wanted to lead the Australians to victory in the Ashes tour, he would have to accept Miller for what he was. For cricket lovers all over the world, thankfully he did, or else the legend would probably have spent the rest of his career in England, as Cec Pepper did.

If the dressing room provided characters like Cec, staff rooms did not, and in Rochdale the Catholic Schools were now being re-structured in the early 1960s, with plans for Secondary Schools to be built, leaving the all-age schools to become Junior Schools. During the first stage of this St Joseph's opened, taking all 3rd and 4th year pupils, but it could not accommodate many 1st and 2nd years, so while I continued to teach at St John's I was now teaching 2nd year pupils. I had no problem with that, and under the new system I had the freedom to teach how and what I wanted, but I became aware that any ambitious senior school teacher needed to be specialising, and thus to teach in a more modern school was essential. I was in no hurry to move because I was enjoying my time in the classroom – but move I did during the spring term 1961 – house, not school.

My parents had been looking at houses for some time, and finally decided that we were leaving Queen Street. My mum had already sold her wool shop, and Junction Flyer Repairs was still thriving, so after toying with the idea of moving to the seaside, they plumped for Hollinwood Avenue, Chadderton. We were moving from our terraced house to a three-bedroom semi, with its own drive, front and back gardens, and a telephone! No longer did we have a front room, but a lounge, indeed two, front and back! The biggest shock, though, was the noise. Whereas the only noises we could hear in Queen Street were the clog irons, or the horse and carts, here we were living on a main road, with cars, lorries and buses changing gear as they approached or left the Broadway traffic lights. I certainly did not need an alarm clock now. I was still enjoying my social life with Richard, Jim and Alan, but I was also spending quite a lot of time with a young lady, Sheila, which made my friends speculate as to whether the relationship might develop.

During November, however, everything changed. My dad suffered a heart attack, and was taken into Boundary Park Hospital, where he spent the next six weeks. He had rarely talked about his health, at least not in my presence, but obviously the angina he had suffered from for quite some time had had a debilitating effect on him, and now my mum, Winifred and I were full of anxiety, especially for those first few days, as we visited him in his hospital bed. All a family can do, however, is to hope and pray, and try to get on with their lives, when a sudden life-threatening attack occurs. My mum must have been distraught, and have felt very lonely, as she spent virtually every day alone at home, living on an avenue where she felt a total stranger. Thankfully our two next door neighbours were very comforting and friendly.

By contrast to my mum's more solitary days mine became rather hectic, with Junction Flyers having been added to my teaching role. Every afternoon I would end up on Shaw Road, where Fred Colman, my dad's sole employee now, would be repairing the flyers. My job was to visit the cotton mills to collect flyers needing to be repaired, or delivering them back to the mills. It was during those first two or three weeks of my dad's illness that I realised why he had taken me round to all the mills, and had introduced me to the people who mattered in each mill. I was now making early morning, lunch-time, or late afternoon visits to various mills to enable Fred to keep the business going. Fred, however, although he could do virtually all the repair work, could not 'balance' the flyers, and that final and very important task was a skill that not many textile engineers had been trained to do. It was rather an elite skill, the training for which was only given to mill owners' family or managers' sons. My dad must have done well, and been fortunate, to have had the training. So in addition to my going to the various mills I also drove to Taylor's in Bolton at least twice each week, where all our repaired flyers were 'balanced' ready for returning to the mills.

It was during those weeks that my dad was recovering that I became aware that I was now a part of a corrupt textile industry, if only a very minor part. Every night I would take my mum to the hospital, and during the time we were there I would keep him up to date on the work coming in and going out. He would tell me what I should 'slip' the carder, or whoever signed the delivery note. Sometimes it would be a £1 note, sometimes 20 cigarettes, sometimes more. As Christmas approached I had to make sure I took whisky, cigars, cigarettes, and cash to thank them for their business. This was a totally new world to me. My parents had always brought me up to be absolutely honest, and I had never been aware of the way of life one had to lead in this textile environment. I had also become aware how crucial the delivery notes were in making a profit on the work done. Soon I would be delivering a skip with say, 50 flyers having been repaired, but the carder would be signing the note for 75 or 80, happily slipping some cash or cigarettes into his pocket. I had to make sure that the delivery notes were signed when there was no-one else present. Nothing was ever said. They signed, I thanked them; they me. Every time.

There was also another lucrative fiddle. Every flyer had a 'presser' attached to it that also needed to be polished. These were rather delicate slim pieces of metal, which could easily break, either at the mill while in the frame, or when being removed for cleaning and polishing. Fred would hand me a piece of paper telling me how many flyers were in the skip, and how many pressers he had replaced. However, when I made out the delivery note both figures were very different for the carder to sign. As an upstanding Catholic teacher all this was something of a dilemma for me at first, but the circumstances in which I now found myself left me no option. Later I would realise that it was just the tip of the iceberg, and back-handers and corruption generally on a much bigger scale was simply normal. Meanwhile, my dad had come home on Christmas Eve, and would be resting and recovering for a few weeks before making a gradual return to work, so during January and February I continued doing my two jobs, but was beginning to look at the teaching posts being advertised, feeling that it was now the right time to move on.

I spotted a post I fancied at the recently opened St Joseph's School, Rochdale, specialising in English and Games. It seemed perfect for me, so I applied for it, and within a fortnight I had been interviewed, offered the job, accepted it, ready to begin after Easter. I handed in my notice just before the closing date, and had now only four or five weeks to go at St John's. It had been a good starting point for my career, and it had been a very happy staffroom too. Perhaps somewhat surprisingly I had got on very well with the very strict Miss Randle, whom I had expected to frown on my outgoing style, as I had with all the other members of staff, including my RAF pal Peter Greene, and the recently appointed Mike Henstock, another cricket and football fanatic like myself. So I was sad to be leaving St John's, whilst eagerly looking forward to my new post at St Joseph's.

It nearly did not happen, though. George Devlin told me that the Education Officer wanted to see me, hinting that it was probably about my leaving St John's before they had found a replacement. That gave me enough time to consider things, and after school that day I went to the Education Office to speak to the top man. He told me that my letter of resignation had come at a difficult time for St John's, and that as St Joseph's were not understaffed they could defer my appointment until September, so it would be better if I put back my resignation until the summer term. He asked no questions, merely outlined his decision. He was the Education Officer and he gave the orders. I waited a moment or two, and then said, "Is that it? Have you 'owt else to say?" He was utterly taken aback. People did not talk to him like that! "Er. Pardon?" he muttered, hardly believing he had been spoken to so rudely. I carried on as before, explaining to him straightforwardly that I had given my notice to leave St John's at Easter, and that if there was not a post available to me at St Joseph's, I would apply for one of the many posts currently being advertised in the Oldham area, nearer to my home, but that my resignation had been made, and at Easter I would leave St John's. I paused only a few seconds and bade him "Good Afternoon."

"Beauty is truth; Truth Beauty." Good old John Keats!

On the way home I called at the house in Royton where Mr Jack Hilton, St Joseph's Headmaster, lived, in order to explain the situation I was in, and to discover what my next move would be. Mr Hilton told me that he had been having his arm twisted by the Education Officer, but that he retained the right to employ me from Easter, and he assured me that he would go ahead and enforce that. We shook hands, and I went home smug and happy. I told my dad all that had happened, and what I had said in the Education Office, and he replied, "Exactly what I would have said. Well Done!"

It was about that time that my dad felt well enough to return gradually to work, which meant that I was back to a less frenzied daily routine. I was relieved and pleased to have been able to keep his business going during those three months, and in so doing, fulfilling the promise I had made in my recently discovered letter from RAF Benson. But had I fulfilled it? Anyway, the final weeks of the Easter term slipped quickly by, and I was now looking forward to my new post at St Joseph's, and the oncoming cricket season. Then at 5 o'clock, on the morning of what was to be my last day at St John's, my mum burst into my bedroom, woke me up and asked me to look at my dad. He lay there in bed, cold and stiff. No words can describe the shock and grief mum, Winifred and I felt at that moment. It was Friday April 13th, 1962, a day and date I shall always, sadly and emotionally, remember.

6 St Joseph's and Junction Flyers

My dad having passed away on the final day of the Easter term meant that both Winifred and I were off school, and therefore able to provide mum with some support during those upsetting moments while arrangements were being made for the funeral, which took place the following Thursday. Almost every minute of our time was spent looking back, remembering, re-living, in sorrow, and trying to come to terms with our situation. But after the funeral our focus had to be on the future. The house was paid for, so my mum had no debts. Both Winifred and I had what were modest teaching salaries, ample enough to pay for our lives on Hollinwood Avenue, but my mum was only 51 and she was going to feel very isolated and lonely when she would begin to be on her own all day as the new school term started. I also wondered if she might have been troubled by the thoughts that she might soon be losing me too – for quite different reasons. After a few years of dating many different girls, I had been going "steady" with Sheila for a few months. No mention was ever made of our courtship, but the effect it might have on my mum's attempt to overcome her grief made me uneasy, so I decided, somewhat reluctantly, to say goodbye to Sheila.

I was about to take up my new post at St Joseph's and would be hoping to stride forward in my career. I was also hoping to do well in the cricket season, which was about to start that weekend with net practices, and it was during one of them that a comment a friend of mine made that would give an added dimension to my mum's future, and to mine too. Players were offering me their condolences and expressing goodwill, but when I was speaking to John Cartmell, he asked me if I was going to carry on the Junction Flyer Repairs business. Without really thinking I instinctively said, "Oh no!" and explained that I was about to start at my new school and would be very busy with all my new teaching responsibilities.

It was only after I had arrived home, and with the question constantly coming back into my mind, that I began to wonder. For the past week I had not really had a moment to think about Junction Flyers. On the day of my dad's death I had called to tell Fred, and to give him his wages, as I also did during the week of his funeral, but there had not been any conversation about what was to happen next. It had, after all, been the week during which we had been looking back. But not now. Very soon it would have to be decision time, and John's question had put my head in a whirl.

Suddenly the future began to look different. My mum said that there was a ladies wear and wool shop for sale, no more than two hundred yards away, on Owler Lane, the very same type of business that she had run for ten years or so in Royton, and she was very interested. It seemed a good idea, which would enable her to be fully occupied, doing what she was familiar with, and moving into the future. It seemed as if in no time at all she had agreed a price for the business. I arranged for a five-year loan for her, but the monthly repayments would probably be a huge chunk of the shop's takings, so that was when Junction Flyers came back into the equation. If I could keep it going, it would provide my mum with the income to repay the loan, and keep Fred in a job. As for Fred, as he came back to work after Easter, he must have been pondering over his future too, and worrying about his prospects in a declining textile industry if he lost his job.

Some decisions work out, some do not, but for my mum to be walking down to a shop only two minutes away, doing what she was good at, standing on her own two feet, not sitting at home in isolation all day, would obviously be a good move. I weighed up my own circumstances, and decided that as I had coped with doing two jobs during my dad's illness, I could also do so now, even in different school circumstances. Fred was happy to learn that I would do my best to keep the business going, and he was eager to continue repairing the flyers, no doubt thankful that he would still have his job. But for how long? I knew that busy times lay ahead, but little did I realise that if I had been living in top gear for the past six months, I would be living in overdrive for the next five years.

Turning up at St Joseph's was like walking into the next century, with all its modern facilities. Whereas St John's simply had eight or nine classrooms, here were state-of-the-art science laboratories, art rooms, woodwork, metalwork, domestic science and music rooms, a huge gymnasium and a very large playing field. All the teachers specialised. I knew that I had made the right decision to apply for the post, and was determined to be successful, largely impressed, as I was, with the whole environment, and by the staff too, many if not most of whom were in their middle twenties. There were no Miss Randles at St Joseph's. I was made welcome, particularly by the Headmaster Mr Jack Hilton, who had helped me out of my difficult situation with the Education Officer a few weeks earlier, and now he was to help me with my new problem, of having to combine starting my new teaching post as well as running the business. He fully understood my circumstances, and assured me of his support, which I greatly appreciated. Jack was a very popular man, well respected by his staff, and I remained on good friendly terms with him all his life.

It was the summer term, of course, which meant cricket, but it meant athletics too, something I had not expected. At first my games teaching colleague, Eddie McLean, took athletics while I organised the cricket, in lessons, net practices and the Saturday morning inter-school matches, but I began to take part in athletics too, and was very impressed by the benefits pupils can gain from one or more of the many facets of this multi-sport, jumping, throwing and running. So impressed was I that I gladly attended after-school coaching courses, learning the techniques required for such events as high jump, throwing the discus and javelin, putting the shot, and baton changing in the relay races – and lots more. I even gave the impression to some of my Royton teammates that I preferred athletics to cricket, so enthusiastic must I have been. All in all, the first term was an eye opener, everything happening so quickly, but I felt as if I had hit the ground running.

In the classroom I taught English, my own favourite subject, to pupils of different ages and abilities, according to my timetable, all very different from the one class all week at St John's. I was now part of the English Department, led by Mike Cannon, who encouraged initiatives and ideas. There were monthly staff meetings, a totally new experience for me, there never having been one in all my time at St John's. And then there were parents' evenings. The school had its own full-time groundsman, and during that first term I was delighted to see how well he prepared the cricket square and the nets, enabling the boys to have good wickets to bat and bowl on. There were many lunchtime and after school hours spent in the nets, and on some of them Ray Reynolds, Royton's new professional, another Australian, but very different from Cec Pepper, very generously came along to coach the boys, who were thrilled to bits by his presence.

Not every lunch time nor after school hour was I on the field, though, but in the van visiting Cotton Mills or Shaw Road, Oldham, where Fred was grinding away on his own. I had to make the Bolton trip once or twice weekly, to take the flyers for balancing, and every day I would end up at Junction Flyers at about 5 o'clock, have a chat with Fred, having unloaded some flyers I may have collected from a mill that day, and perhaps loaded a skipful to be delivered to a different mill early the following morning. Then I would give Fred a lift home. It was overdrive, all right, but I was managing to keep both balls in the air, as they say. It did become slightly easier for me during the summer when Fred told me that he thought he was cable of balancing the flyers himself, which would cut out my journeys to Bolton, so I went along with his suggestion. Had there been any problem when the flyers were put back on the spindles

I would soon have been told, but there were no complaints, so Fred's idea had worked. It was only later when I thought that perhaps in those final few weeks during March when my dad had returned to work, that he might have shown Fred how to do the balancing, in case of another emergency. It seemed highly likely, just as he had prepared me for my possible future role, much earlier.

My mum was now enjoying her time behind the counter once again, and her shop was taking the money that the previous owners said it would, and it also gave her the opportunity to get to know her customers, some of whom she would also see at St Margaret Mary's, which was our Parish Church. Both Winifred and I looked for opportunities to do something interesting with mum on Sundays, and once or twice I took her on the Motor Club Treasure Hunt rallies. I was still writing the monthly newsletter, and enjoying my Monday evenings at the Roebuck Inn.

Saturdays, in summer, were cricket days, of course, and I spent much of the first half of the season in the 2nd XI but there was one game when I perhaps wished I had not been promoted to the first team. It was the Wood Cup Semi-Final away at Middleton, on a Monday evening following a weekend when Basil D'Oliviera's bowling had been hammered all over the field, and the club decided that their professional had sustained an injury and therefore they had to find a deputy. So who did they get? Gillie! Yes, Roy Gilchrist, against whom I had played, but not batted – thanks to the rain – two years before. Was D'Oliviera injured? Probably not, but that was the way it was, and I was not very happy as I arrived home that afternoon to read about the team change in our Oldham Chronicle.

Having lost the toss we were put into bat, and were soon 24 four 4, with Gillie not having taken one of the wickets. Our batsmen had tried to fend off his fiercely fast bowling, and got themselves out trying to score off the left arm spinner Eric Price at the other end. Following a good stand between Ray Reynolds and Brian Smithies we recovered to 84 for 6, which was when I went into bat, and when Gillie bowled his first ball to me I simply never saw it. I did my best to keep him out, managed a cover drive for four off Eric Price, until, with the score on 93 for 9, he had me LBW for 7, his sixth wicket. On the following night Middleton reached 96 for 6, with my old Xavarian College friend and rival Paul Rocca not out 0. No doubt he went to Benediction that night! As for Gillie it was the first and last time I faced his bowling, and I have no regrets about that. Those were the pre-helmet days, and batsmen could have been killed by the speed of his bowling. For the rest of the season I remained in the first team, somewhat surprisingly, as I hardly ever reached double figures, but my best season was to come the following year. The cricket season had ended earlier, of course, at St Joseph's, and I completed my first term there having happily blended into my new surroundings, and now had a few weeks to devote more time to Junction Flyers.

Going back into the cotton mills following my dad's death I wondered whether some of the business might be lost, but thankfully the carders at all the eighteen mills he had done all their flyer repairs for, continued to phone in when they had work to be done. The difference for me now, of course, was that it was I, not my dad, who had to decide what to tip the carders, and what to write on the delivery notes. Not that I ever considered attempting to change things. I was now part of the "real world," as people described it. If I wanted business it had to be at a price, or another company would soon be getting it. The carders and under carders were all genuinely likeable and friendly men, and I got on well with them. I continued to back-hand them money or cigarettes, and weighed up any additional opportunities if a carder might be tempted to co-operate even more. During my first few weeks making deliveries, as my dad lay in his hospital bed, I may have felt a twinge of guilt at fabricating the number of flyers and pressers I was delivering, on his instructions, but not any more. If a back-hander, or a fictitious delivery note, meant more work – so what? My job now was to make a profit for my mum, a wage for Fred, and free transport for me. I never received, nor wanted, a penny for myself during the five years the business survived, and indeed, thrived. As far as I was concerned my free travel was a bonus, whereas my mum's loan repayments were the number one priority. Little did I realise then that I would average 60 miles a day in the van, making over 400 mill visits each year. It mustn't have been overdrive I was doing, but supersonic speed!

Perhaps it was gathering some of that speed when the new school year opened in September 1962. On the playing fields now it was football for me, and rugby for Eddie. On Saturdays were the inter-school matches, and I managed the first team, but I appreciated the back-up and support I received from my friend and English Department colleague Damian Maloney, who was happy to arrive at the school, home or away, where the game was being played, before me. I left home very early, of course, but I would have some flyers to deliver or collect first, and if there was an unexpected delay, I was covered by Damian who always enjoyed refereeing the games. It was during a games lesson that season when one of the most memorable examples of enforcing discipline took place. Discipline was very good at St Joseph's, when the use of the cane was still permitted, but rarely used, for there was a genuine respect for authority on the part of pupils, with the staff very rarely, if ever, overly strict. Eddie carried out his effective punishment once on the rugby pitch, and an effective impromptu punishment it was too.

Eddie and I had been called to attend to matters outside the changing rooms as the Fourth year boys had completed their weekly games lesson and were showering before the lunch break. We went back in after the boys had all left the room, only to find it reeking with cigarette smoke. We said nothing until the following week after they had changed, and then we reminded them of the smoke filled room, and asked every one of them to stand side by side with their backs to the wall. They did. Then we told them that if they were one of the smokers, to take a stride forward, in total silence. After a moment of stillness, out strode Leonard Kane, a tough and proud lad, his head high. Hesitantly, perhaps, others followed suit, until twenty or so had admitted their guilt, whilst another twenty still had their backs to the wall. Eddie and I asked each one, "Were you smoking last week?" and accepted the "No Sir," including that from Fred Collins, an absolute rogue, obviously lying through his teeth and infuriating the honest smokers who were prepared to accept their punishment. Their facial expressions at Fred's claim of innocence said it all. Their punishment was to run round the edges of the large playing fields twice, within a limited number of minutes. Failure to do it on time would mean starting the run again. Once again Kane led the way and they set off. As they did so the non-smokers began a game of football. Fifteen or twenty minutes later the smokers completed their running, all within the time limit, and we allowed them a little rest. Then Eddie took rugby players on to the other pitch, selected two teams, but very astutely. Most of the smokers formed one team. Eddie himself always took part in the games, acting as coach and referee, and he played scrum half for the opposing team, selecting Fred Collins as his out half, with instructions to stay near him, ready to take a pass, whenever Eddie had possession.

Top left Jimmy Kinsella, Top right Me, with a group of senior pupils at St Joseph's.

Fred was a well-built lad, more a prop forward than an out half, but this was today's team. Eddie got the ball, and as the opponents moved towards him he passed the ball to Fred, who was tackled just after catching it. Eddie would call out "Ready Fred," or "Keep going Fred," as he got possession, and after three or four last minute passes swung to

Fred, the smokers began to realise what an invitation this was. They had stood up to be counted, taken their punishment – but here was Fred, too sly to own up, thinking he had got away with it, now in the firing line. The tackles came in harder, but Eddie insisted that all tackles should be fair. Soon Fred was getting up very slowly, and visibly aching from the robust tackles. The smokers were happy. They had accepted their punishment, and were now administering theirs. As the boys showered and changed Eddie related the events to me, and I could see the looks of delight in their eyes as they trooped out of the changing rooms, glancing approvingly at Eddie as they passed.

Attempting to maintain discipline in the classroom these days must be a nightmare. It amazes me that so many teachers remain in the profession when pupils know that their bad behaviour is virtually untouchable. I also believe that this increasing contempt for authority has made its way into society generally, as increasing numbers of unruly pupils have left school, and having grown up in an environment where there was no effective control, they commit crime with the same feeling of certainty that they will never be caught or punished. The longer it takes for politicians and lawyers – usually the same people – to realise that our society is on its way to anarchy, the worse it will be, and the harder to tackle. Children, both at home and in the classroom, need a fair and firm authority that is not undermined by lawyers. The very rare instances of bullying by over-strict teachers have been blown out of all proportion, and those people who have campaigned for the changes that have been made, when any allegation made by a pupil, with or without evidence, automatically leads to a teacher's suspension, I regard with contempt. Fair and firm authority is needed in a civilised society, just as it is on a football or cricket field, and after my first football and rugby season at St Joseph's, it was the cricket season again, and at Royton too.

The 1963 season was the only one in which I never played a second team match. I might have done if I had followed the duck in the first game with another one, but instead, against the team I had made my successful debut in 1958, Littleborough, I was not out 36 when we declared, having shared a stand of 46 with Derek Stuart. My next good

Royton First XI 1962.

Back Row: (L to R) Kenny Lees, Me,
Alan Howarth, Reg Langton,
Stuart Anderson, John Cartmel

Front Row: David Shannon, Jack Scholes,
Ray Reynolds, Trevor Turner, Derek Stuart

innings was in the Wood Cup at Walsden, where I went to the wicket on 43 for 4, and hit 37 out of the 49 scored while I was out there. Thanks to Vibert Rodney (5 for 25) and Stuart Anderson (3 for 33) we won – and thanks to my top scoring innings too! But I was back to earth with a bump the week later, out for a duck to Depeiza, Heywood's West Indian pro. The most surprising, if minor, success of my season was not with the bat but the ball, at Castleton Moor when our pro, Ray Reynolds, captaining the side, put me on to bowl. I bowled nine consecutive overs, taking 2 for 27, including their opening batsman, Lou Pountain. I doubt it he would have been proud of that moment! Later in the season I made some scores in the teens and twenties, but the best was a gritty 12 not out against Stockport on a difficult wicket, hitting a cover drive for four to pass their 97 all out. Perhaps the most famous pro in the league that season was Sonny Ramadhin, then at Radcliffe, and he had me stumped, but not before I had hooked him for two boundaries.

Not only had 1963 been a success for me at the wicket, but at the altar too. Having arrived at St Joseph's the year before, I was pleased to see that there were at least four very eligible and attractive young ladies on the staff, and, of course, they soon all fancied me! I rather fancied them, too, and though Susan was not the first one I dated, she was the one I was really fancying, and I think we were both soon playing hard to get. Two people can get to know each other quite quickly when in each other's company every day as teachers are in the staff room, when characters and personalities are easily recognisable – whereas meeting for the first time during the last waltz on a Saturday night followed by a number of dates, takes a good deal longer. We continued to play hard to get, but subtle flirting was happening increasingly, but whether others on the staff noticed it or not they never said.

Anyway, I made the first move, or rather I couldn't move, because the van had broken down, and I needed a lift if I was to go out that Saturday night. I rang Susan who had her own car, so she picked me up and we went for a drink. Our romance began then, and blossomed. We were both regarded by our colleagues as strong personalities, and we could agree or disagree about anything and it made no difference. There is a common perception that opposites attract. We were certainly not opposites but we did attract. No one has a crystal ball, of course, and one never knows the future. Many years later things would turn out differently but in 1962 we fell in love, and by the summer of 1963 we had bought a detached bungalow in Moorside and tied the knot. Ours was not the first wedding, though. Jim Murphy had married Marjorie the year before, and was now firmly under the thumb, never going out on the traditional "lads' night out" every Friday for a pint or two. Richard and Judith had married in February, so his bachelor days also came to a glorious end the same year as mine did.

It had certainly been an exciting summer, but on the business front things were beginning to look gloomy. Cotton was a declining industry, and mills were being closed down. My initial involvement was in collecting flyers from a mill following a carder's telephone call to say he had a full set of 140 flyers to be repaired, polished and balanced. The mills routinely maintained their spinning frames, turning out their work efficiently. But as business declined some frames became idle, and there was less money spent on maintenance. Gradually the carders only required the "spares" to be repaired, perhaps 40 or 50, as they broke down on different frames. The other problem for me was that our stock of pressers was running out. Replacing broken pressers was the most profitable part of the business for us, and my dad had been shrewd enough to obtain unwanted pressers at mills that were closing down, where all the metal would be sold as scrap. A back hander to a carder would see to it that a full skipful of pressers could be acquired thus ensuring his supplies for the coming months.

I began to realise that I had better go out to knock on doors, call to see the carders, rather than wait for them to ring, and to make enquiries for pressers and flyers that a mill no longer needed. Getting on well with the carder was the key to these situations, and one good turn deserved another. Calling at the mills to see if they had any work often prompted a carder to promise to find some work the following week, usually as an act of kindness when they realised we were quiet. Going to try to obtain work at "new" mills was not easy for me, but there was no other way but to try. I wrote letters to managers, had business cards printed, and at half terms or in the Easter or summer holidays I would be suited up, calling at a mill office, requesting to speak to the manager. Mostly it was a "No thank you," but I did manage to find new work and our overall income rose, despite the intense competition. It took an increasing amount of my time, and a study of some of the notes I made in the diaries I recently discovered, provide an insight into the way my mind reacted to the circumstances I had found myself in, and the way the cotton industry was, as I strove to keep Junction Flyers on the go. For obvious reasons the names have been changed.

SPRING MILL	*Collected a skip full of old rovers. £1.*
ELK	*Brian helpful. Must give him some fags soon.*
HARBOUR LANE	*Delivered. Harry 50 fags. Very pleased.*
VALE	*Alex starts as manager next Monday. Two under carders to be given a run for carder's job. Took pies and custards. They loved 'em.*
MONARCH	*Got 30 inters. Just right for Vale. Bert £1.*
DAWN	*Under carder ok. Gave him 2/6 – looks a good bet for us.*
VALE	*Took pies.*
AQUA	*Joe 10/- Derek 10 fags.*

MONARCH	*Got 60 pressers. £1. Bert.*
VALE	*Very disappointing. Alex cagy. I think we've lost it. George on our side. Said Alex had been told to look for a cheaper firm. Alex said nothing.*
ELK	*Brian 10 fags. No rovers for a while. Things looking gloomy. Visited 15 mills this week to find new work. Mostly "nothing doing" "doubtful" "manager busy" "could be" etc.*
VALE	*Chat with Alex. Doing his best for us. Took pies. Friendly. Going for a pint with him next Monday.*
MONARCH	*Got 60 pressers. £1 Bert.*
VALE	*Alex confirmed we were back. Our work is definitely better.*
ROY	*Granville 10/-*
	34 mills visited in week before new term starts.
AQUA	*Derek 10 fags. He's getting used to them, I think.*
VALE	*Took Easter Eggs.*
MONARCH	*Bert £1 for 30 inters – just right for Vale!*
BARCHANT	*Carder a curious chap. Signed note then said, "We all know that carders make a bob or two." I ignored it. Gave him 10 fags. Cheeky beggar.*
DAWN	*News of its closure announced yesterday. Went to see if I could get some pressers.*
LILAC	*Collected spares. Seem to be modernising soon. Outlook not rosy.*
BARCHANT	*Booked 10 extra flyers. Carder 5/-*

AQUA	*Strange experience. Manager reprimanded me for taking 3 flyers off a frame. Also reprimanded Derek and Ted for letting me. Made Derek ckeck to see if any unauthorised flyers were in my van. Two delivery notes had already been signed. Hope the manager does look to see how many flyers I had delivered! Fingers crossed.*
DAWN	*Got three sets of roving pressers. Bob 50/-*
OLDHAM TWIST	*Frank signed note. No flyers! £1.*
DAWN	*About 200 inter pressers. Bob 30/-* *Half Term 29 mills visited in four days.*
DAWN	*Got 3 frames of inters. £3/10/0. Met Tom 9pm. Signed note. £3!*
NEWBY	*Delivered. £1 Bernard. 10 fags Dave.*
BARCHANT	*Met Frank in Oddfellows. Signed note! 50/-* *Gave Fred 10/- and 20 fags. Took him for drink. He's done well this week.*
VALE	*Alex in a queer mood.*
BARCHANT	*Delivered! Frank 50/-*
VALE	*Collected. Alex ok today.*
MONARCH	*Picked up about 200 rovers and 25 inters. Just right for Tower.*
MONARCH	*Delivered. As per note, for a change!*
HAWTHORN	*Collected spares. Signs of hope of steady work here. Fingers crossed!*
MOSTON	*Carder said we would be getting some work soon.* *Mid –Term. 14 mill visits in 2 days. New van. LBU 50E*
BARCHANT	*Carder fast asleep! Must call Monday.*

ELK   *Tommy off ill. Gave Frank a lift home*
End of another year. Outlook gloomy in trade
generally, but an unusually large number of
one – off jobs have cropped up, and continue
to, which have cushioned the general
position. Time will tell. Much talk of more
closures soon. Outlook poor. We shall see.

Also contained in my 1965 diary is the list of presents I had bought to give to various managers, carders and under carders, for Christmas.

2 x 100 Senior Service. 30 x 50 Embassy Tipped. 18 x 50 Players Plain. 40 x 40 Embassy Plain. 5 x50 Park Drive. 4 x 10 Manekin Cigars. 2 Milk Tray, All Gold, Weekend, Ballerina, Devan Milk, Quality Street. 2 Advocat, 2 Dubonnets 3 Whiskies, 1 Rum, 1 Vodka, 4 Good Sherries, 5 Cheap Sherries, 1 Burgundy.

I must not have kept a record of the cash I back-handed that Christmas, but there can be no doubt that some pound notes were part of the "Happy Christmas" tradition. All these randomly selected comments above are exactly what and how I wrote them into my diaries between 1964 and 1967, reflecting as they do the role I played in keeping the business going, and the double life I had to live. During the day I was the Catholic schoolmaster living an honest life, doing my best to ensure that my pupils did so too, whereas when I visited the cotton mills I was living in another world, and had to adopt its different morality if the business was to survive. Thankfully it did.

If life was fast in the St Joseph's and Junction Flyers' worlds, it was accelerating in Sholver Lane too, wonderfully so, when Richard was born. What a difference my becoming a dad made to me! I had never been a person who fussed over other people's young babies, but now I was suddenly a sensational softie. My friends couldn't believe it, nor could Susan, when they saw me drooling over Richard when he was only days, then weeks, or months old. His birth had brought out things in my nature that I never knew were there. I am sure that virtually every new dad will have experienced the same shock to the system, but when it happens it is wonderful, as it was the following year when Lucy was born. Now I had both arms full during the evenings, giving Susan a rest from her all day mothering role, including nappy changing and bath-time duties. I was becoming an expert!

By that year, 1965, my day time duties continued at overdrive pace, and having organised a number of fund raising social events at the Cricket Club I became an elected member on the General Committee. My earlier experiences at High Moor Motor Club in taking part in Route Card Car Rallies had prompted me to organise them at the Cricket Club, and they were very popular. I went round the shops and various businesses in Royton and asked them to donate prizes, which, generously, many of them did, so there were some happy faces in the club house after the rallies as they collected their prizes. The biggest event I organised, though, was the Single Wicket Competition in 1965 when sixteen good amateur and professional cricketers took part in this novel competition, an idea I had got having read about the first one that had taken place the year before at Lords. I was supported in putting forward my idea by George Lees, who was an excellent club chairman, and Bill Varty, a wise and well respected committee member who, more than a decade later, became the CLL President. Months of planning went into the organising of the event, which invoved a lot of hard work done by a large number of members, especially on the day when there were about thirty fund raising stalls and competitions on the car park, tennis courts and around the pavilion, and hundreds of people came to see this exciting new cricket competition. Thankfully we had a sunny day, and we made record takings. It was the first of my three years on the Committee, and in both 1966 and 1967 I also organised the competition, which quickly became a big event for professionals and amateurs to take part in.On the field myself though, since my successful 1963 season, I had done less well. I had looked forward to the 1964 season, and although I was selected for the first team for most games I only topped 20 in four or five occasions. Two of these were against Ashton, and it was in the home game when I was put on to bowl and I took the third and final wicket of my career. I must have terrified the Ashton skipper because after I had bowled my first ball of the season, which dismissed the batsman K. Kelly, the innings was declared closed – denying me a hat-trick perhaps? Highly unlikely! The other match I recall was our professional's benefit, in which The Manchester City star, Francis Lee, played. He was lively in the dressing room and on the field too, bowling fast and hitting a quick 38 runs. All in all I was fortunate to keep my place in the side even though I did manage to attend net practice on most Tuesday evenings despite my increasing workload.

During 1966 I was also busy in a totally new project. I had found it remarkable, in the weeks following Lucy's birth, how many friends and relatives bought her baby clothes as presents. I was also mindful that Susan, who enjoyed being busy and involved herself, seemed to be finding it rather difficult to adjust to being at home all day. My business brain must have switched on, and I broached the idea of our opening a children's wear shop, which Susan could run. Then just as night followed day we eventually found premises in Ashton, a town where the main suppliers of top quality children's wear manufacturers had a "vacancy," so we went ahead. In those days top suppliers restricted each town to two or three outlets, so Ashton was the nearest we could find, and as Warrington Street was near to the market and bus station, we went for it. The premises had been a shoe repairer's, so there was a lot of physical change to be made before it could be opened as a trendy and fashionable baby and children's wear shop, which would be called Kiddie Boutique. Joinery, plastering, papering and painting were needed in abundance, and I spent most nights labouring away, along with friends who were better than me at DIY skills, and the shop began to take shape. My St Joseph's friend Damian was exceptionally helpful and generous with his time, and was a very good handyman too. Susan was in contact with the various manufacturers, doing her best to buy the best selling lines, and with the new furnishings in place Kiddie Boutique opened on the day we had planned for, 22nd July 1966.

Susan initially worked two or three afternoons, and Saturdays, with Joyce employed full-time, and our fashionable new business was on its way. It is difficult to predict the takings of any new business, so if it pays its way and makes a profit from the start, things can, one hopes, only go better. We were pleased with the first few weeks, not only because of the takings, but because Susan was not now just a mother, but busying herself in the shop, busy in all manner of ways on the learning curve that a new business presents. My roles had increased too. In addition to the 400+ mill visits I was making every year, my responsibilities at St Joseph's had increased when I was awarded a promoted post, as the School was slightly re-organised following the opening of the new upper school, which took some our top year pupils. I became the Careers Adviser, in addition to my English and Games curricular roles, so this meant I was attending various meetings and short courses to become acquainted with this new work. Junction Flyers was still big part of my life, of course, but with mills closing down and work becoming even harder to find, I felt under increasing pressure to keep it going. Despite the gloomy outlook the overall takings had increased every year, so I must have been doing something right. As we approached Christmas, 1966, with only six months' repayments still to be made on my mum's 5-year loan, the Junction Flyers profit would soon cease to be of crucial importance, but I remained determined to do my best to face the textile industry challenges.

A successful Kiddie Boutique would be ideal as the additional income for us, were my free transport to go, so we were happy with the progress during the first six months. My daily routine had an extra chapter now. Instead of going home when I dropped Fred off I would drive to Ashton, collect the day's takings from Joyce, then give her a lift home to Failsworth, and finally drive back to Moorside. Busy though the many aspects of my life were, family, business, and cricket, I was an increasingly totally committed teacher at St Joseph's, where I never put my responsibilities to the pupils or my colleagues second. It was there that I began two of the initiatives I would develop more in later years, the first was in editing a school magazine (echoes of the monthly newsletters at the Motor Club), and other was in taking pupils to the theatre.

My memories of having enjoyed our Saturday evening family visits to the Coliseum Theatre would have influenced me in arranging the first school visit to a matinee performance, which the children thoroughly enjoyed, most of them never having been to a theatre except to see a Pantomime. The other visits I organised were in the evenings, taking a group of 4th year pupils who wished to go, and whose parents could afford to pay for their ticket and bus fares. There was no way we could have hired a coach. Looking back now on the way I made the totally acceptable arrangements then, seems unbelievable. The thirty or so pupils, living in or around Rochdale, caught the 6.00pm bus from the town centre, totally unsupervised, and they travelled to Barker Street, Oldham, where I met them, having parked my van nearby. I then walked with them, all in line, through the market place, and then down Yorkshire Street, to the theatre. The pupils knew that there was to be no talking during the play and definitely no toffees being noisily unwrapped! After the performance I escorted them to the Star Inn, caught the bus with them to Barker Street, bade them good night, and they carried on to Rochdale where, perhaps, or perhaps not, they were met by their parents, as they alighted. They behaved well on the bus, knowing that I had told the conductor to contact me at school the following day if any misbehaved. How times have changed!

I arranged many theatre visits at my next school, but at St Joseph's the visits were well appreciated by the pupils and their parents, because there was not a weekly theatre company in Rochdale, so attending a theatre to see a play was a rarity. The pupils also enjoyed helping to produce a school magazine, which I first edited in 1965. That edition was a photocopied booklet of articles written by 4th year pupils, but the 1966 and 1967 versions were commercially printed magazines entitled "The Worker" based on the real St Joseph's occupation. They included photographs and were financed by local businessmen who placed advertisements in them.

It also provided a good opportunity for the pupils in their final year at school, preparing for the world of work, to experience the commercial and business aspects of the project. I arranged for them to go out during the school day, usually in groups of two, to different shops and businesses, to seek advertising, and successful they were too. Our 1966 edition had

29 full, half or quarter page adverts, and in my editorial I praised the work done by the pupils and named John Mills, John Taylor, Anne Marie Grant and Julie Motelevich, "who were particularly successful and who were told they would make good salesmen and saleswomen. I offer them my thanks and congratulations." In the following year another set of pupils had entered the 4th year, and the magazine was equally successful, and I singled out for special thanks and praise Marie Gillis, Catherine Shields and Alfie Riley.

Probably my five years running Junction Flyers had given me more business acumen than I would otherwise have had, which was useful in my role as a careers adviser, as was the art of writing persuasive letters of application. It was a skill I did my best to instil into them, and there were a number of pupils and former pupils who were later told by their employers that the good letter they had written had ensured an interview, often leading to their being offered the job.

It was during the 1967 summer that I wrote my own such letter. I had seen a vacancy advertised for the Head of English Department at North Chadderton Secondary Modern School, a Grade B post, so I applied. I did not feel optimistic because I expected there to be many applicants who would have more experience then me, perhaps already on Grade A, and looking for promotion. I was delighted to be invited for an interview, and stunned when I was offered the job. Mr Graham, the Headmaster, later told me that he had been impressed by my letter of application. I think he would have been even more impressed by the reference I had been given by Mr Jack Hilton. I could not have had a better one if I had written it myself.

To Whom It May Concern:

Mr John Cleary was appointed to the staff of this School in April 1962 and since that time he has been a very valued member of the English Department. In class teaching and management Mr Cleary has always shown a very high level of skill and in all his work there has been sustained interest and success.

As a teacher he is firm and tactful. He has the respect of the children and is held in high esteem by all members of the staff as a most valued and loyal colleague. He is a man of original thought and ideas and keeps abreast of the changing educational pattern by constantly attending courses and lectures. In September 1965 Mr Cleary was appointed to a post of special responsibility for Fourth Year pupils. Here he is responsible for Careers advice, liaison with the Youth Employment Service, reports and references for school leavers. He has been of considerable assistance to me personally in the help he has so freely given in the planning of Fourth Year Courses. The school fully appreciates the amount of time Mr Cleary has spent in extra-curricula activities – assisting with school teams, organising Fourth Year and School Dances, the running of General Knowledge Quizzes and the publication of the annual School Magazine. I know him to be a man of the highest integrity and ideals. It is therefore with confidence that I can recommend him for the post for which he has applied.

J Hilton
Headmaster

So as the school year ended I would have one final term in Rochdale before taking up my new post in January 1968, teaching up to 'O' Level, CSE and soon 'A' Level too, responsible for a department of eight full or part-time teachers of English. A new challenge awaited me. Meanwhile I was facing a new challenge at Junction Flyers too, even though we were coping, mainly thanks to "one-off" jobs that I had managed to get, but it was taking an increasing amount of my time, especially on Saturdays, half-terms and holidays. Two factors stood out. My mum's loan had been paid off, so she no longer needed the income, but the prospect of my turning up at a new school as a senior member of staff with a textile business to run as well, seemed wholly unacceptable.

Fred was now 63 and without him there would have been no Junction Flyer Repairs throughout the past five years, so I felt I owed him something, which is why I went to see Mr Taylor at Bolton. The overall outcome was that he agreed to buy the business, having given me his assurance that he would continue to employ Fred for the two years until his retirement – but only at a price! That was to be a payment of ten pounds per week! It seems a strange deal as I look back on it now, and it seemed a strange deal in 1967, but I was happy to put his £10 note in my pocket, drive back to Oldham, and hand over the keys to Fred, and thank him profusely for all he had done. He thanked me for keeping him in a job and we parted on good terms.

During those five years I had succeeded in increasing the number of mills we did work for from eighteen to twenty nine, and raised the annual income by more than 50%. This had meant my making an increasing number of mill visits, of course, and up to August 17th, when I made my final one, I had already made 280. I looked back over those years with great satisfaction. I had put a lot into it, and it had given me considerable business experience that teachers can normally never acquire. Above all, I had fulfilled the promise I had made to my parents in my letter from RAF Benson, ten years earlier.

Kiddie Boutique was now a year old, and Susan was into the swing of things, but by the autumn she was not swinging quite so fast, as on October 9th she gave birth to Sarah. I was a doting father once again! The bungalow on Sholver Lane was now becoming crowded. Richard was a lively three year old, Lucy was two, both sleeping in the same bed, with Sarah in the cot. I was at home more now. I had organised the single wicket competition during the summer but gave up the committee work, so apart from my regular visits to Ashton to collect the takings I did not have quite so many outside responsibilities, becoming almost a full time dad.

At the end of the term I said farewell, but not goodbye, to St Joseph's. I remained on very friendly terms with all the staff, and for many years would meet up with Jack Hilton, Damian Maloney, and Liam Ryle for a pint or two in Royton. The six years had been very valuable to me, all of which had hinged on that visit I made to Jack's home on the afternoon of my meeting with the Education Officer. Had that not happened who knows what direction my life and career would have moved in? Thankfully it did happen, and after six good years I was eager for the next challenge.

7 North Chadderton, Abersoch and 505

This, my second career move, was a much larger stride forward than my first one; it could have been quite daunting, but thankfully it was not. I walked in as a senior member of staff, head of the largest department, and a total stranger to all the staff. I looked forward eagerly to my new challenges and adjusted to my different responsibilities very quickly. I was based at the newer Hunt Lane building, where all the 3rd, 4th and 5th formers were taught, the 1st and 2nd year pupils remaining at the original Broadway building.

The next four and a half years enabled me to develop and fulfil many of the ideas and ambitions, both in and out of the classroom, that had been growing whilst in my Rochdale schools. It was at North Chadderton that I first took a group of pupils outside the classroom, to a more scenic location, a field through which a stream flowed, to develop their descriptive writing. I would do that even more in my final school, Limehurst, always based on my belief that William Wordsworth would never have been inspired to write his "Daffodils" poem whilst sitting in his study.

I also extended my theatre-going idea to a level I could never have imagined whilst at St Joseph's. Nor could I have imagined that within a year of my taking up my new post that I would not just be teaching to

GCE "O" Level, but to "A" level too, as the school developed a 6th form, leading to my Grade B post being upgraded to a C.

In the classroom during the first few days at North Chadderton I became aware of a different atmosphere than that at both my Rochdale schools where the pupils had been mostly from working class families, with some parents struggling to feed and clothe their children. Here the pupils came from a mainly semi-detached locality and their behaviour was more mature. Discipline had been good in Rochdale, but had often to be enforced. At North Chadderton it was much more relaxed. I quickly adapted to the different challenges, teaching the top stream in all three years as well as the bottom stream, where, as one would expect, there were one or two trouble makers, but I enjoyed the work immensely.

I was full of ambition – not for promotion – but for my pupils to do well and for me to be successful in this new higher level challenge. I remembered the days when I began to study in Manchester's Central Library, where my love of literature had blossomed; and now at my new School I must have been re-living the experience, for the benefit of my pupils. In turn their well behaved and mature approach to their work made my task both easier and more rewarding, and I was delighted when in August their "O" Level and "GCE" results were very good. However, on the day the first results were published I went into the school with my fingers crossed, knowing that my reputation in the school rested on the level of success my pupils had achieved. Thankfully I came out smiling, as did the pupils, some of whom were returning in September to become the first "A" level students in the school.

By now my theatre visits idea had taken place, too, beginning with one to Oldham Coliseum, when the tickets were snapped up and more or less paid for within two or three days, not at the 3p per week system at St Joseph's. I arranged visits to the Coliseum, Manchester's Library Theatre, The Octagon in Bolton, The Everyman in Liverpool, even The Regent in Stoke. Occasionally there may have been a matinee visit, but mostly they were evening performances, always travelling by coach. It was the success and popularity of these theatre visits that prompted me to plan for the most ambitious one. In the Autumn term of 1969 I arranged a 3-day visit to Statford Upon Avon. The coach journey began on Tuesday morning, enabling us to spend the afternoon visiting Shakespearian places of interest in the town, and after an early evening meal we took our seats for the evening performance. An overnight stay at a nearby youth hostel was followed by a morning spent writing, as the pupils again visited the River Avon and theatre area. We then attended both the matinee and the evening plays, and the superb acting, outstanding scenery and the sheer magic of the theatre itself made it a memorable three days. There were more visits and time for writing on Thursday, before setting off on our return journey.

I believe that well prepared visits of this kind, always managing to persuade the theatre staff, when I booked the tickets, to provide us with seats close to the stage as possible, with my assurance that the pupils would remain absolutely still and quiet, are wonderful experiences for young people, who will grow up with not the slightest prejudice against the Bard, and will, hopefully, go on to encourage their own children to enjoy his plays many years later. Occasionally I meet up with former pupils who have been on one of my Stratford visits, and they will invariably remind me of how memorable the occasion was.

In the School Magazine "Breakthrough", which I edited in 1969 and 1970, I included some of the pupil's writings which they completed by the River Avon or on their return to school, which reflect their appreciation and enjoyment of their visit.

The River Avon
The weeping willow dipped its weary branches into the stagnant water. Gliding gently under the bridge, the barge disappears into the dark dismal tunnel. The noisy town traffic drowns the gentle whispers of the trees; from the overhanging branches leaves whirl silently, landing delicately on the water, where lilies float in clusters. Looking up on the ash, seeing its branches entangled like a person in pain, the mushroomed shaped oak stands, looking like the king of all trees, holding its branches proud and stiff. Pigeons are perched at the water's

edge, staring vainly into the rippling water; on being disturbed they flutter to the other side. White frothy looking swans turn, showing off to their land admirers. A beige-grey coloured church towers up from the well-cut hedge. The smell of freshly cut grass fills the air, while the privet hedge, cut so professionally, look like stone pillars. All is peaceful, except for the tiny birds, which frequently give a little chirrup.

Pauline Hopwood

Peace

The mood is placid; maybe this is because the river, which is so tranquil while everything else seems to be sad, but beautiful. Ripples roll over each other like tiny fish at play, and a few forlorn leaves bob along and seem to be toying with the water. Rows of trees stand amongst the primly cut lawns, with no movement, apart from the crunchy leaves being whipped along by the slight breeze; showing signs that autumn is approaching, throwing over its cloak of orange and brown, and casting aside the summer. A great willow dips low and rests upon the ground, throwing out its branches and spreading them about the lawn. One particular tree, an ash, winds and twists itself so that the branches resemble arms searching or feeling for something they may never find. A little further along the river a host of swans coasts along the water, waggling in the most dignified manner. They are watched by ruffled pigeons which seem to be stuck to the bank. A slight rustle of trees is all that can be heard in the peace and solitude of Stratford.

Ann Turner

Stratford's Royal Shakespearian Grounds

The celestial grounds of Stratford's Royal Theatre are decked with colourful gardens and leafy trees, between which flows the River Avon. A little beyond this twining river, with its wooden bridges, stands Hamlet, gazing wondrously at the skull of Yorick. Hamlet's marbled body, clad in period costume, renders a nostalgic feeling, enhanced by his fellow stone companions. Prince Hal stands majestically placing a crown on his head, a triumphant smile across his face, which none can erase. Lady Macbeth views everyone with icy contempt, her glowering eyes seeming to ridicule the beauty of the surrounding scene, as she stands erect, her back turned on the drunken Sir John Falstaff. This rogue stands forever in his element, with a tankard of ale at hand, and a smile for all who come to view these epic characters. The most magnificent statue of all is of the master Shakespeare. He proudly sits, casting a watchful eye over the ever-changing scene, a book and pen at hand, yet chained to silence by the black marble.

Lesley Cunliffe

Atmosphere By The Avon

Willow trees hang relaxed over the water's edge; others reach Heavenwards. Large gaps of green stand on both sides, housing more of this tall majestic wood. The trees, now shedding their summer plumage, embellish the scene. On the right bank stands a complex of brick, which is the home of the performing of Shakespeare's plays. In contrast, a gaily coloured barge chugs into the lock, arousing curiosity among the tourists. An harmonious gathering of swans paddle elegantly down river, their reflections shimmering on the rippling water. The serenity of this place could not be more charming and comforting.

Lynne Dawson

Interval Reflections

I remember the theatre at night during the interval. I stood with my elbows leaning on the railings, stirring the fizzy contents of my drink with a candy-striped straw, contemplating the events of the play, like many other people. I was recovering from the fierce heat of crowded bodies, and reviving for the second half. The cool darkness hit my body as I got on to the balcony. White swans glowed in the night; they grouped together as though they were magnetised, floating through the cascading lights glinting on the Avon, a glowing blaze of light connected with dark shadow. Trees decorate the building, a ball of green foliage, the reflection speckled with swans. The effervescence in my drink clouded the bottom of the container. Groups of people clustered round tables, talking about the play and commenting on the players. The Royal Shakespeare Theatre glowed and shone, bringing the darkness to life like a candle. The oranges, yellows, blues and greens contrasted, giving a very abstract picture. Swans buried their poised heads, their necks arched beneath the expanse of colour, in order to replenish their appetites. The beautiful life of Stratford at night, the chaos of hot breathless bodies squeezing to get back to their seats, began. I waited, breathing cool, fresh air, before I submerged into the crowds. The glowing night would eventually die out, and the darkness would pervade the river. A barge lay at anchor sleeping in the tumult of the night, a black silhouette. The dark blue sky lay above, quiet, and living over this busy hive of life.

Christine Lightfoot

An Image Of Stratford

The glistening water gently flows
With the silent breeze.
The sky darkens,
Shadowing the now still water.
Leaves fall from gigantic trees
Rustling lightly in the quietness.
Shakespeare's home town,
His name on a golden plaque,
Will remain there in years to come.
The silent nights show what a calm
And peaceful town
Stratford is.
Its quaint little pubs and houses with
Lights shining, shows the warmth
And friendliness of these people.
Shakespeare's monument stands
Triumphantly in a beautiful garden.
Like everything else in Stratford
It is
Beautiful.

Irene Christy

Autumn In Stratford

The wind rustles the leaves.
Silence; peace; for autumn has come
And summer has passed quietly away.
The last roses are fading,
Their splendour and beauty ebbing,
Alone, their silent blossoms die.
Autumn, your colour and beauty
Nothing can surpass,
Your endless breezes, your morning blushes
As the piercing rays of the sky's own daughter
Smiles down upon you.
Your warm evening passions
Fill the heart with joy,
To see the night's lantern shine
Upon the silent waters.
To watch with love the elegance
Of your silent friends.
Autumn; Stratford; a memory I hold most dear.

Gail Mayes

The 1969 visit was such a huge success that I also arranged others in 1970 and 1971, each time being able to include both an "A" level and "O" level set play in our schedule, so the theatre visiting rarity in Rochdale had become a regular event for the North Chadderton pupils. Their examination results, each August, were good too, including those taking the first "A" levels, when once again I felt the pressure as I walked into the school in the summer holidays. The sixth form was gradually growing and my promotion to a grade "C" made me the only member of staff at that level. I had worked hard to achieve my success, and had enjoyed virtually every minute of it. It was certainly a busy four years or so with most evenings and much of my weekends taken up by marking homework and assessing pupils' work.

By 1972 my role in the school was very settled, Mr Burton having become Headmaster following Graham's sudden death. The English language and literature results were good, and I did not think in any ambitious way about the future, until it became apparent that there was not going to be a third Chadderton Grammar School, for we were now entering the Comprehensive era. As a successful head of the senior department my salary would be assured in any change over, but at the time I regarded my chances of holding on to my status as nil. In any Comprehensive School involving the mixing of a Grammar School and Secondary Modern School the Head of the English Department would almost certainly be the teacher from the grammar school, who would have a degree. I had no degree, of course, so I reached the conclusion that it would soon be the time to move on, before the amalgamation took place. I did consider the idea of taking an Open University three-year degree course, but that, I was informed, would require 15-18 hours of study each week, so with Richard, Lucy and Sarah being an increasingly lively part of my life, I decided against it.

I was in no hurry, nor was I under any pressure, but when I spotted a post advertised at Werneth Junior School, where I had completed a month's teaching practice more than a decade before, I applied for it. It was the first promoted post in an Oldham Primary School, and I hoped that my experience in leading a department of eight teachers might be seen as an advantage, which would, hopefully, lead to my eventually becoming a Primary School Head Teacher. Following my interview I was offered the post, to begin in September 1972, bringing to an end a very exciting four and a half years in which I felt I had fulfilled all the ambitions I had had since the first day I walked into the school.

The total of four and a half years at North Chadderton had indeed been very busy ones, but so had life outside the classroom. The children had started at school, of course, with Susan being more or less full time at the Ashton shop, and then in 1969 we made two big moves. In February we moved from Sholver Lane into Birch Avenue, Chadderton; then in June whilst on holiday at the Warren Holiday Site in Abersoch, I purchased a new 3-bedroom chalet on one of the loveliest beach sites in the country. Two years later, as I became a member of Royton and Chadderton Round Table, and with Susan becoming a member of the Ladies Circle, our social lives grew in leaps and bounds.

It was my decision to buy the holiday home, however, that stunned most people. We had enjoyed our Oldham Wakes holiday weeks of 1967 and 1968 in North Wales, where we had stayed in a farmhouse near to Nefyn, and enjoyed spending our days on different beaches on the peninsula. In 1968 we made our first visit to Abersoch, but being only mildy impressed by its rather stony beach, we decided to move on. By sheer good luck as we left the town we spotted a narrow lane leading towards the sea, and found ourselves passing lots of caravans, before parking the car only 25 yards away from what we later realised was the Warren Beach, where we spent a lovely afternoon. The sand was spotless, the sea calm, a perfect setting for young families.

We had been fortunate that day in that the barrier at the site entrance had not been in operation. Alas, it was on the following day when we tried to return, so we made some enquiries and only a few days after our holiday was over we had decided that the following year we would hire a caravan on the Warren for a week. Our friends and next door neighbours, Cyril and Margaret Huxley, decided they would too, with daughter Johanna, and we arrived there on a lovely June Saturday.

Every aspect of the site was attractive; the beach, caravans, the services, facilities, the club, and the general friendliness that everyone conveyed, and so by Monday lunchtime I decided I would buy a caravan there. Two years earlier I had negotiated the sale of my mum's Junction Flyers to Taylor's at Bolton for £10 a week, and my mum decided when the final payment had been made and there was £700 in the account, that since I had never received a penny for my keeping the business going for those five years, I must have that money. She insisted that I take it, and I could see her logic, so with caravans then being generally valued at four or five hundred pounds I thought I could comfortably afford one.

So I went to see the site manager Harold Roberts, but he informed me that no more caravans were going on the site, only chalets. Caravans were gradually being replaced by chalets in all the top holiday sites, of which The Warren was regarded as the best. They cost nearly £3,000 including

Our chalet, K24 on The Warren

the concrete base, annual rent and initial siting costs. There was no way I could afford £3,000, so I spent the rest of the day looking round at other nearby caravan sites to see if I could buy one somewhere else. However, none of the other sites that I looked at came anywhere near to the attractiveness of The Warren, so I felt it had to be The Warren or nothing, and went back to ask if I could pay by HP. Apparently that was how most of purchasers paid for their chalets, so I would have to pay a deposit of £405 and pay off the rest at £55 each month for five years. By the Friday we had agreed on the exact plot where our chalet would to be placed, on a quiet corner on K Site, with a field behind us, and it would be only another week or so before the chalet would be in place, with water, electric and gas all installed.

During that week we were on a different holiday site in mid-Wales enjoying our second Oldham Wakes week with the Huxleys, when Susan was busy working out what items we would have to buy as soon as we arrived home, to furnish the chalet with, such as blankets, cutlery, crockery etc. I also needed to make sure I could find the £55 each month, so I knew I had to hire the chalet out, and placed an advert in the following Monday's Manchester Evening News. We spent all day Saturday buying various items Susan had listed, and I then drove down to Abersoch during the following week with a handyman friend from my local pub to fix everything up, get the keys from the office, and generally make sure that everything was in working order. It had to be, because it was hired out from the following Saturday. In fact it was hired out for four weeks before Susan and the children had even seen it, never mind not having spent a night there.

The first full year of owning the chalet on The Warren was especially exciting for us. First we went for a weekend as the site opened in March, then for the Easter and Whit Bank Holiday weekends, two weeks at Oldham Wakes, at least a week in August and finally the Autumn half-term break prior to the site closing at the end of October. Then as we became increasingly familiar with the site's facilities, and gradually got to know people in other chalets and caravans, K24 had indeed become our second home.

Lettings had to be done successfully if I was going to be able to afford the monthly repayments, but I worked hard on it to try to ensure we only let it to people likely to respect it and not leave it a mess. I also had to become not quite the world's worst DIY man because there was a lot of work to be done over the first two years to make the garden area both attractive and semi secluded. This involved dry stone walling and flag laying, which took up quite a lot of my time, but was well worthwhile.

A lot of time was, of course, spent on the beach with the children. In those first two or three years we would be sand castling, paddling in the sea, playing various ball games, and as time went on more time would be spent swimming, playing in inflatable boats as the children made friends and generally enjoyed themselves. Soon they each had a bicycle there too, and enjoyed riding round the various paths and roadways which weaved their way up, over and around the sand dunes to the many secluded parts of the huge Warren site. It really was a holiday home, only a short walk from the Warren Club which opened every day of the week, including Sunday, which was a rarity in that part of Wales at that time.

We gradually got to know and became friendly with people in nearby chalets, especially Roy and Julie Wadsworth, and Alan and Jean Harter. People spent different weeks of the year there, but most chalet owners were there at Bank Holidays, when it became the custom for us to share a huge barbeque, usually in our garden, with a few glasses of wine too. Our next door but one chalet owner never joined in our barbeques however, because he was rarely there – Gordon Banks, the famous England goalkeeper who came to The Warren in 1970, following the famous World Cup save he made from Pele. Gordon and his wife were friendly neighbours, but his many football commitments probably restricted their usage of the chalet. We used ours as much as we could and I often looked back to the day in 1969 when I risked such a huge amount of money for a "glorified caravan," with absolute delight, the best £405 I ever spent, plus the monthly repayments of course! We also enjoyed the company of friends who came to visit us at the Warren, perhaps just for the day or staying with us for a night or two.

We also met many people whilst enjoying a drink in the Warren club, and we became good friends with Maurice and Jean Rothwell, who lived in Royton. Maurice very kindly took Richard out on his speedboat, and helped him to learn how to water-ski, for which Richard always walked to the shop every morning to collect and deliver his newspapers. Then one day, when Maurice told me that he was trading in his speedboat for a new one, I decided to offer to buy it from him, and within a few days our time at The Warren had a new dimension; we were speedboaters now. The children loved the experience of accelerating around the bay, and occasionally, if the sea further out was calm, going round St Tudwal's Island. Sand castles were just a memory by the late 1970's. Ours may have been one of the smallest and slowest of speed boats on The Warren, but the children, especially Richard, couldn't get into the boat fast enough, and he loved his skiing across the bay. It was wonderful. Our happy days at The Warren, however, were for about six weeks each year, the other 46 being spent in Chadderton, where in 1971 I became a member of Royton and Chadderton Round Table.

Richard Murphy and I had discussed the good social life he said that one of his colleagues was enjoying since he had joined Oldham Round Table, and following our interest in also doing so Richard said he would make some enquiries. Two or three weeks later I answered the knock on the door to find that the Vice Chairman of Royton and Chadderton Round Table, Barrie Coop, had called to meet me. He explained the activities of the club, what was involved and expected of members, and was happy to answer any questions. Following an interesting discussion he invited me to attend a number of fortnightly meetings, enabling me to decide if I would like to become a member, and at the same time to enable all the thirty or so members to get to know me and make up their minds whether to offer me the option.

Attending my first few meetings was a real eye opener for me. The Club was made up of men under the age of 40, with restrictions on the number permitted to join from any one occupation, so there was a wide range of professional and self employed, clerical and manual, present, everyone respecting and being respected by each other during the friendly pre-meeting meal, and in the business being debated afterwards. As a teacher accustomed to addressing a roomful of pupils and students I sensed how different, and indeed how much more difficult it felt to do the same before an adult audience. These Round Table members simply took it in their stride, showing oratory, persuasion, commitment and humour, usually in the best balance. As a guest I was not really expected to speak much, but to absorb the atmosphere, but I knew that unless I contributed appropriately by asking a question to a guest speaker, for example, my silence would not be regarded as an asset.

The induction process for new members takes two or three months, and I was delighted to receive my badge from Barrie himself, who had become Chairman at the AGM. Membership involved two meetings per month and the Ladies Circle, to which Susan was then invited to attend and join, once a month. Over the course of the year there would be plenty of social and fund raising events to enable everyone to mix purposefully and enjoyably, thus developing friendships. Happily there were no cliques in "505," as the Table was always referred to, and this was especially noticeable at the meal which was served before each meeting, where members positively adopted a policy of not sitting in the same place or with the same members each meeting. Another excellent policy, adopted throughout the whole movement, was that no-one discussed religion or politics at any meeting of members.

Apart from my teammates at Royton Cricket Club in my playing days, and the friends I had made in my late teens and early twenties, mostly over a drink or at football and rugby matches, as a teacher my opportunity to meet people from other walks of life was inevitably very limited. Suddenly I was surrounded by a wealth of diversity of working backgrounds, and the experience was enhancing. Members respected each other for what they contributed, not for the status they either had or did not have, nor for their wealth or lack of wealth! Everyone was on a level footing, and those whose ideas worked most successfully, who could persuade others by their oratory, were respected accordingly. Similarly Susan enjoyed the Ladies Circle meetings and became good friends with them, which also lasted a long time, and we fitted into the social life very well.

There was a strong community service ethos in the club, and events would be organised in order to make donations to worthy causes, many of which would be local to which members of the public were pleased to contribute. One of these was an annual summer gala day in Royton Park, with hundreds watching and betting on the donkey races, and having a go on the many stalls, all sideshows and competitions all around the park. Members never claimed any expenses and the trust that the public had in the Round Table movement was well deserved. Every night for two weeks in December we would walk the streets of Royton and Chadderton partaking in the annual Can Collection. This was a joint effort with

Royton & Crompton Rotary Club, who provided the float which their members pulled through the streets. There would be a Father Christmas seated high at the back, waving to the people who would stand at their doorsteps as the float slowly wheeled by, playing Christmas Carols as it did so. We would have nine or ten of our members slightly ahead of the float, knocking on the doors, asking for cans to be donated to the needy and impoverished, usually elderly people, and it was customary to see that they had their three or four tins ready before we even knocked, maybe having seen the feature in the Oldham Chronicle, and pleased to participate in this traditional charitable event.

Also at Christmas time we arranged an annual Christmas Party, to which perhaps 50 or 60 deprived children would be invited, taking place in a school hall, after which the children would receive a present, following two or three hours of games and a supper.

Whilst some of the community service and fund raising efforts were arranged annually, nothing was ever fixed, and new ideas were welcomed, with every incoming Chairman encouraged to express his preference for individual causes, a tradition established by the very founder members themselves.

Those founding members of 505, by their unparalleled achievement in setting up the Honresfeld Leonard Cheshire Home, began the strong community service ethos that all subsequent members inherited and maintained. Way back in its formation year 1955, however, when every single one of its founding members were just beginning to get to know each other, for them to even have attempted such an ambitious challenge was creditable enough, but to have so demonstrably succeeded thanks to their unstinting physical and mental effort, countless hours of their leisure, and in many cases business and professional time, influence, persuasion and the determination to see it through, simply beggars belief. The names of Royton and Chadderton Round Table and the Honresfeld Leonard Cheshire Home will always be indelibly linked, and all the members of 505 who, such as myself, joined The Table in later years, continued to admire and respect the outstanding achievement of our founder members.

We also regularly raised funds for charities by our Bottle Stall, which was our traditional speciality, with people paying for the chance to draw out a winning number to try to win one of the whisky bottles on display. Not all our community service involved money, however, and we would, on a rota basis, start to redecorate an elderly couple's home on a Saturday morning and by the Sunday afternoon the house had been transformed, with all the members doing their bit for three or four hours. There was no publicity involved, but there was a widespread respect for what members of 505 did. Taking part in such events would often mean that there was a "winding down" informal get together at, say, the Chairman's house, afterwards, and the presence of maybe not all but many of the members and wives did much to strengthen the friendships, as newer members began to get to know, and become known by, the more long serving ones.

On the more formal side of things I was surprised and flattered when Barrie Coop asked me if I would be interested in being nominated as Assistant Secretary, having only been a member for 10 or 11 months. He persuaded me to let my name go forward, and I was elected to the office, with the automatic progression to Secretary for the following year. Ian Wolstencroft was elected as Vice Chairman, so he and I spent considerable time in the first of those two years becoming familiar with the details of what undertaking the roles involved, both of us hoping to carry out our duties successfully in the year of office. That often involved visiting and welcoming members of other clubs in Area 40, to which our Table belonged. We had quite close links with Saddleworth and Oldham Tables, and members of these and other nearby ones such as Middleton and Rochdale would exchange visits, maybe in groups of three or four, all of which not only helped to bond the clubs and also widening our circle of friends even more.

Charter nights were some of the most memorable evenings, according to the ambitions of the clubs concerned, but it was in a way the kind of event which spawned the Sportsman's Dinners, which developed strongly in the 1980's. My first Charter Night experience was when Barrie Coop was Club Chairman, and he booked Bernard Manning, whom I had never seen until that night. Needless to say I was more than impressed, and there was quite a close affinity between him and our members, and be turned out at more than one of our fund raising efforts and charged us a lesser fee than his normal one because he knew that it was for local good causes. We also managed a Table visit to his Embassy Club, and we reserved our seats by the side of the stage for us, and Bernard made sure that no one pinched them. We had a superb night. Each year there would be an "Area Rally." This was a social event arranged in a different town usually on the last weekend of October at a reasonably sized hotel in Blackpool, Harrogate, St Annes or whichever town the organising Table decided. We organised one at the Norbreck Hydro, Blackpool, and it involved a lot of hard work, but once again the voluntary participation undertaken by various members increased their friendships.

At the Club level I was soon to be the one writing the minutes of the meetings, once Ian had taken over the Chair, with me as his Secretary. It was quite a shock to the system, in a way, to realise that the Secretary could never afford to switch off during a meeting. Whilst everything that was said didn't have to be written down, every matter raised the Secretary has to note it, even if he does not decide to include it when he sits down to write up the minutes following the meeting. I tried to make sure that I accurately recorded every formal proposal, and during the year I learned quite a bit about procedures of meetings, which came in handy over subsequent years. One letter I wrote to Fred Trueman, however, caused me some unease, when I booked him to speak at the Charter Night Dinner, attended by more than 200 guests, all in evening suits – all except Fred, that is! As Secretary, I had written to him providing full details of the evening, and explaining that the event would be "in formal dress." What Fred had read was "informal dress." When the whole room is crowded with men in bow ties, and the only person walking in wearing a lounge suit is the Guest Speaker, there arises the question of who got it wrong? Did the Club not inform the speaker, or does the speaker not care? Fortunately Rory Hartley, a past Chairman of considerable standing in the club, and acting as M.C., explained to those present that there had been a genuine misunderstanding, which was quite true, but I appreciated the way that Fred Trueman had just accepted the situation. It was he, after all, who was the odd one out, and could easily have reacted critically, but he just took it in his stride and was not troubled by it. I have always noted the lesson I learned that night. "Dress will be formal" was how I wished I had written it. Some years later at a Royton Cricket Club dinner I spoke to Fred about my letter and he said that it had happened to him on numerous occasions, and he just got on it with it. It never troubled him. It had troubled me, though.

I got on with my year as Secretary without any serious blemishes that I can recall, and two years later I was successfully proposed as Vice-Chairman. If having been nominated for Assistant Secretary so soon after having joined 505 had shocked me, the very idea that I might aspire to becoming its Chairman nearly floored me. Once again I spent a year in preparation, learning and listening as Keith Chadwick took over the Chair from Roy Mayall. This included visiting quite a few of the other local Tables, and becoming acquainted and friendly with their vice chairmen, in preparation for our year office, when each would invite the others to their big nights, such as Ladies Evening and Charter Nights. We would in most cases also include informal house parties, all of which again widened our circle of friends. Susan loved such evenings, back at others' houses as well as at ours, where she would, of course, always make a superb meal. Our social life, for which reason I had originally enquired abut joining the movement, was now at full speed, and I never detected any deference to wealth or disdain for lack of it, at this inter-table level.

Having become 505 Chairman it meant that 1976 was a special year for me, and it was a special year for my mum too. Having bought her shop in 1962, she had settled very well into the local community, largely thanks to the many ladies living nearby who were regular customers and with whom she had become good friends. Following Winifred's marriage to Tony in 1966 my mum decided to look for a smaller house, and settled for a bungalow on Kirby Avenue, an equally short walk from her shop. Whilst she always enjoyed her five or six days in the shop, she enjoyed her Sundays even better, when she could spend time with Richard, Lucy and Sarah. On virtually every Sunday I would take them to see their grandma, who fussed over them and spoiled them as every loving grandma does. She was a willing baby-sitter too, when Susan and I were enjoying our Round Table social life, and she would have them for a full week-end at least once a year. She was invariably tired out though, when we called to collect them, doubtless having been run off her feet by the lively three.

By this time, in the middle 1970's, she had retired. Having enjoyed ten or eleven years in her Owler Lane shop, she decided to put it up for sale. Way back in those difficult days following my dad's sudden death the purchase of the shop had seemed a good idea. Indeed it had been, and it helped her to rebuild her life during the following years. And while, during this time, she made many new friends in Chadderton, she always kept in touch with Edith Kenyon, her best friend from our days in Royton. Tom and Edith had moved from Royton to Stockport, where they had a shop for a number of years, after which they bought a house in Bredbury, before finally moving to the St. Annes area to a private caravan site. During all her years in the shop my mum would go to Manchester every Wednesday to visit various wholesalers to purchase stock, and on many of those days she would meet up with Edith, and they would spend many an hour in each other's company. They continued to meet up following Tom and Edith's move to the seaside where, sadly, Edith became ill, and passed away. During the following two years or so Tom and my mum kept in touch, and in 1976 they decided to get married. Norman had crossed the Atlantic, of course, to be the best man, and I gave mum away, as it is said, at St Margaret and Mary's Parish Church. I had not seen Norman since he and Pat moved to New York over a decade before but it was good that our boyhood friendship had been renewed, and that we were now step-brothers. Meanwhile mum and Tom were now enjoying retired life in Kirby Avenue and were very happy.

I was happy too, having just taken on my 505 Chairman's role, which involves chairing some twenty five meetings in addition to twelve

Council meetings during my year of office. That experience of chairing so many meetings at a fairly young age gave me valuable experience, both in my own teaching career, especially during the six years as the Choral Speaking Association Chairman, and later in countless meetings I chaired at Royton Cricket Club. I thoroughly enjoyed my chairmanship of 505, and as I handed over to John Emms at the AGM I was only three months away from my 41st birthday, which would have meant that I was leaving the movement that night had I not been eligible for one additional year in my capacity as Immediate Past Chairman, and so I did what a number of others enjoyed, spending a relatively relaxing final year whilst being available to offer support and advice when required by the current Chairman, I also continued to cement the good friendly relationships with members in other Tables, especially such as Rochdale, where Ron Wolf was a member. Ron was married to Ann, Susan's school friend, and thanks to our Round Table link up the four of us enjoyed a close friendship for many years.

Then it was goodnight and goodbye 505 at the 1978 AGM, when Richard Murphy, my best man and best pal, also came out, as did Geoff Broadbent, with whom I had also become a good friend. Geoff and I were members of Crompton and Royton Golf Club, where we played at least once a week, me after a day at school, and Geoff after his day at the bank. One good thing about leaving Round Table, however, was the immediate opportunity to join 41 Club, namely the club of former members of 505, some of whom had retired from 505 before I had even joined, but others who had retired over the previous six or seven years, and so the monthly meeting was not only nostalgic but very enjoyable and positive as it provided a pleasant evening amongst friends, with none of the heavy fund raising business to organise. The eight years or so that I had just completed, however, resulting from that knock on the door when Barrie Coop had followed up Richard's original enquiry, had added richly to our personal and social lives.

8 Werneth

My membership of Round Table and having a chalet at Abersoch may have made my social life extremely enjoyable, but things were to change abruptly in my teaching career. Having spent four and a half marvellous and successful years at North Chadderton where I had, as it were, climbed Everest, I suddenly felt as if I had dropped down a coal mine when I arrived at Werneth Junior School. It was as if I had not just turned the clock back to when I began my career at St. John's, but more like my days as a boy at St. Aidan's. Having taught in modern buildings with excellent facilities was something I had come to take for granted over the previous decade, teaching 13 – 18 year-olds, but I was now sitting in front of a class of pupils aged nine, in an environment I had forgotten existed. There was nothing wrong with the school – it was me, and the unpredictable decision I had made some months before, and I came home after that first day there full of despair, bitterly regretting what I had done, but knowing that there was nothing I could do about it.

It has always been my belief, though, that there is no point in looking back. What's done is done. The only way to go is forward, but it seemed as if I had a long journey ahead. And having been specialising in English I was now going to teach Art, P.E. Geography, History, Maths, and even Breadmaking! I had been appointed to the first such promoted post in an Oldham Junior School, but I had never taught a Junior pupil, except in my training college days – shades, perhaps, of my college tutor situation? Thoughts of this kind may well have been in the minds of some of my colleagues, but I never detected any resentment in the staff room, and as I settled into the school I got on well with them. I was determined to give 100% to the challenges facing me, despite the culture shock on that first day.

Now I was refereeing again, in charge of the football team, enjoying coaching them and delighted when they topped the league. Thanks to my wider involvement in the school I felt rather more settled, and following Miss Baker's retirement, the new Head was Mr Tom Jones, who was very keen on football and cricket, and we got on very well. He was eager to maintain the high standards that the school had achieved, being regarded as one of, if not the, most successful Junior schools in the town. I also managed the cricket team, which won the cup in two of the three seasons I was at Werneth. Cricket was always exciting for the pupils because Werneth Cricket Club was, and still is, literally, over the playground wall, and the club officials traditionally invited the school team to play their matches and to practise on their ground, The Coppice. At Junior school level the teachers who umpired the inter–school matches would more or less captain the side too, arranging the field and making bowling changes. This did not happen in the play off final, however, when the schools which finished top of each of the town's two groups, met. In 1973 the final was held at Moorside, where we won fairly comfortably.

In 1974 and '75 the finals took place at The Coppice, and both were memorable, but for different reasons. Our opponents in both games were the Hulme Prep. School. They were the winners in 1974, when we had a relatively young team, but which had not played at its best. At the end of that game their team manager came to shake my hand and condescendingly complemented our team for having been their toughest opponents of the season, but his demeanour indicated that he had expected to walk all over us. But it was not to be the same the following year. Our team had matured, somewhat, with the previous season's 3rd year pupils now in the top class, including very good players such as Andrew Milnes; another who would in later years play for and captain the Werneth club team, David Ainsworth; and the one who was the star on the day, Emil Hacobean, a strong, well built lad who could bowl powerfully. So in 1975, having elected to bat, again we did not fulfil our potential, and were bowled out for just over 100. The Hulme Prep. team were slowly but surely scoring runs, and I had no doubt that there would be a repeat of the condescending comments, as their parents prepared for their victory parade, as it were, before Emil Hacobean struck.

He bowled a ball which lifted sharply and hurt the batsman's finger. There was a delay as he received treatment, and it was whilst this was happening that Emil did something I can still see in my mind's eye. He stood at his bowling end, going nowhere near the injured batsman, his arms resting on his hips. I was sitting by the boundary looking towards him, when he stared knowingly at me, slowly and reassuringly nodding his head. I was not sure what his facial expression meant, but I did the next ball when Emil bowled a yorker to uproot the batsman's wicket! Emil had been trying to reassure me that he had remembered what I had told them to do when such a circumstance arose. He knew that the batsman would be looking for another short ball and be hesitant, after his injury, so Emil had bowled a fast full length ball. I was proud of him, and, smugly perhaps, proud of myself too, for the type of coaching I had done with the team. All the new batsmen seemed scared stiff of Emil's strong bowling, and we had soon bowled them out to win by twenty or more runs. It was particularly pleasing to compliment their coach for giving us our toughest game of the season! Their parents quietly made their way out of the ground, trying to cope with the unexpected, whilst everyone from Werneth, players, staff and parents, celebrated a memorable victory. I have never seen Emil since the school year ended later that month, but that nod of his head I shall always recall with appreciation and amusement.

Cricket and football were not the only after school involvements I had at Werneth. Most of the teachers were spending some lunchtimes or late afternoons on activities such as a choir, gymnastics, orchestra, dancing, acting, etc. so I decided to start a chess club. It was not that I had ever been chess player myself, having learned how to play by reading a book so that I could help Richard to enjoy it at home when he was about seven years old. At school the enthusiasm grew as more pupils came to my classroom at lunchtimes, and I arranged a game between our best players and those from St. Mary's, Failsworth, where chess was also very popular. We played them home and away, and as the events had been enjoyed by the pupils, decided to call a meeting of teachers from all schools interested, to see if we could develop chess playing in this way. The meeting took place and the Oldham Primary Schools Chess Association was officially formed, and within a few months I had become its secretary, with Mr Marsden, Headmaster of St. Mary's, the chairman.

I worked hard to promote the Association's growth, and after only two years the original seven schools had grown to forty, with four leagues and a cup competition. As a virtual non-player myself I never attempted to become involved with the formation and development of a Town Team, which was far more appropriate for those teachers who were good players themselves. I remained the secretary for five years, and continued to be involved at school level to the end of my career, and the fact that the Association is still going strong and has achieved high standards over the years pleases me, having helped to instigate its formation.

Whilst chess, cricket and football were my main out of school involvements I began to toy with the idea of arranging a school trip. The success of the North Chadderton visits to Stratford-upon-Avon motivated me to think of visits appropriate for 10 and 11 year olds, and London seemed the best place to start. Whenever an idea takes hold of my brain I simply cannot let go, so a London visit began to take shape. Eventually it was a three days' educational holiday to the capital city, staying in a 4 star hotel for two nights, travelling by coach, which we would use at arranged times during the three days, all of which would take place during the first week of the Easter holidays. In other words, the teachers who took part would be giving their time voluntarily. I arranged visits to as many of the London main tourist venues as possible, trying to obtain a balance of entertainment, history, culture and sightseeing.

For most of the pupils it was their first visit to London, and to walk into Westminster Abbey, listen to the guide explaining the significance of the many historical features around and high above them, was marvellous. Similarly at the Natural History Museum, Tower of London, St. Paul's Cathedral and the Planetarium, the pupils, and the teachers too, were enthralled. It was also quite a culture shock for most of the pupils to stay in such a posh hotel, as it was to have spent three days away from their parents, which was a maturing experience in itself. Much of one day was spent walking from Trafalgar Square to Parliament Square, over Westminster Bridge, and other places of interest, and in the evening we went to see 'Showboat' at a London theatre. We never wasted a minute during our time in London, and everyone returned delighted to have taken part. It was the first of many such visits I would organise, and it prompted me to think about other places which might be equally successful and beneficial to visit.

The following year then, I arranged a West Country tour, beginning at Warwick Castle, then on to Birdland, at Bourton on the Water, to see Red Pelicans, King Penguins, crowned cranes and hundreds of other colourful birds, making a lovely afternoon, before our visit to the impressive ruined remains of the 13th century church, Tintern Abbey. We stayed at a hotel in Bath, and on the following day visited Slimbridge Wild Fowl Trust, established by Sir Peter Scott. Visits of this kind are mind-boggling for children. They see hundreds of species of ducks, geese and birds in their resplendent colours, and simply cannot believe their eyes. They have the freedom to walk along the winding paths, throwing nuts to attract the creatures to come closer, feeling thrilled to see so many species for the first time. Later we travelled to the Roman Baths, which must have been the most exciting history lesson they had ever had, and from there to a local museum. Other visits were made on the third day before and during our return journey, and as we arrived back at Werneth Susan was one of the mothers who were all waiting to welcome their children, because I had found Richard a place on the trip, he being the same age as the other pupils. I was glad that he had enjoyed it just as much as all the others did.

Both educational holiday visits had been appreciated and enjoyed by pupils and staff, and thankfully there had been no hitches. I was not too sure whether my third venture would turn out quite as successfully, however, and many of my colleagues seemed to have serious doubts, too. Stratford-upon -Avon having always been of special interest to me, I began to consider the idea of arranging a visit there in 1975, when I realised that Macbeth was being performed at the Royal Shakespeare Theatre. Most people, myself included, regard Shakespeare as a subject not appropriate for very young children, because of the language problems they have in reading his plays. However, I had seen such enthusiasm shown by many pupils of all abilities at North Chadderton, that I began to believe that if eleven year-olds were properly prepared they would love Macbeth. Not that I thought that very many of Shakespeare's plays would excite them, but with ghosts, murders, witches, ambition and jealousy being in almost every scene, I was convinced that Junior School pupils could really enjoy it.

With Tom Jones' full support I made all the necessary enquiries at the theatre, and after the letters to the parents had been dispatched we soon had over forty tickets sold. I borrowed a set of texts from North Chadderton, and during lunchtimes told all the pupils about the play, and fully prepared them for all the exciting aspects of this savage play. One of the biggest problems a teacher has in introducing Shakespeare to young people is prejudice. Once that has been removed by the right kind of preparation the pupils concentrate on the plot and characters, and the rest comes easily. Thankfully that is exactly how it worked at Werneth. We had a splendid day, had a tour of the lovely town, strolled by the River Avon and saw the matinee performance from the excellent seats in the stalls that I had persuaded the management to allocate us, on my solemn promise that the pupils would be perfectly behaved and well supervised.

It was ironic that I had assured the theatre staff that our pupils would be silent during the performance, because during the play an increasing number of children from other schools, sitting very near to the stage had begun to talk, and as the noise increased the audience began to feel distracted. Suddenly one of the actors sprang up and shouted to the offending chatterboxes to behave, keep quiet, and let the audience enjoy the play they had come to watch in respectful silence, whereupon he received an appreciative round of applause, and he switched back to his role in the tragedy. It worked, too, for there was no more noise, apart, that is, from Tom Jones, seated amongst a group of our pupils. He must have dropped off to sleep and began to snore! I could hear him from where I was seated across the centre aisle, but there was nothing I could have done without making a noise or causing a disturbance myself. The pupils next to him were looking round, puzzled and embarrassed, but must have been too afraid to nudge him to wake him up. Thankfully he suddenly jerked his head and sat up, and the snores ceased. The pupils probably remember that with amusement just as I think they will still recall their enjoyment at having seen their first Shakespearian play at such a famous theatre, with all the prejudice they might have acquired against his works removed before it could even have begun.

I had moved to Werneth in 1972, but I was not the only member of the family to change schools around that time. Lucy and Sarah had been attending Werneth Convent for a few years, but Susan and I had begun to think about their future prospects of gaining Grammar School places. Loretto Convent in Manchester was the one we hoped they would go to, and we were advised that in order to improve their chances of being accepted for a place when they were eleven, it would be best to get them into the Loretto Prep. School. So when Lucy was nine and Sarah seven we did just that. We had been reasonably happy with Richard's progress at St. Herbert's until, after beginning to wonder if he was being pushed sufficiently, he came home one day to tell us that he had been knitting all afternoon. That was it. I had had enough. One or two enquiries were made, and following a few phone calls Richard was offered a place at Xavarian Prep. School, so as the next term began we were all getting out of bed an hour earlier, to make sure they caught their buses to Manchester.

My daily routine was to drive the girls to the 82 bus stop on Manchester Road by 7.45am, then drive down to Failsworth where Richard boarded his bus, from where I drove back home to eat my egg and bacon breakfast which Susan had cooked, and then I was off to begin my school day. At the end of the afternoon the girls would arrive on the 82 bus at Manchester Road, not far from my Werneth school, where I collected them at about 5 o'clock, whilst Richard would catch the bus to Chadderton from Piccadilly. But whereas my move to Werneth had at first seemed disastrous, the children's moves were all successful, as they quickly settled in and did well in their work. Richard obtained a place in the main college, as did Lucy at Loretto a year later. Sarah, however, lost out because of changes in the Manchester Education policy changes preventing pupils living outside the city boundaries being eligible for a place, so she went to an Oldham Prep. School for her final Junior School year. Changing schools meant changing holidays too, with Oldham Wakes no longer our Abersoch abode. Manchester schools also reopened early in September, and it was in that first week of term as I sat waiting for the girls to step off the 82 bus that I saw a newspaper advert that would radically change my way of life.

A footwear stall on Skipton Market was up for sale, and I began to think about the idea. Perhaps the five years I had spent running Junction Flyers had implanted a business urge in me that I was now missing, but whatever it was the idea of my having a market stall buzzed in my head all night. On the following day I was not collecting the girls, but going to watch Richard play in a football match, which gave me the opportunity to speak to Tony Buckley, himself a footwear wholesaler, who was the father of one of Richard's friends. His advice was that I should not pay for a stall, but go and buy some 'gear' and find a stall for myself, thus saving some money. I spent virtually all and every day for the next week, before the term started, looking at footwear stalls on indoor and outdoor markets, and realised that there was no way I could attempt to sell the vast range of footwear that I had seen on so many stalls, and thought it might be a better idea to start off by specialising in slippers, and to see how things developed. That was Tony's advice, too, when I next spoke to him, and during the first week of term, soon after the 4 o'clock bell rang, I drove for the first time "up the valley" i.e. the Rossendale Valley, the heart of the footwear industry, and, on Tony's recommendation, went to Spencer's and Tattersall's, spending the £200 back pay I had just received following a recent salary increase.

By now I had part exchanged the last Junction Flyer's van for an Austin Cambridge car, and with its boot crammed full, the back seats packed to the roof with boxes, and two trestle tables on the roof rack, I set off the following Saturday morning to try to find a stall. For three consecutive Saturdays I travelled to four markets each week, only to be told by the 'Toby', i.e. the market manager, the same answer, that there were no stalls available. By now I had begun to wonder if I would ever get started, and spoke to Tony Buckley as we watched the lads playing football after school on Friday. He suggested that I should drive into Cheshire, and begin at Congleton, so on the following morning I set off, along with Richard, down the A34. As luck had it the size of the outdoor market had just been increased, and as a footwear trader had recently retired, the Toby offered me a pitch. Thankfully it was a dry day, so we set up our gear for the very first time, thrilled not only to have finally made it, but also to end up driving home having taken £50, and also having been offered the pitch on a permanent basis. That Saturday in October 1974, I have always remembered, but little did I realise as we drove home that day, that I would be making journeys to Congleton virtually every Saturday morning for the next 28 years, and for 12 years of Tuesday markets too, and that I would become known throughout the town of Congleton as Johnny Slipper.

I remained Mr. Cleary at Werneth, of course, where I was beginning my third year there, having settled in comfortably, my initial despair now a mere memory. I did have some misgivings, however, as the term began, for in the Junior Four class I was now teaching there was John Oldland, the son of a former colleague of mine at North Chadderton, Vernon. We had never crossed swords in any way, but I always sensed that he did not think much of me, and when on the first Parents' Evening Vernon entered my classroom I felt rather uneasy, but his comments floored me. He thanked me profusely for what I had done to motivate his son, who, he said, had professed to be ill with one symptom or another virtually every school day – until he came into my class. I could hardly believe what I was hearing. Having expected a sarcastic five minutes, I was being given the highest accolade imaginable. Their son was a very intelligent and well behaved boy, and I treated him exactly as my instincts and style directed, and it was obviously working. Vernon will never know how much he amazed and pleased me that night. I was also very pleased and proud to receive a letter the following April.

Dear John

By the time you read this letter I am sure that John will have told you about his Governor's free place at Hulme Grammar School and his acceptance by M.G.S. Both Kathleen and I are delighted at his success, but feel that your considerable part in it must not go unrecognised. You must be aware that before you took over he loathed school and spent years dreaming up excuses to keep him away: his work rate was minimal and his progress nil. Since September the change in him has been unbelievable and I don't think that either of us have seen him happier, as busy or more contented with his lot, at school, than he is now. Again, John, many, many thanks for sorting him out and making his success possible; but, for God's sake – don't stop now!

Vernon and Kathleen

Teachers go through their careers being accused of being too strict or too lenient, of having treated a pupil unfairly, especially by the many parents who profess to support discipline, but who complain if it is their child who is punished. So it was very heart warming to receive Vernon and Kathleen's letter, which I must have valued so much that it found its way into my loft, along with so much more that I only recently found.

By coincidence it was in that year at Werneth that I had begun my market trading, and feel that the effort I was putting into being successful selling footwear never detracted from the dedication I always had in the classroom.

My original motivation for my move to Werneth had been to use it as a step towards my ambition to become a Headteacher, and during 1975 I had been applying for posts as a Deputy Head, being nearly successful on two or three occasions. I was happy at Werneth with its traditional environment, desks in rows, and good discipline in every class, but I was becoming increasingly perturbed by the modern teaching methods being expected, and gradually demanded, by education officers. The failed teachers, about whom I made comments during my years at St. John's, seemed now to be swamping the training colleges with their crazy theories, and the newly trained teachers were coming into schools brainwashed by the crackpots who had lectured them. In my time at Werneth I attended many conferences and courses, often infuriated by the nonsense we had to listen to by these self styled experts. Teachers who wanted promotion were becoming under increasing pressure to advocate the modern theories, or they risked not even being considered for an interview, as various newly appointed education officers and advisers had come through the barnpot college life in which any traditional teacher was regarded as a dinosaur.Thankfully I did not have to endure such a situation when I was interviewed for the post of Deputy Head at Limehurst Primary School, and was thrilled to be offered it, to begin in January 1976.

9 Limehurst – Early Years

I walked into Limehurst County Primary School as Deputy Headteacher, a step, as I believed at the time, on my way to a headship that I had been determined to achieve since my resignation from North Chadderton in 1972; but, as events turned out, my new post would be my final one, which I would hold until I took my early retirement in 1990. I had, of course, been trading on Congleton Market for about fifteen months before I left Werneth, and had been really surprised that during that time none of the staff had picked up on the fact that I had a market stall. Now that I was starting my new job as a deputy head, however, I felt it was important for me to try to keep my Saturday activities secret for as long as possible, so that I could become accepted as a committed senior member of staff, one who was willing to lead from the front in such as out-of-school activities for the benefit of the pupils, many of whom came from deprived homes.

This was another new experience for me, teaching on a Council Estate, something of a culture shock, as some of the tales of some of the families were passed on to me by members of the teaching staff who had taught at the school for many years. It would be wrong for anyone to make critical judgements and assumptions about families simply because they live in Council houses, because ever so many of the parents of pupils I taught were striving to do their best to provide a good home and family upbringing for their children, and were also very supportive of the school and members of staff. There were some, however, who caused havoc on the estate and their children were allowed and even encouraged to run wild, defying authority of any kind. Some 'families' of six or seven children each had a different father, and it was no surprise when girls in the households became pregnant at 15 or 16, and thus the cycle began again, with children beginning school whose mothers, never having experienced a family background themselves, were unable, by their very immaturity, to become capable mothers themselves at such a young age.

This meant that the teachers in the infant department had a lot of hard work to do in order to help such neglected small children become capable of adapting to school life. Many Reception Class pupils had spent the first four or five years of the lives sitting in front of a television all day, and had great difficulty in adapting to life in the classroom. How their teachers coped I do not know. Thankfully, as the most deprived of these children worked their way through the school, things changed, of course, invariably for the better, but the whole range of difficulties I was experiencing for the first time in my teaching career placed me on a new learning curve. Another surprise awaiting me at Limehurst was the discipline. I had left Werneth with Mr Tom Jones having told me that my strict disciplinary style would be just what Limehurst School needed, and I expected to have to make my mark in this manner soon after I arrived. I simply did not need to. The discipline in the Junior Department was very strict, if not too strict, which was a strange conclusion for me to have reached, or so many people would think.

It was genuinely good, however, and with three of the Junior staff and the Head being men, it was unusual for the balance of male and female staff to be roughly even. Irrespective of any politically correct views some people hold, I am convinced that it is better for pupils to be taught by men and women, especially in an age when so many children are being brought up in single parent homes, thus having no day to day involvement with a man. Simply by being a man does not make anyone a good teacher or a good disciplinarian, of course, but in the days when discipline in schools was enforceable, virtually every female teacher I knew agreed that growing young boys benefited from the presence and disciplinary influence of a male teacher. During all my years at Limehurst there was David Hindle, who was appointed as the new Headmaster in the term following my appointment, on Mr Jack's retirement, and Danny McLaughlan and Philip Adshead, both of whom were on the staff before I arrived and were still there after I had retired. It was a good school. All the staff got on well, made any new members welcome, were all supportive of each other, and thankfully there were no stick-in-the-muds rejecting changes or new ideas.

When Mr Jack announced his intention to retire I did not think it appropriate to apply for the headship, having only just arrived myself, which also helped the good relationship I always had with David Hindle, as he knew that I had not been a disappointed and rejected applicant for his job. He and I always got on well together. Our views were often different, his softer, safer and perhaps slower; mine aggressive, riskier, and often confrontational; but we both respected each other, and once we had agreed a course of action neither of us adopted an 'I told you so' attitude if it hadn't worked. I think the bottom line for me was that I was not coveting his job. Within two years or so of my arrival at Limehurst my Congleton footwear stall was a steady financial sideline for me, and one day each week the environment of the market was in itself stimulating and enjoyable. All week I was giving 100 % to the wellbeing of the pupils I taught, whereas on Saturdays I was doing it for myself and my family, perhaps also fulfilling the business side of my nature that I first experienced in the five years of Junction Flyer Repairs. I have no doubt, too, that I must have inherited my dad's enterprising nature that had first taken him to London in the post–war slump, and then on his return, inspired him to set up his window cleaning business before going back into textiles. Some of my friends would occasionally tell me that I had the best of both worlds, with the security of the deputy headship, whilst enjoying the competitive world every Saturday. 'A change is as good as a rest' began to make a lot of sense to me in those days.

It was during those first few years as a market trader that I began to advertise in the local paper, the Congleton Chronicle, which was read by virtually everyone in and around the town. I became aware that some people had obviously read my advert, and had come to look at, and maybe buy, the footwear I had publicised. This prompted me to develop my ideas on advertising. As all adverts were printed in alphabetical order, I wrote mine so that they were at, or very near to, the top of the page, and tried to make them interesting and amusing.

At my market stall on a fancy dress market day.

Best Holiday Leisure footwear selection. Trainers Sandals Pumps Slippers. Everybody knows my sales gimmicks – Keen prices, reliable quality, no pressurisation. Courteous service. Everything price labelled. Worth visiting Johnny's Slipperama. See for yourself.

Back to school. White pumps £1.30. Trainers galore. All sizes. Soccer specials. Soccer boots at sensible prices. Slippers galore. Gents and Ladies. Johnny's Congleton Slipperama.

Another Delivery Saturday. Leather football boots, screw-in studs, £5.75. Repeat £5.75. Smart PVC football boots. All sizes. £2.99. Yes – £2.99. Come early – Congleton Slipperama

Avoid Frostbite. Enormous Autumn Slippers Selection. Leather trainer bargains. Why pay silly prices? Everything labelled. No pressure selling. Ask anyone. Visit Johnny's Slipperama

Absolutely splendid Christmas Slipper selection. Umpteen styles. Prices to suit everyone. Everything clearly labelled. Exchanges before or after Christmas. Courtesy. Service. Reliability. Unflappability. Johnny's Slipperama. Congleton Market

Above Average Christmas slipper gift display. Below average prices! Something for everyone

Umpteen styles. See for yourself. Thousands must be right. Johnny's Celebrated Slipperama.

All your men – boy friends, husbands, uncles, fathers, grandads, sons, nephews, brothers. Say it with Slippers! Spoil them. Slipperama selection at £1.35, £1.45, £1.85, £2.40, £2.85, £2.99, £3.75, £4.75, £4.99, £5.25, £6.50. Even greater selection in Ladies Slippers. Children's too. See for yourself. Everything labelled. Johnny's Congleton Slipperama.

Absolutely Eye-Catching Slipper display. Everyone's ideal Christmas gift. Everything clearly price labelled. Exchanges after Christmas. Thousands must be right. Johnny's Slipperama.

It always pleased me when customers made reference to one of my adverts, usually with a smile on their faces. Perhaps it had been the advert that had prompted them to come to my stall. Whether it was or wasn't, I felt it was definitely helping. By my second or third year that I had been trading in the town I had begun to feel part of the Congleton scene, and recognised as a regular trader, not one who might not be there the following week. This meant that they felt confident that they would get a refund if there was anything faulty that they had purchased. I felt that my weekly adverts added to their recognition of me as an established and trusted trader. That also made me feel good, as did writing an eye-catching or imaginative advert. They made my Saturdays increasingly enjoyable.

I also think that my enterprising style expressed itself in many of the various school trips I arranged over the years, ideas which had blossomed with the Stratford-on-Avon visits from North Chadderton, and then the three-day education visits to London and the West Country whilst at Werneth. Particularly enterprising had of course been the Macbeth visit, which had been such a surprising success – surprising to others, perhaps, but not to me. Not long after my arrival at Limehurst I began to think on similar lines. How would Shakespeare go down on Limeside Estate? I fancied the idea, and supported by David Hindle I arranged a visit to see Comedy of Errors, which I had been informed was a huge success with young audiences at The Royal Shakespeare Theatre. Letters were sent to the parents of all the 4th year pupils, and on December 6th we went to Stratford-upon-Avon. All the pupils had been made aware of the importance of good behaviour, and the need to be absolutely quiet when sitting in the theatre – and no toffees! I had sent off my letter to the R.S.C. when booking the seats, with a special request that if there was any chance that they could find us seats near to the stage it would be very much appreciated, and that their behaviour would be impeccable. I followed that up with a telephone call the following day, the result of which was that we were given front seats in the stalls. Absolutely magnificent!

Instead of expressing my views or recollections of this visit I thought it might be more interesting to let the pupils themselves say what they thought about it. I kept many of their writings which they completed in the days following the visit, many of which were exhibited on the classroom and corridor walls, and I think they very aptly sum up their enjoyment and appreciation of what for most of them was their first day trip anywhere. Amazingly I must have kept their writings in a folder which I placed in my classroom cabinet, and at the time of my retirement I decided to take them home, along with hundreds of other literary efforts written over the following fifteen years.

Early Morning
When I got up on Thursday it was like a dream. I had never got that early before.

Catherine Pledger

I had to get up an hour earlier than usual and I was very tired. After I had had my breakfast I took my travel sickness pills. At 7.30 I set out from our house. The roads were icy and I kept slipping. I went across to the paper shop to buy some barley sugars. There I met Colleen and Karin so I walked over to school with them. At a quarter to eight the coach came and picked us all up.

Carol Garner

At The Motorway Halt

When we stopped at the service station to use the toilets we got off the coach and went through the main entrance. After that I went downstairs where I saw a lot of one-arm bandits and other amusements. We were not allowed to go on the amusements, but the temptation was too much. I wanted to play on the one-arm bandits and the other machines. I thought that the service station was like Paradise. Then I glanced round and saw another bit of Paradise, a toffee shop, and who should be in it but Walter buying some chocolate. After that we all lined up and went out of the service station and back on to the coach.

Darren Page

Lunchtime By The River Avon

After we had all walked round the town and looked at the ancient buildings, all those in Mrs Towse's group began to feel a little peckish. Luckily we managed to reach the River Avon to eat our packed lunches before we starved to death. We watched all the ducks squabbling over the bread we threw to them. The ones that ate the bread got pecked by the others. I watched for all the greedy ones and I only threw the bread to the timid ones.

Colleen Gray

When I had eaten my first sandwich I got another one out and threw some bread to the ducks. Then I saw a swan and threw some to it but unfortunately two ducks pushed the swan away and got it. I felt sorry for the swan so I tried again but it was no use, the duck kept getting the bread. So I threw some bread out in the river and all the ducks went after it, and then I threw the swan some. At last the swan had got a piece of bread.

Paul Fitzpatrick.

Why I Enjoyed The Play

I enjoyed the play because it was a comedy and the actors made it look as if it really was happening there and then. When Shakespeare wrote this play he really did capture what it was like at the time. The play itself is very funny and the producers have changed it into musical. Altogether I think that The Comedy Of Errors is fantastic.

Christine Dennett

I enjoyed the play because the scenery was superb. Every bit of it matched the actors' costumes. It also made the place real, although I have never heard of such placed as Ephesus and Syracuse. Another thing is the way they did the acrobatics. I couldn't do them to save my life. It was marvellous. I also liked their costumes. I thought they had the right kind of costume for the right kind of person. They also had exactly the right actors for the different roles, and I thought Dromio performed a miracle on the stage with all the acrobatics. I think without him the play wouldn't be half as good.

Wayne McCarthy

The Comedy Of Errors is a hilarious play about people who get mixed up because they look the same. I enjoyed the play because of the actors' enthusiasm to make it as enjoyable for us as it is for them. The play was very exciting to me because I have never seen a play before in my whole life. It must be very exciting to be in a play. If I ever was and I had five hundred people watching me I would be as nervous as a mouse about to be eaten by a cat. The characters I liked best were the two Dromios because they were very funny and could do lots of tricks. When the Syracusan Dromio was jumping on and off the table it seemed as if we were at the pictures and the special effects man was doing it all. I think they were superb.

Colin Forster

The best part in the play was when Dromio came on stage with an ice-cream and Antiphalus pushed it in his face. Then he sat on it. At the end of the play Dromio jumped off the stage and he shook hands with me. I was the only one in our class he shook hands with. The play was great all the way through.

Dale Robinson

At The Wimpy Bar

When we arrived at the Wimpy Bar we had to sit two boys and two girls at each table. First we had tomato soup. It was delicious. Just right. Walter put mustard in his soup. I thought, "My God". Then I had chips and fish burger. I tried to put some ketchup on my chips but it came out slowly at first, so I shook it harder and it nearly all came out. After we had finished they took our plates away. They served us very well. Then came my banana longboat, and it filled me up. Everyone had smiles on their faces when their sweets were served. Altogether my meal came to 97 pence plus 10 pence for a tip. I had to borrow 10 pence off Dale, so I was all right. Then we went to the coach and set off home. I said to myself it had been a great trip because no-one was sick on the coach.

Anthony Green

When the lady came I ordered fish and chips and she went into the kitchen to make it. Ten minutes later she brought my meal and asked if I wanted anything else. I said, "Yes, I would like a knicker bocker glory". About ten minutes later she came with my sweet and I had to stand up, because if I had remained sitting the glass would have been too high to eat out of. When I had eaten it I could hardly walk because it had filled me up so much.

David Abbot

My dinner cost 46 pence. Then we had to order a sweet. Both me and Christine ordered banana longboat and a drink of coke. When I had finished that I was full up. The whole meal was lovely. The two boys opposite us were very ill-mannered. Walter was putting French

Mustard in his soup with salt and pepper. When he got his sweet he said he was going to put French Mustard on his chocolate nut sundae. That is just typical of him.

Julie Standley

What My Parents Said
When we arrived back at school my mum was waiting for me. I said goodbye to Mr Cleary and we started to walk home. My mum said, "Did you enjoy yourself?" I said it had been the best school trip I had ever been on. She said, "Did you like the play?" I said, "Yes. It was great." By the time we had arrived home and was ready for bed my dad had come in. He also asked if I had enjoyed myself, and I told him it had been great. Then I kissed him goodnight and went to bed.

Tina Myers

I believe that the above extracts from the many pieces that the pupils wrote following the visit aptly reflect the wholehearted enthusiasm that all those who took part in the visit enjoyed, and leaves no doubt that they fully understood and appreciated their first Shakespearian experience. The success of the visit had thrilled me too, of course, but it had not been my first initiative at Limehurst, because I had started a chess club, following the interest that the Werneth pupils had shown there. I was still the secretary of the Oldham Primary Schools Chess Association, which was beginning to attract ever more schools into membership, and I was playing a leading role in arranging league and knock-out competitions. So it was a particularly happy occasion for me, being a very inexperienced chess player myself, to watch my Limehurst team win the very first inter-school knock-out competition. But in no way did I ever claim credit for their success, but attributed it to a teacher who had moved to another school a year earlier, and who had introduced the pupils to the game and had coached them to the high levels they had reached. It was a huge success for the school and sheer delight for the members of the team.

Out of school activities figured prominently at Limehurst, and in those days, before the many changes that Governments have introduced, many of which I believe have had detrimental effects on the education system, teachers looked forward to giving their own after school time to provide extra benefits for their pupils. On at least two or three days each week I would be running my chess club with my classroom almost full; out on the field Philip would be coaching football to another twenty and more boys; Danny would have taken another large group to his gymnastic club in the main hall; and out in the playground Janet Long would be coaching her netball group. Indeed, when the home-time bell rang on most afternoons fewer than half the pupils would be going home. There was no pressure from head teachers in those days for members of staff to undertake such tasks, just the enthusiasm of the teachers themselves. Now, all the form filling and red tape, introduced in recent years, have significantly reduced after school activities, much to the disadvantage of many pupils.

At Limehurst there was an excellent atmosphere. The staff got on well, and with the odd exceptions there was strong parental support for the teachers. It was also good for the school that so many of the staff had spent many years there, and that stability, adding the mutual respect that everyone had for each other, made for a successful school. And in his own quiet way David Hindle made his contribution very strongly. He was not one who followed the trendy management techniques that the people running the various education courses propounded. His style was genuine and trusting. If a member of staff had set out to abuse the system, taking time off for fake illness, for example, he or she might have got away with it. But no-one ever tried. David's trust contributed to everyone's sincerity and dedication. There were bound to be occasional hiccups in staff relationships or about changes that had to be made from time to time, but in the fourteen years I worked with David, I felt that the goodwill that existed in the staff room permeated through to the classrooms where no teacher ever felt under pressure.

Such a good atmosphere is a bonus when the pupils come from a disadvantaged background. And whilst I have made mention of the strong support so many parents gave to the school, everyone knows how difficult it is to deal effectively with disruptive pupils from the homes where anything goes. But when all the staff work well with each other, none backing off from dealing with problems, and being supportive, most of the difficult behavioural problems can be overcome. In most cases once a pupil realised that the teacher was being strict but also being fair, he, for invariably it would have been a boy, would gradually fall into line. I can remember quite a number of disruptive pupils, once they realised that they were not going to win, began to behave. They might look for a chance to mess about, but they knew that I never took my eyes off them, so that chance was not going to happen.

Classroom discipline, though, is based on the assumption or knowledge that the teacher has the authority to enforce the rules or level of behaviour. Sadly, not only for the education system, but for society as a whole, this has gradually eroded, and every pupil now knows that a teacher simply cannot enforce anything, and in an increasing number of schools chaos reigns as the disruptive pupils make hell, not only for the teacher, but for the other pupils too. I believe that the changes in the law brought about by various court cases have damaged the very basis of our society, where young people have been denied the childhood experience of being educated in an enforceable environment. There is no doubt that a frustrated teacher can act rashly in a moment of provocation. There can be no doubt that some teachers might have been too strict, almost bullies. But I believe these have been rare exceptions. Now we have a situation in which teachers are afraid of restraining a violent pupil, even to protect another pupil, never mind himself or herself. There have been too many high profile cases to testify to that, and they are just the tips of the iceberg.

For a pupil to be able to accuse a teacher of assault, even without any evidence that the accusation is true, and which invariably if not automatically leads to the teacher's suspension, is simply unjust. Pupils have lied, made deliberately false accusations, and those teachers will have gone through mental hell whilst under suspension, worried that their colleagues and friends will conclude that there is no smoke without fire; and even when in many cases, after months of waiting for the outcome of the enquiry, the case is either dropped or the teacher is declared innocent, how will it have affected them?

For the past decade and more the pupils going through school have grown up with total freedom to ignore rules, because they know that they are unenforceable. Year by year, this downward trend growing all the time, these pupils have entered their adult lives with the word "authority" totally out of their experience, and a notion to be rejected. Hence, in my opinion, why daylight crime is on the increase, whatever the statistics are said to be. They are convinced that there is nothing anyone can do to stop them. After all, that is how they grew up in school, so why stop now? No wonder so many teachers took retirement as soon as they were financially able to do so, and why there is a greater percentage than ever before of newly trained teachers leaving the profession after only two or three years in the classroom. Pessimistic though my opinions may be, I believe that the problem can only go worse, in the legal quagmire created by do-gooder and lawyers, which is severely damaging the fabric of our society. I regret having to express these opinions, but I do so honestly and truthfully.

Thankfully, during my teaching career, this decline had not yet taken place, and I was able to develop my individualistic style of teaching without the constraints that exist today. If they had I would never have been able to arrange so many outings and visits. As I have described earlier I believed that there were many benefits that pupils could obtain by taking part in such educational visits as I had arranged at Werneth, and as I had previously done on subject basis at North Chadderton, to Stratford-upon-Avon. Here at Limehurst I believed that such three–day breaks to London would be even more beneficial, for most of those pupils would never have had the opportunity to see the famous London landmarks, and the thrill of staying in a 3 or 4 star hotel, visiting a London theatre, among countless other memorable travelling experiences.

Beginning in 1976, when I set about planning the first London visit, there would be nine or ten consecutive years when such educational holidays took place, alternating between London and the Bristol and Bath area, for the nine to eleven year-old pupils in the upper junior classes. I made the arrangements months in advance, which often enabled me to negotiate better deals, and it gave the parents plenty of time to make their weekly payments, the only way they could possibly pay for their child's place on the coach, which always left Limehurst no later than 8am, to arrive back at 8pm two days later, where a mob of parents and family members waited excitedly to welcome their children home.

Not a single minute was wasted on any of our visits, and while there were variations in our itineraries from one year to another we almost always went to The Natural History and Science museums on Sunday afternoon, followed by a coach tour of the London highlights before our evening meal, before returning to our hotel, which had been our first stop on arriving in the capital. On Mondays we would begin at Trafalgar Square, walk down Pall Mall, then go to Westminster Abbey, where I had always pre-booked a good guide, thus guaranteeing a more informative and meaningful understanding of the famous Abbey features. From there we would go across to the Houses of Parliament, then walk across Westminster Bridge to enjoy its spectacular views.

We then travelled by boat up the River Thames to the Tower of London, which was an absolute 'must' visit, one for which I invariably had obtained free tickets available on 'first come first served' basis. The Crown Jewels and countless other exhibits always made for a wonderful afternoon, after which we travelled by coach or tube to our hotel where there would be an hour or so for everyone to have a bath and get changed, after which we would go for an early evening meal before taking our seats at London Theatre.

In 1977 we went to see Danny La Rue at the Palladium, where we had been allocated front centre seats in the stalls, achieved, perhaps, by my persuasive telephone calls, and some of our pupils were invited to go on the stage during the show, which made it a very special evening for them all. In other years we saw Pirates of Penzance, Little Shop of Horrors, Starlight Express and on two separate occasions saw Cats, which was absolutely brilliant. On Tuesday mornings, after breakfast in the hotel, which was a feast in itself for the children, it was time for them to pack their cases before boarding the coach, and we would always go to St. Paul's Cathedral, where we would climb the steps to the Whispering

Gallery, and even more excitingly climb the hundreds of steps above the gallery, between the inner and outer domes, to stand high in the London sky enjoying the truly magnificent views around the city. From there we would usually go to the Planetarium, with its tilting seats enabling everyone to look up into the starry sky, learning ever so much about stars and planets. Next door was Madame Tussauds, a popular venue, though not my favourite. In the afternoon it was Matinee time at another theatre, and after that everyone, pupils and staff, was ready for a restful journey home following a hectic three days.

The writings which the pupils completed following the first London visit are amongst those which I have kept, and the selection I have chosen to include reflect their reactions to what was for virtually all of them, the first visit to London and their first overnight stay in a hotel, and how enjoyable the experience was.

The Morning I Woke Up
On Sunday morning the alarm clock started to ring, so I got out of bed to turn it off. When I was dressed I was so excited at going to London that I forgot to wash my hands and face. So when I went downstairs my mum said to me, "Have you washed your hands and face?" and I said, "Oh, dammit, no" and went back upstairs. My mum made me egg on toast, which I ate very quickly, then I grabbed my suitcase and jumped into the car. My mum and dad drove me to the school yard. Soon we got on to the coach, and when we had all calmed down the coach set off.

Sharon Thorley

What I'm Looking Forward To
Mostly I am looking forward to going to see Nelson's Column, because it is so big. In our house a lot of preparation is going on. I've got new clothes, shoes, pumps and underwear. I am also loking forward to seeing Danny La Rue. He's the man who dresses up like a woman. We are going on the front row of this theatre in the best seats so we are having a big treat. London, I think, will be my best ever trip, so it will be very enjoyable.

Peter McGann

The Rembrant

Soon we were at the hotel. It looked like a palace, and even better than on the photograph. We took our suitcases to our bedrooms, changed into some fresh clothes and had a wash. At night time the place looked beautiful; the lights of London were shining like a great ball of fire.

Jason Montgomery

Groups Of Three

We were in groups of three in the hotel, and when we were getting ready to go to the London Palladium it was James' turn to have a bath. He was being a bit awkward and said he wouldn't have one, so Richard pushed him. James stumbled and fell into the bath. He then went out of the room to tell over Richard. Richard then started packing his clothes in his suitcase, remembering the warning that Mr Cleary had given us as we arrived. He then slumped on the bed crying, thinking he would be sent home. I felt sorry for him when I saw his miserable face, peering from behind his glasses. Then he got up to look through the door to see if James had really gone, and to Richard's relief he was just having a bit of fun.

Philip Smith

In The Hotel

On Sunday when we had our bath we ran it and Wendy got in first. After she had finished it was my turn. I got in and it was lovely and warm. I washed myself, then got out and dried myself. Then Lynn got in and the water was rather black when she had finished. We put our nightclothes on and climbed into bed. On the Monday when we had our bath we went in the same order as on Sunday, but when we had finished we didn't go to bed but got ready for the London Palladium.

Brenda Hayes

160

The London Palladium

On Monday night we went to the London Palladium to see Danny La Rue. He was Aladdin's mother called Widow Twanky. During the show he said, "Would any boys and girls like to come up and sing?" My hand shot up like a rocket going to the moon. Really I didn't expect him to pick me, but I was wrong. I was the first up on the stage. We had to sing "Oh I ain't half proud of my old mum." As soon as I was on the stage I wanted to go to the toilet, but I couldn't really say "Please can I go to the toilet?" Then I got separated from the others in our group and had to sing with complete load of strangers. It ended up in a draw, so we all got Quality Street and chopsticks, or Roses and chopsticks. It was a great night.

Dawn McGann

The Most Exciting Visit

The most exciting part of the London trip was when we went to the Science and Natural History Museums. As soon as I got in I was speechless. It was so good to go inside the museums, and see the prehistoric dinosaurs. I was as excited as Mr. Cleary was to see the Blue Whale. It was huge. I took a lot of photographs; it was so exciting. In the Natural History Museum it showed how a baby was born. They had telephones which you picked up and asked a question like, "When was this museum built?" and it would say something like, "It was built in the sixteenth century." In the Science Museum they had flies about twice the size of our hands. The buildings are so big it would take a week to look at everything, including reading the writing.

Roger Eyres

The Planetarium

I was very interested in the Planetarium. I never knew that all the other planets travelled backwards except for Venus, which travels forwards. Nor did I know that Venus sent out acid when it rained, and not water. It was very impressive as they showed us what life was like in outer space. I knew nothing about life in space until I went to the

Planetarium. Now I have learned a lot. I thought it was brilliant to be told so much about space. When we came outside it took five minutes for my eyes to adjust to the light.

Barbara Pogorzelic

The visits to the West Country offered many more variations. On the journey south we often visited Coventry Cathedral and Warwick Castle, both superb venues, and Birdland, Ironbridge, Berkely Castle and Stratford-upon-Avon were often included too, on our way to Bristol. On two occasions we were able book in at the luxurious Redwood Lodge hotel, with its splendid indoor swimming pool, available to our pupils during the evening. This was a 4 star hotel in sumptuous surroundings, and by telephone and my follow up letter I persuaded the owner to do a good deal for us, with my absolute assurance that the pupils would be impeccably behaved, and he offered us the £15 per night per person for £5. It was one of the best deals I ever did, and perhaps no wonder that the staff in the secretary's office and many of my teaching colleagues soon regarded me as spiv or a conman as they overheard me bartering over the telephone. Visits to the Roman Baths, Cheddar Gorge, Wells Cathedral and Blenheim Palace were all very popular, but one we always included and allocated ample time for, was Slimbridge Wild Fowl Trust, established by Sir Peter Scott.

I have usually described these visits as educational holidays, but really it is a misnomer, because the three day programme of visits to historical, wild life, scientific and religious places of interest was simply mind boggling for these young children, most of whom would never have had the chance to see or visit any of these places, stay in a hotel, or travel through so much of the country with their families. It is impossible to quantify what benefits each pupil gained, but I know from my occasional meeting with former pupils that they still look back on them with affection today, twenty and more years later. The only set of written work completed by the pupils who went on the west country visit was that in 1982, which once again captures the way they appreciated the new world they were experiencing.

Gough's Cave

When we went into the cave I looked up and saw a huge hole in the ceiling, it was like a giant chimney. As we moved further on we saw stalactites and stalagmites. Stalactites are spikes of lime hanging down from the ceiling. Stalagmites are spikes rising from the floor. The next part of the cave was where lime was slanting the walls. They had been given names, such as The Frozen River, and Niagra Falls, which was the most beautiful structure of them all. Then we looked up the twirling chimney we could see a giant stalagmite ten feet high, which must have taken over ten million years to grow.

Darren Gilleece

Slimbridge Wildfowl Trust

This is a trust which looks after ducks, geese and swans. The birds are allowed to fly in and out as they please, as they are not caged up, so they can live just as they did in the wild. Before we went to look around we saw a slide film describing feathers and their many uses. For courtship displays, waterproofing, nest insulating, and even just for plain flying, without feathers they couldn't do any of these things. The Wildfowl Trust was built to provide a home for the birds, at the same time letting people see them. They have grown incredibly tame over the years, and not afraid of people any more. At this time of the year, the mating season, the birds will be nesting. We saw two ducks trying to find a nest. We also saw two other birds, male and female, with the male trying to warn off others from his mate by honking as loud as he could to scare them away. We saw many land birds too, such as Canada Geese, which our guide told us were quite rare in this country. In the middle of a large lake was Barnacle Island, named after the colony of Barnacle Geese which lived there. There were some ducks and geese in pens to protect them from the crowds of people. These included Eider ducks, used for making eiderdowns, and Flamingoes, which are a type of goose which get their pink colour by eating a pink liquid. To enable us to see the birds a long distance away the Trust had built a hide, which we all went up. At the top was a marvellous view of all the scenery, When we came down we finished looking around and bought our souvenirs and postcards, which ended our tour of Slimbridge.

Frances Turner

The Roman Baths

My first thought whilst we were approaching the building was what colour the water would be. As we arrived it looked like a Roman Temple, with plans of the Roman Empire, and maps of the city. In the East Bath we could see mosaic floors with all patterns and gods on them. The bath had green water, with fish swimming around. The guide told us that the baths were heated by hot water springs which came from under the ground. There were several baths, and we saw all of them. The West End Bath was a small cold water bath for men only. I was pleased to see the Roman Baths.

Daniel Lambert

The Roman Villa

On our way back after visiting Slimbridge and Berkeley Castle we went to Chedworth Roman Villa. As soon as we walked in we could see a model of what the villa would have looked like in its heyday, and a complete plan of the villa. We then watched a film showing us more details, after which we met our guide who explained everything. He first showed us a mosaic made of stone from a nearby quarry. This was almost complete, showing the four seasons. Then he showed us some pillars which once held the floor up. This was because the Romans had a kind of central heating called hypocost. Then he showed us more mosaic floors. The villa itself was discovered quite by accident. The people from the nearby villages had always known there was something unusual about that certain place. Then one day a huntsman was chasing a rabbit when it went down a hole. He then put his ferret down the hole, but it never came out, so he started digging and found a few stones, and after that the discovery was made. Today, right in the centre of the villa is a Victorian house.

Darren Smith

The S.S. Great Britain

At Bristol Dock we visited the famous S.S. Great Britain. This was the first iron ship to be made and to sail successfully. It was salvaged at the Falkland Islands where it had been abandoned, and finally towed back to England, and placed in a dry dock at Bristol so they could restore it. S.S. Great Britain is very big so it will take until the end of the century to complete it. When people visit the dock they are allowed to go underneath the ship to look around. Underneath is a very big propeller, which is a replica of the original one. The guide who took us round told us that "The ship was probably the First Wonder of the World." On the deck was a huge funnel which towered above us. Below the deck was the machinery. The space needed for all that machinery was vast. After we had completed our tour of the ship we went into the souvenir shop. The people in the shop were supposed to shut up at 6pm, but very kindly stayed open for a little while longer which I think was very kind of them.

Samantha Prestwich

Wells Cathedral

Wells was another superb visit. I think it was built in 1187. The front of the cathedral was smothered in lovely carvings. As soon as we stepped through the door we could see masses of arches, and a dome shaped little room at the far end. Our guide told us a story. She said that some boys had been taught up near a balcony-like platform. She said that they were so hungry that when the gong went for dinner they used to go to one side of the balcony and jump off the edge on to a pillar, then slide down it so they would be first in the queue. Many of the pillars are carved. One carving is of a little man holding his mouth open because he has toothache. It looked so real. There is an arch called the Scissors Arch, because it just looks like a pair of scissors. Apparently it was built there for a reason, not for decoration. Somebody had decided to build a tall tower, but unfortunately it was too heavy and a crack appeared in the wall, so they built the Scissors Arch. On the left hand side is the famous clock. At the top there is a small ledge, where two men come out and one knocks the other off his horse every quarter of an hour.

The most beautiful thing of all was the carving of Christ. It looked so lifelike, as though he really had clothes draped over his arms. There are 297 surviving statues in Wells Cathedral, the greatest statuary in Europe.

Tracey Smith

Our Lovely Bedroom

When we arrived at our hotel I thought that the bedrooms would just have beds, a sink and a toilet. But it had a colour television, three beds, a shower, kettle, cups, mirror, milk, a sewing kit and other things. The beds were very comfortable. The pillows were so soft you could just sink into them. The carpet was soft too. There was a radio in the headboard that had ten channels. The showers were so beautiful, and the water could be hot or cold or any temperature you liked. The bedroom was very posh indeed.

Donna Durose

What Lovely Countryside

On our way to nearly all the places we visited we travelled through the countryside. It was lovely, with wild flowers, trees and various ruins all making the landscape look beautiful. All the houses in the countryside look nice, with their white walls and lovely oak framework. There are flowers in the fields, lovely trees, and with the sun shining on the sparkling early morning dew, it all looks very nice and very neat. The people working in the fields waved as we went past. I was quite sorry to have to leave the wonderful countryside as we reached the motorway for our journey home. Wells Cathedral had been our final visit. The structure and art, inside and out, is magnificent. The stained glass windows are lovely. Some are assorted because they had been smashed in Cromwell's time, but a faithful servant had collected all the bits of glass and stuck them together. The main feature is the clock. It is astronomical and tells the faces of the sun and moon as well as the time. This year Wells Cathedral is celebrating its 800th birthday.

Lisa Cook

It was important for the success of our three-day visits that virtually every minute was planned for in advance, and that the pupils conducted themselves in an orderly and disciplined way, so that they could benefit from and enjoy the whole experience. They were understandably very excited. Being away from home, staying in luxurious hotels and visiting so many places of interest, must make every ten year-old child excited, which was why it was important that they behaved well. We were never regimental, but we did exercise strict control throughout the visits, and with the total support of their parents. Everything was fully explained at the meeting for the parents of all those taking part, in the week prior to the visit. One point I always made was that it was important that every pupil got a full night's sleep in the hotel, in order to be refreshed the following day. I explained that the excitement of sleeping away from home, and being in a hotel with their friends, might make it difficult for them to fall asleep, but we had a golden rule. This was that at 10pm the television and bedroom lights must be switched off, and then absolute silence! There was not to be a word spoken, so that one restless pupil did not keep another awake. They would all have my room telephone number in case of emergency, but that if and when one of the teachers walked quietly past every bedroom door and heard any talking, all three pupils in that room would be put on the train to Manchester early the following morning. This strict policy was always accepted by the parents who, in the few remaining days before our departure, constantly reminded them to do exactly as instructed. What they were not to know, of course, was that none of the staff ever did walk down the corridors. We did not need to, because the bluff always worked – well nearly always!

By being well behaved during the visits had advantages too. I always tried to make sure that on visits where guides were available, that I booked the best and most experienced one, in order to get the most out of it. When guides are explaining the features of an abbey, cathedral, castle, etc, and all the pupils in the group are attentive, listening, and quiet, they are so pleased that they go to extra lengths to make the visit even more enjoyable, and end by thanking them and praising them for their good behaviour. On one of our visits to Warwick Castle more than one member of staff told me that our pupils had been the best behaved group that day. Complimentary comments were also made in theatres too. On a number of occasions, as we guided our forty or more pupils to their seats, I detected expressions of unease on the faces of the adults seated in front of, or immediately behind us. I sometimes went across to reassure them, and at the end of the performance we were often approached by those seated nearby to thank us for the pupils' excellent behaviour.

An essential feature of every school visit is ensuring that every pupil is present. For this the group had to stand still in order to be counted. It would happen as we left the hotel, came out of the building, or wherever, before moving on. Occasionally we would find that one or two were missing, perhaps visiting the toilets, or still queueing in the souvenir shop, unaware that the others had left the building. It normally only took a few moments before we were all on our way to the next venue. And with such meticulous thoroughness we were totally unprepared for the moment when we realised that we had lost a pupil! We had just stepped off the Tube train on our way back to our hotel from the Tower of London when we suddenly realised that Jeanette Timmins was missing. The obvious explanation, so we assumed, was that she was still on the train, so we quickly alerted the station staff to contact colleagues at the next two or three stations to check the passengers. As the minutes ticked by we were becoming increasingly worried, especially when the messages being received were that there was no single girl passenger on the train.

Thankfully our next move proved successful. Our only logical assumption was that we must have set off from the Tower without her, and when we made the phone call the answer was, "Yes, she's here." I had been counting the pupils as they left the Tower souvenir shop, and my colleagues were assembling the group on the pavement outside, and once the last one, so we thought, had left the shop we walked to the nearby station, and we would probably have done a routine count on the platform had not the train arrived just as we did. Hence the first count was as we stepped off the train. Philip took a taxi to the Tower where he found Jeanette being "entertained," as he described it, by the Beefeaters. She had been allowed to ring the 'clear-out' bell at 6pm. Apparently it was a regular occurrence for pupils to be left behind at the Tower. It was the first and last time we ever experienced such a worrying half hour on our visits.

After every such visit we arranged another night in the school hall for parents and pupils, to enable them to watch the cine films and photographs we had taken during the three days, bringing the event to a conclusion. The parents very much appreciated the opportunities and benefits the visits had provided for their children, and many commented that it had been a very maturing experience too, when for the first time in their lives, their son or daughter had been away from home, and how they seemed to have grown up in those three days. The parents also very much appreciated the willingness of the teachers for giving up their time for such visits. Danny McLaughlan and Philip Adshead came on every one of them, and Margaret Ownsworth, came on the first four or five, with a number of other lady members of staff taking part over the ten years, and to all my colleagues I was, and still am, grateful for their support.

10 USA ×2

All the "holidays" I had arranged at North Chadderton, Werneth, and now at Limehurst, had been, of course, for the benefit of my pupils, but in 1978 I decided it was now the right time to arrange an adventurous family holiday. We had been going virtually nowhere except Abersoch since 1969 and enjoyable though it always was I felt that a change would be a good idea. As the children were moving towards their teens they had begun to ask, "Do we have to go this week end?" as many of their friends were spending their holidays in Spain. Freddie Laker had done much to bring down the air fares, and the thought of a holiday in America began to buzz. For years I had dreamed of going to the Grand Canyon, following a book I had read in which there were some wonderful photographs, so in the autumn of 1978 I asked the children if they fancied the idea of going to Disneyland, Las Vegas, San Francisco and the Grand Canyon. They were simply over the moon at the thought of it. At first we decided to make it a west coast holiday, but after discussing it with my step brother Norman when on one of his visits to see his dad, we were persuaded by his suggestion that we fly to New York, spend three days with his family, perhaps also visit Washington, before flying out west.

It all fitted into place perfectly, and soon I had booked the flights, car hire in Denver, and our accommodation at the Grand Canyon. So with passports and visas, at the beginning of August 1979, we flew to New York, landing at the J.F. Kennedy airport, where Norman was waiting to collect us as we walked out into what felt like a red hot oven. For Susan, myself and the children this flight had been our first, and the experience of boarding the jumbo, feeling nervous at and before the take-off, then experiencing the thrill of speeding across the world, was wonderful. Norman drove us to his house near the New Jersey boundary, where we met Pat and their two boys Nicholas and Christopher.

Norman took us on a full day tour of the Big Apple, including the United Nations Building and up to the top of the famous Twin Towers, tragically no more, and countless other places of interest. The biggest attraction for the children, though, was their first visit to a McDonald's. Having a Big Mac was something special, as were the huge ice creams they could order in the many ice cream parlours, another new concept, as was the Pizza Hut. All the children got on very well and our three days flew by very quickly. Finally, after enjoying their hospitality and friendship, barbeques, drinks and visits to so many places, we were driven into the city by Norman where we boarded the Greyhound bus to Washington, some three or four hours away.

In some ways our two nights in Washington were the start of our holiday, in the sense that we no longer had Norman guiding us and explaining the American way of doing things. Now we were on our own, and I felt the responsibility lay on my shoulders to ensure that everything went well. We enjoyed a bus tour of the city, which included a visit to the Arlington National Cemetery, where so many Famous Americans had been laid to rest. We also enjoyed our visits to the Smithsonian Institution, which houses some remarkable museums, including the Air and Space, and National Galleries. Then we joined the long queue to visit the White House, seeing many luxurious Presidential rooms, finally leaving the famous building through the front door. A wonderful day! Also wonderful for the children was the chance to visit a McDonalds as we walked back to our hotel. We had seen the Lincoln Memorial, The Pentagon, and the Arlington Memorial Bridge, and as we strolled down Pennsylvania Avenue I tasted a nectar for the first time in my life, bought from one of the street traders who dotted the busy tourist routes. How lovely it tasted, far better than that first banana in 1945!

Having enjoyed our time in the capital city we made our way to the airport for our flight to Denver, where we would begin our tour of the Western States. Excited once again at the moment of take – off on what, after all, was only our second flight, but one that became our third, fourth and fifth, as the plane landed at Memphis, Dallas and Kansas airports on our way to Denver. We had become experienced flyers already. It was early evening when we arrived in Denver, to be collected by our driver from the Holiday Inn, where we were booked in. Up bright and early the next morning, and having had our massive American breakfast, we went to collect the hire car, and what a car it was too! My driving experience had been mainly small vans and an Austin Cambridge, my 'motorised armchair.' But now I was hiring a New York plated limousine with a 3.6 litre engine with all the trimmings, air conditioning, tinted windows, and what was difficult for me to adjust to, an automatic.

As we climbed in and set off we felt like royalty, but driving on the right hand side of the road made me tentative, and as we drove along the freeway I made sure I kept to the 55 m.p.h. maximum speed limit. I was one of only a few who did, though, as cars overtook us on either side. We were on our way to the Rocky Mountains National Park, and we had a splendid day, through lovely countryside to Estes Park, and up to different vantage points in the Rockies until we reached the Continental Divide. My main problem in adjusting to the car was slamming on the brakes. Not that I meant to, of course, but my instinctive action was to put my left foot on the clutch to enable me to change gear, but as there was no clutch every time I did it the children, who were in the back seat, were being thrown forward as I slammed on the brakes. Eventually we made our way back to Denver for a long sound sleep, having experienced some of the vastness of America for the first time.

So we were rather late getting up after our long day touring the Colorado Rockies and Denver city, and it was time to begin our journey south towards New Mexico. Once again we drove through vast open spaces, of which we were to see so many in the following two weeks. We had been in the USA for a week and by now the days had no identity; we were simply enjoying every minute, looking forward to the spectacular places of interest ahead of us. The road was wide and quiet and gradually my foot pressed harder on the accelerator pedal and our speed rose. It felt safe in the wilderness of our journey south, and we even touched the 100mph mark, but I began to slow down as we seemed to be approaching a town. Alas, too late! Suddenly a police car began to follow us, but at 55 mph I thought little of it until Richard noticed that its lights were flashing. I pulled into the side of the road to see what the matter was. As I got out of the car the two policemen both had their hands at the ready on their guns as they leaned on the roadside barrier watching my every move.

"Is 'summat' up?" I asked. One of them looked at me, glanced at the car I was driving, with its New York number plate, and said, "Where are you from?" "Oldham" I replied, "Near Manchester." When they realised we were from England, and not some flash New Yorkers, they relaxed, but they told me I had been driving at 78 mph. I professed to be shocked at this, whilst acknowledging that I had been doing about 60mph. It was lucky for me that they had not seen me a few minutes earlier. They instructed me to follow them to a police patrol area, which I did. The officer who was then dealing with my case told me to sit in his car, and that as it would take a little while, "Maybe your wife might like to do a little shopping?" Eventually, after the forms had been completed he told me that he would only 'do' me for 74mph, thus allowing me not to have to 'go down the station.' He was very friendly, and I handed him my fine of 20 dollars which he placed in an envelope and for which I received a receipt.

All this had delayed us by nearly an hour, so we got on our way, this time definitely not exceeding the limit. But another surprise awaited me an hour later, when another police car began to follow us, also flashing its lights. I immediately pulled in, this time furious that I was about to be victimised. Once again the policemen were quickly out of their car and as I approached them I simply said, "What's up now?" "Has your wife lost her purse, sir?" he asked, and sure enough Susan had put one of the shopping bags down where we had been parked, and had forgotten she had done so. The patrol man gave me directions to a service station parking lot about four miles back, to where the other policemen would bring the shopping bag. Half an hour later the officers came, handed Susan the bag, which some honest person had found and handed in, and the two officers very generously had driven some fifty miles to return it to us. What a wonderful gesture, for which we expressed our appreciation.

It had certainly been an eventful day, and soon we had booked in at a Best Western in Alamosa, thinking that if in the next fortnight there were to be more unexpected incidents we might never make it to San Francisco. Thankfully there would not be, and having been up bright and early the next morning we were soon on our way to the historic and ancient city of Santa Fe, to spend two nights and the best part of three days absorbing its unique atmosphere. What a contrast with New York! Here in Santa Fe, with its mixture of Spanish, Indian and Anglo cultures, are some of the oldest buildings in America. We visited the famous St. Francis Cathedral, the Palace of the Governors, and the fascinating Loretto Chapel with its legendary 'Miraculous Staircase', an absolute masterpiece of carpentry, one that is believed to have been constructed by a passing stranger, none other than St. Joseph! All round the Plaza Pueblo Indian women were seated on the floor selling their pottery and jewellery, and the whole atmosphere as we followed the recommended route through the centre of the city was awesome. Its architecture and culture belonged to ancient times. We were absorbed by the galleries, crafts, and countless cafes specialising in New Mexico flavours. We certainly found no Big Macs!

Having spent three days in the ancient Pueblo atmosphere we began our journey to the west coast, stopping briefly in Albuquerque, before making our way west along the freeway towards what was for me to be the highlight of the holiday, The Grand Canyon. Once again the landscape was attractive, and as we moved towards The Indianlands we marvelled at the spectacular sandstone monuments rising into the sky.

(L to R) Richard, Sarah, Me and Lucy on my 60th Birthday

Emily and John

Me, Jony Jo (M.C.) Bob Uttley (Sponsor) Nick Hopwood,
Neil Crompton, Tony Spence, Brian Johnston, Andy Brookes
(Sponsor) John Holder, Roy Kerr.

The 2007 CLL Dinner
Alan Wright (Secretary) Dean Redfern (JW Lees Director)
Howard Dronsfield (Chairman) Me, Neville Fletcher
(Vice Chairman) Alan Stuttard (M.C.)

Being presented with the gift to mark my 15th and final
Sportsman's Dinner 1999.

Alan Taylor, Mike Bamford, Mike Craig (Comedian) Me,
Neil Midgley (M.C.) Denis Law, Tony Spence, Trevor Lewis.

Richard, George Best and Me at our 1994 dinner.

My final day at Congleton Market when the traders presented me with the Acctim Clock

Trevor Veg, Johnny Cheese, Café Ron, 'Blusher' Stuart, Rocky Thompson, Me, Towel Rick, Leah, Trevor Sparks, Pictures Johnny

Blusher and I holding the £10 note I won from him on my final market day.

At Machu Picchu 1997.

A sea lion on a Galapagos Island 1997.

The Great Wall of China.

The Twelve Apostles.

The Grand Canyon, as seen from Hopi Point as the sun sets.

The Colorado River, as seen through the helicopter window.

181

Richard, Sarah and Lucy in 1969.

K24 our chalet on The Warren.

We were travelling near to Navajo Indian territory, but did not have the time available to explore it, committed, as we were, to our timetable. We did make one detour, however, after we had seen signposts directing travellers to Meteor Crater. This is the world's best preserved and first proven meteorite crater. It was an unbelievable sight. It is deeper than the Empire State Building is tall, with the circumference of its rim three miles. The meteor is estimated to have been travelling at 30,000mph. We spent an hour or so looking down from the rim, listening to the details described by the guide, and walking through the museum and shop. The whole place was truly fascinating, yet before that day neither Susan nor I had ever heard of it. It certainly buzzed in my mind as we drove to Flagstaff, having covered some 400 miles from Santa Fe. After an evening meal we went to an ice cream parlour, then back to our Best Western before our visit to the Grand Canyon, early the following morning.

All went according to plan and we were on our way immediately after breakfast, reaching the Grand Canyon village before lunchtime. We booked in, took our bags to our rooms, and walked towards Mather Point to take our first look at what most people regard as the 'most sublime spectacle on Earth,' as expressed by Major John Lesley Powell in 1895. What an awesome sight! I had long been impressed by the beautiful photographs in the book, but this was the real thing, and simply fantastic! The canyon is not one wonderful sight, but hundreds, stretching, as it does, 277 miles, and at the Grand Canyon village there are countless vantage points, each with their special attractive views. There is a free bus service every fifteen minutes, enabling visitors to travel from one end of the village to the other, each stopping at every vantage point to allow passengers to walk to the rim, enjoy the views for as long as they want before going back to await the next bus. That was how we spent all afternoon, making our way to the vantage points, looking down a mile to the River Colorado, and marvelling at the spectacular rock formations on all sides. Finally we went to Hopi Point, where all visitors gather to see the changing colours on the rocks as the sun sinks in the sky – a most awesomely beautiful sight! Finally we made our way back to the village, where we enjoyed an organised barbeque as the rangers presented their evening programmes in the amphitheatre, much of which is prepared for children, and which Richard, Lucy and Sarah all enjoyed.

They also enjoyed the following day too, when we all climbed into a helicopter! I had decided that this was a once in a lifetime occasion, so never mind how much it cost, go for it. For the next fifteen minutes we enjoyed the most memorable flight of our lives. From the moment when the helicopter flew over the edge of the rim, as we were able to look out of the windows or through the glass floor to see the sights below, it was unbelievable. The pilot described the many canyon features the whole time, and he took us down towards the Colorado River, which also enabled us to see many spectacular rock formations, many sparkling in the sun's rays. He also twirled us around some of the peaks and 'temples' that can only be seen from the air, and we also saw the geological wonder of the inner gorge. They were the most memorable fifteen minutes of my life, rounded off as we flew back over the rim, close enough for us to see the innumerable historic layers, before gently landing once again on Mother Earth. None of us will ever forget the experience.

We made our way back to the village with the feeling of satisfaction that we had seen virtually everything, but there was still one thing I wanted to do. It was to see and photograph the complete sunset at Hopi Point. I decided to be there early, in order to stand at the best vantage point, and arrived at about 5.30pm. I was one of the first there, never moved from my position by the railing for over two hours, taking pictures of the rocks every few minutes as the sun began to set, and as the crowds behind me grew. The rocks changed from bright orange to deep crimson over the two hours, providing the pictures of a lifetime, and rounding off such a wonderful day.

After another evening barbeque and ampitheatre display we called it a day, and on the following morning said goodbye to 'the most sublime spectacle on Earth' as we drove toward Las Vegas. By lunchtime we had covered quite a distance and decided to book in at a motel and spend a lazy afternoon by the pool. It was a good relaxing day, after our many hectic sight-seeing days, and Richard really enjoyed himself swimming and perfecting his diving skills off the high diving boards. On the next morning we set off towards the gambling centre of the world, on a route which took us past the enormous Hoover Dam. It seemed too good to miss, so we took a guided tour, which was very informative and interesting. We went from top to bottom, inside to out, realised what an enormous task its construction had been, and then climbed back into 'our' limousine to make our way to 'Casinoland.' We were driving mainly through desert country but it was surprising to see so many impoverished townships so close to the city where people gambled day and night. Soon we had made it to the centre of this enormously large city, where we drove down the famous 'Strip.' It was so thrilling that we drove up and down two or three times, soaking up the atmosphere and taking photographs.

We booked in at our Best Western hotel, and soon we were walking along the 'Strip' until we reached the only casino in the city that we as a family were permitted to visit, Circus Circus. We spent all afternoon there, enjoying having a flutter on virtually everything in the huge building. It catered for people of all ages, with an atmosphere rather like a cultured fairground, and the children enjoyed spending their money – and some of mine – on various machines, competitions and stalls. The casino staff were very tolerant, often pretending not seeing those under age playing the machines. Eventually, having spent our allotted quotas, and with the children clinging to the prizes they had been thrilled to win, we made our way during the early evening back to our hotel, having had another great day.

Once again, as we made our customary early start, for the long drive towards the children's favourite resort, Los Angeles, which meant Disneyland, we passed through more poverty stricken townships in the isolated countryside, and by now I had reached the conclusion that America must be a wonderful place to live in if you are comfortably off, but not for the many thousands, if not millions, who are destitute. These forgotten people do not seem to accord with the worldwide perception of the American dream. The dream for Richard, Lucy and Sarah, however, was to make it to Disneyland that day, and we covered some 250 miles to Anaheim in California, the last of the eight States of the USA that we had visited, with another nine exciting days of our holiday ahead of us.

We made our way to the Alamo Motor Lodge, which I had booked a few days in advance, as I had done throughout the holiday, and on our arrival were pleased to discover that we were only a short walking distance away from The Magic Kingdom. This was the children's dream come true. Virtually none of their friends back home had ever been to the USA, and they were delirious with excitement that our twelve months of talk, planning and dreaming had become a reality. They couldn't get through the turnstiles quickly enough. Disneyland belonged, as it were, to the children, as Susan and I were simply delighted to watch them enjoying themselves, going on as many attractions as possible. On some rides all five of us enjoyed, but on the more adventurous or scary ones they went on by themselves. Then, as the daylight faded, the lights came on, and there was an even more exciting atmosphere. The highlight of the evening was the 'Main Street Electrical Parade' where apparently more than half a million twinkling lights are used on a long parade of vehicles and Disney characters illuminated in a sparkling procession, which was described as 'night-time enchantment.' Indeed it was, being the highlight of a truly great day.

On the following days we went to Sea World, did the Universal Studios Tour, Marineland, the Wax Museum in Hollywood, and numerous other attractions on a coach tour, not wasting a minute on either day. By now we had decided to stay for an extra day in Los Angeles, having allowed room for some flexibility in planning our holiday, according to the way things might unfold, so all day Thursday, apart from the afternoon by the hotel pool, we spent at Disneyland, where we enjoyed another wonderful day before packing our bags to say goodbye to L.A. early Friday morning, to begin our long drive north towards our final destination, San Francisco.

Our first stopping place was Santa Barbara, where we caught our first glimpse of the Pacific Ocean, and in a race to reach the water first Richard just made it before Lucy and me. We enjoyed the scenic coastal journey along Route 101 until we arrived at Morro Bay, where the ocean waves battered the rocky coast, for an overnight stop, then moved further north towards Hearst Castle, which we had hoped to visit only to find it fully booked. We arrived at Carmel, the home of the rich and famous from Hollywood, before moving inland to San Jose, for the last night of our travels, finally arriving on Saturday morning at San Francisco, the city where Tony Bennett had left his heart. I could leave mine there too, such an attractive holiday city it is – the best in the world, I believe.

Now that we had finally reached the end of our long journey, having covered a few thousand miles in those twenty days, and exactly on schedule, I felt relieved and relaxed. All the planning had been worthwhile, and now, even if the car were to break down, we would be fine, with three days for us to spend exploring San Francisco. What surprised us, however, when we opened the car doors for the first time, was how chilly it was. For three weeks we had enjoyed unbroken sunshine and lovely hot weather, but now, although it was a clear day, we were almost shivering at midday. But the temperature was certainly not going to stop us from enjoying ourselves, and after we had booked in at our hotel on Market Street we began to drive up and down the steep and spectacular hills for which the city is famous, and went in search of Lombard Street, which the children were especially eager to drive down. As we slowly wound our way down 'The Crookedest Street in the World' there were smiles on all our faces. "Let's go back and do it again," shouted the children, and so we did, three or four times, before parking the car and spending the rest of the afternoon at Fisherman's Wharf, with its mixture of entertainments, games, restaurants, marina activities and shops galore.

On Monday we enjoyed a coach tour, crossing the Golden Gate bridge, travelling to the top of some of the 49 hills, and to many of the city's famous sites, but were disappointed that we were unable to travel by Cable Car, because the system was in the middle of a repair programme; nor could we visit Alcatraz, as the tickets had already been sold out. We very much enjoyed our final full day in the U.S.A. though, when we drove across the famous bridge towards Sausalito and on to Muir Woods, to see the giant redwood and sequoia trees, before once again crossing the Golden Gate on our way to Chinatown, and then going on a Bay Cruise, where we saw how large San Francisco Bay really is.

Our holiday was now coming to an end, and on Wednesday morning I handed over the keys for the superb limousine at San Francisco Airport for the start of our long journey home. First we flew to Los Angeles, changed planes to fly to Bangor, Maine, where we had to sit on the runway for hours, finally crossing the Atlantic to Heathrow, after which we caught two trains before arriving at Piccadilly, where Sim, Susan's brother collected us, on Thursday evening. We felt as if we had been travelling a whole week! Not that it mattered how tired we might be, for we had just enjoyed the holiday of a lifetime, one that none of us has, or will ever, forget.

The children's only visit to Abersoch following our holiday was in the half – term break before the site closed for the winter, and so by spring 1980 they were all excited at the prospect of going back. Perhaps absence had made their hearts grow fonder, for they were certainly looking forward to returning to The Warren. By now Richard had been successful in his 'O' levels, enabling him to move into the 6th form at Xavarian College; Lucy was about to begin her final year at Loretto College, which was now an 11 – 16 school; and Sarah had moved to Our Lady's Comprehensive in Royton, where Susan had taken up her teaching post a year or so earlier. At Abersoch everything had gone well. I had become a better DIY man as I endeavoured to keep the chalet and its garden in good order, continuing to be successful in hiring it to people who did not leave it a mess, and we enjoyed our holidays ourselves, renewing our acquaintance with our friends there. The children enjoyed their weeks there too, and growing up as they were, began to hint that soon they would like to go for a holiday there on their own, with friends, not with mum and dad!

I had been doing some thinking, too. In the near future family holidays would become a thing of the past, and with the thrilling memories of

1979 still alive in me, I began to think of the options for 1981. It was now or never, I believed, so in the autumn I put my ideas to them. Susan wanted a less hectic holiday than our first one, and we all agreed on a mixture of something for everyone. We would begin in Florida, then fly to New Orleans, after which we would fly to San Antonio, Texas, where in a hire car we would see as much of that Pan Handle State as possible, including popping into Mexico, before ending our three weeks in New York with Norman and Pat.

By the end of July 1981, all the necessary arrangements and bookings having been made, or so I thought, we signed in at Manchester Airport, but for quite a few hours I did not think we would be flying. The first problem was the news coming from the USA that the air traffic controllers had gone on strike, so there would be a delay. As we sat around waiting I went as far as to telephone my insurance company to see if we were covered in case the holiday was cancelled. That was the first problem, which seemed to be easing as it was announced that we would be boarding soon.

There was no way I could have anticipated the other problem, though, having done everything to ensure our papers were in order, including, once again, going to London to obtain our visas. But as we made our way through the boarding area the airport official looked at our family passport and informed us that only Susan, Sarah and I were covered, because Lucy was 16 and Richard 17, and needed their own passports. I was distraught. I was staring at a disaster, and at what was my fault. The official suggested, as he glanced at his watch, that there was time to go to Liverpool and back before the plane took off, in order to obtain their passports. "But what about their visas?" I asked, to which he replied, "Oh yes," and after pause, during which I feared the worst, he said, "I must advise you that you are travelling illegally," before allowing us to move through the gates. This whole catastrophe plagued me throughout the flight, and as we approached Miami I began to speculate on the possibilities facing us if the airport officials were to spot the 'illegality.' By now it was early evening, our flight having been delayed over six hours, and thankfully the official handed back our passport and visas with, "Have a nice day." and we felt more relieved than delighted as we left the airport.

We were delighted, though, when having collected our hire car, we were soon on our way to Fort Lauderdale to spend two nights, before driving north to Palm Beach, and from there to the Kennedy Space Center which was outstandingly popular that year, as only three months earlier the first space shuttle had been launched there. After that we moved towards Orlando for two hectic days at Disney World and surrounding attractions, once again thrilling the children no end. So having enjoyed our week in Florida we drove to the airport for our flight to New Orleans, and what an exciting city it was. Sadly I feel I must use the past tense in describing New Orleans, following the widespread damage that Hurricane Katrina did in 2005, but the city that we saw and enjoyed in 1981 was unique. Our first impression, however, as we walked from our hotel towards the River Mississippi, was that it seemed to be nothing special, and we were surprised to see such filthy water flowing past us as we stood on the levee. Jackson Square was lovely, though, and St. Louis' Cathedral simply magnificent.

We then went for a meal, and by the time we left the restaurant it was becoming dark, and New Orleans was waking up. It was a city that slept by day and throbbed by night. The whole of the famous French Quarter buzzed both on the streets and in the bars and clubs, and we had a terrific evening listening to the jazz bands, soaking up the atmosphere we had never experienced before. On the next day we enjoyed a meal in the famous Top of the Mart Tower, in a revolving restaurant, with panoramic views of the whole city below. We went to Preservation Hall, the home and birthplace of jazz, and went on a tour of the city visiting such places as the Sugar Bowl Sports Stadium and the famous city cemetery where all the bodies were in graves above ground level. It was an exciting three days, and particularly nights, in a memorably bustling and vibrant city, and as we arrived at the airport to fly to San Antonio with anticipation of more places to see and enjoy, it was mingled with sadness in leaving its very special and magical atmosphere.

We were soon on our way to San Antonio in the largest and friendliest state of the USA, Texas. The city is famous, of course, for the Battle of the Alamo, with Davy Crocket and Jim Bowie amongst those revered and remembered. One particularly attractive feature is the Pasco del Rio, the River Walk, with countless cafes, shops, bars and restaurants, with tables outside and in, all overlooking the calm waters. River boats glide by, and the evening atmosphere is exciting and romantic. Texans are very friendly people, genuinely pleased to hear an English accent, and invariably say, "Come back and see us some more," their way of saying goodbye. After two nights we set off in our hire car to Corpus Christie on the Southern coast, and visited the swelteringly hot North Padre Island, before setting off the next day towards the southern most tip of the USA, Brownsville, where we crossed the bridge on to South Padre Island, a place of sheer holiday luxury.

Here I fancied hotel luxury too, and managed to book in at the Hilton hotel, where we spent four relaxing days, enjoying the hotel's many indoor and poolside facilities, barbeques and bars, with the most splendid private beach just yards away. We did drive a few miles in order to see more of the island's scenic attractions, but the only time I crossed the bridge was when I decided to drive to a Rotary Club meeting, and as I drove through Brownsville a police car began to follow me, with his lights flashing. This brought back memories, of course, but I was taken by surprise when he told me that I had been doing 40mph in a 30mph district. He asked to see my passport and seeing my address 'Oldham' he said, "Is that Oklahoma?" in his distinctive Mexican accent. I was dumfounded. English is the second language in that part of Texas, with all road signs showing Spanish first. Anyway, I paid him my 25 dollars, for which he gave me my yellow ticket, and went on my way.

Then after four splendidly luxurious days on South Padre Island we made our way to Laredo, in order to cross the Rio Grande and step into Mexico, just for the thrill of it. It was instantly recognisable to us as a third world country, even though we only ventured in the souvenir shopping malls close to the border. It would have been risky to have gone probing any further inland. It had been an interesting eye opening experience for us, though, and an enjoyable afternoon, and we returned to the Laredo, a city teeming with cockroaches, even in the Hilton hotel. I had noticed that hotel prices varied in different parts of the country, and that in the outskirts of Texas the Hilton prices were much lower, hence our up–market accommodation!

Soon we were on our way again, this time through the wilderness of the Lone Star State, where cactus seemed to be everywhere, as we passed isolated farms with their oil wells, and seeing cotton fields galore. As we drove through the many miles of emptiness I began to appreciate why Americans demand the right to own a gun. The wide open roads, meanwhile, were so deserted that I even asked Richard, who had not yet taken his driving test, if he fancied taking the wheel for a few miles. He didn't need asking twice and jumped into my seat. It was not long before he had his left elbow dangling out of the window, and steering with one finger. It could have been a risk too many, so he was soon back in the passenger seat, having enjoyed the experience. We went on to enjoy our four days, spending an afternoon at a rodeo, visiting the Lyndon B Johnson Ranch, travelled through different towns, many with interesting characteristics, such as one with all German architecture, and staying one night in the state capital, Austin. Then we arrived back in San Antonio for our final night in Texas, in another Hilton hotel!

We enjoyed another lovely evening on the River Walk, but before we departed the following day we made a tour of The Alamo, regarded as one of America's most important shrines. Then with even more souvenirs packed in our bags we made our way to the airport, to fly to New York. But there was to be yet another surprise awaiting us, another speeding ticket! As we were making our way from the city centre we must have made a wrong turn and we had been driving up the freeway for some time before we realised it, so at the next junction we went up and over the bridge to set off back towards the city. By now we were struggling for time so I put my foot down, or we would miss our flight. Then as we speeded along we were spotted by the police in a car parked on the far side of the other freeway. Straight across the road they drove, over the grassy stretch, and with their lights flashing they were soon behind us, now at 55mph, of course.

I feared the worst, especially when, after handing the policeman my passport, he opened it to check my details and found the yellow ticket I had received in Brownsville! I had to sit in his car to answer his questions, and explain our situation. Then very much quicker than I had expected he took my money, handed me my yellow ticket, and said he hoped we would make it to the airport in time. Off we went, and thankfully managed to return the car, clock in our luggage to catch the slightly delayed flight. It must have been our lucky day. There were three more to come in New York where Norman once again collected us, and we were soon barbequing in his spacious garden, both families delighted to have met up once again. Once again Norman drove us into the city to see some of the landmarks we had not visited in1979 including going to the top of the Empire State Building, which was tremendous. All in all, our three days with Norman, Pat and the boys were the ideal way to round off what had been another adventurous three weeks holiday in America. But I had one more ace up my sleeve. With the children now in their teenage years there were not likely to be any more family holidays, so I had made a provisional booking for our final night at the most famous Hilton Hotel of them all, The Waldorf Astoria.

Both families climbed into Norman's car for the last time on the Wednesday morning, when I had dressed as smartly as my holiday clothes would allow, for our drive into the city, finally turning into the hotel car park. We made our way through the plush corridors and hallways and I reached the Reception desk, where I introduced myself. "Mr and Mrs J Cleary. Room for two?" the man said. "No." I replied, "We have three children, so there are five of us altogether." "Never heard of five in one room." he said, and walked out of sight. Knowing that I had the paperwork from the San Antonio Hilton in my pocket I waited confidently until he came back, pressed some more buttons, then handed me the keys. We all went up to the 27th floor to find our room. In we went and after a few moments Richard asked me where that other door led to. Suddenly we realised that we had been allocated a suite, normally 375 dollars a night, for 135 dollars. Another lucky day!

Norman, Pat and the boys enjoyed the afternoon with us, as we wandered through the many lounges and bars, in one of which was the piano of Cole

Porter, and then we said goodbye to them, and thanking them for their hospitality once again. In the evening we decided to have our evening meal in Oscar's, one of the six Waldorf restaurants before retiring to our luxury suite, feeling like royalty. On the following morning as we ate our breakfast I slid a Waldorf teaspoon into my pocket, a memento of my most treasured hotel experience, ever. Then as I tipped the porter for carrying our cases to the taxi we said goodbye to our final Hilton Hotel, New York and the USA, on our flight direct to Manchester, where we arrived early Friday evening, with everything having gone so well, with our good fortune at the tricky moments, especially as we had travelled 'illegally.'

Twelve hours later Richard and I were travelling again, this time to Congleton Market, selling footwear all day. Understandably we felt tired by the time we arrived home, to find that Susan, Lucy and Sarah, thanks to the jet lag effect, had slept almost 24 hours, waking up just before Richard and I returned. We were on our family travels again the following week end, to spend a few days at the Warren. It was, of course, nearing the end of the season and there were some bargains on offer at Land and Sea, the main boat dealers in the town. I thought it would be the right time to buy, and got a good deal as I traded mine for a larger and newer one, and with a bigger engine. If Lucy and Sarah were delighted then Richard was simply thrilled, because he knew that it would be he who would be behind the wheel the most – when he wasn't on the water skis, of course.

Here we were, then, coming to the end of the 1981 summer, and after another memorable American holiday, all three of them were looking forward to their holidays at the Warren the following year. Their love of the Abersoch had returned. It was back to school for all of us in September, of course, with Richard entering his 'A' level year, while Lucy, having passed her 'O' levels, joined Richard at Xavarian College, in the Lower 6th.

11 Limehurst Memories

By 1981 I was in my fifth year at Limehurst, and yet none of my colleagues had yet realised that I was 'Johnny Slipper' at Congleton. If that was remarkable it was to become unbelievable over the next four years. The council had been building a new indoor market hall on a nearby site, and this was to open on Saturdays and Tuesdays in September, with all new outdoor stalls in place. I was one of the two footwear traders, but the other one already had a Tuesday market, so I realised that if I did not take a stall the 'Toby' would look elsewhere for a shoeman, who would doubtless soon claim a Saturday stall too, thus increasing competition.

For the next four years, then, my Tuesdays began at 6am, when I set off with my neighbour and friend Alice Wood, who had happily agreed to work for me. It took us about an hour to reach Congleton, and another half an hour or so to unload the stock, before I unhitched and parked my trailer before beginning my journey back to Oldham, exchanging my sweater for a jacket and tie, to arrive at school just after 8.30am, looking just the same as on any other day. The other traders at Congleton believed that Tuesday was my buying day, hence the need for Alice to run the stall for me. At Limehurst they knew nothing either, even though I did no after-school activities on Tuesday afternoons. So whereas on most afternoons I would not normally leave school for an hour or more after the final bell had rung, I had to be fairly quickly away on Tuesdays, especially with the roads being busier at that time than on the early morning journey. On arriving in Congleton I would soon load up the boxes that Alice had already filled, and we would normally arrive back home at about 6 o'clock, when I would have a quick shower and shave and rush to the Rotary Club meeting. Tuesdays were certainly busy days.

Meanwhile, in exactly the same way that I described my days at Werneth in the year I started trading on Saturdays, I always endeavoured to make sure that my market business did not in any way detract from my work in the classroom. This might seem an audacious statement, but I believe it to be true, as, for example, the many out of school visits that I organised testify. But it was my day-to-day ambition to do my best for my pupils that drove me, being determined to try to motivate them to want to learn and to enjoy learning. My philosophy might be best summed up by one of the education officers who used an expression I have always cherished, "Children are not cans to be filled, but candles to be lit." As I first heard her say it I felt how perfectly it matched my lifelong beliefs.

I have referred earlier to how I did my best to make mathematics as attractive as possible and to remove the fear of failure in the no-hopers, and that how my efforts had by and large been successful. At Limehurst I also developed imaginative ways to motivate my pupils to write well, and to explore language. This is always a minefield when it comes to marking their essays. Should I ignore mistakes in spelling, punctuation and grammar in the search for imaginative writing, and therefore anything goes, or should I underline every single mistake, which is sure to discourage those with lesser ability but are trying their best? I believe the best solution is somewhere between the two, and if in my judgement I thought a pupil was genuinely trying to do well, I would try to emphasise and praise the good points while not ignoring the errors. All the very good writings would be exhibited on the classroom or corridor wall, but it had to have been correctly edited by the pupil himself, or herself, before it could be displayed, and I could see their determination to make it perfect, as they used their dictionaries in their desire to achieve the status of having their writing on display.

I enjoyed teaching the persuasive and descriptive types of writing equally. Whenever an incident occurred which I thought offered a good opportunity for them to write a letter about it I was on to it in a flash, be it a poor television programme, about a dog having bitten an innocent passer-by, or anything deserving thanks, praise or genuine concern. The most successful letters would be sent off, and the response awaited eagerly, usually by letter but sometimes by a visit by a policeman or the company representative, always in a constructive and appreciative way. Thus the pupils could see for themselves that if in their own personal or family circumstances they wished to make a complaint about an unsatisfactory situation they would know how to do so. I also looked for opportunities for them to write letters of thanks and appreciation, as the first of those I have selected indicate.

1 – 11 – 88

Dear Sir,

I am writing to thank you for giving us some new furniture in our school dining hall. The furniture is nice and soft, and it is warm and comfortable. It is better than the old ones. It is not as noisy as before. The new tables are better because we have more room to eat our dinner, as the tables are bigger. I also think the dining hall is nicer with the boards with the pictures on them. Now that you have given us some furniture the room looks like a restaurant. Thank you for your kindness.

Yours faithfully,

Suzzanna Bryer.

16 – 3- 83

Dear Mr. Carrington,

I am writing as one of the pupils from Limehurst School, and would like to take the opportunity to thank you for letting us watch the preview of the musical 'Calamity Jane', yesterday afternoon. It had all the ingredients a good show wanted, bright lights, colour, glamour and fun, and we enjoyed the result thoroughly. I especially liked the dancing girls with their lovely dresses, Francis Frier as the dressed up woman who had us all in fits of giggles, and of course Calamity and Katy, who would have been great if only they had let their hair down and spoken up a little. I would also like to congratulate the choir for their well scripted, catchy-tuned songs which I think they acted out superbly, but perhaps the funniest person in the cast, to me, was the little man with his straw hat, who was always in the background. I thought he was really cheeky and funny with his part, and played it very well. Maybe it would help if the actors and actresses looked as if they were enjoying it, even if it was nerve wracking being on the stage in front of the audience. If they had a smile and forgot about their shyness I think it would help a lot. Please don't think my criticism rude or too harsh, though. Apart from these points I thought that the show was very intresting and great fun, and I am sure the public will think the same. Once again, thank you for letting us watch the rehearsal, and I wish you good luck for your performance tonight, and every best wish for the future.

Yours sincerely,

Frances Turner.

31 – 10 – 88

Dear Sir,

I am writing to ask you if you would come to chop one of the trees down in our school playground because we think it is dead. We think it has been dead for about two years and is about 12 metres high. When a strong wind comes it might fall down and do one of these things. First of all it might fall down on children and kill or injure them. Secondly it might fall down on a car while it is passing on the street, and thirdly it might fall down on the Old Folks' Home across the way. We don't want *any of these things to happen, so please would you come and cut the tree down?*

Yours faithfully,

Luan Saint

29 – 10 – 88

Dear Sir,

We have a dead tree in our school playground and we will be very pleased if you will chop it down. The tree has been dead for about two years now and is about twelve metres high. It is not only a danger to us but there is a road near our school and cars come up and down every day. Twice a day children play near the tree and it could cause a serious accident. We will be very pleased if you will chop the tree down.

Yours faithfully,

Samantha Davenport.

21 – 4 – 88

Dear Chief Constable,

I am writing this letter to tell you about a dog which lives on Higher Lime Road which so gruesomely bit a six year old girl, a ten year old girl and an older woman for no reason at all. The younger girl was only going to her friend's house when the dog attacked her, and now, two days later, the bruises look worse than ever. Then the mother of the victim found out that the dog had bitten two other people, one being a girl who was playing with her friends when the dog pounced on her and bit her on the leg. Blood was everywhere, streaming down her leg, as she screamed in pain. It was absolute chaos. Both girls, Joanne and Leslie, want the dog put down before it bites a little baby and the result ends up fatal, but if you are against that idea put it in a home for a few weeks where it can be trained to do things on command.

Yours sincerely,

Steven Booth.

19 – 3 – 84

Dear Chief Constable,

I am writing to report that a little black and white Jack Russel on St Chads Crescent on Limeside is attacking and biting people, but especially children. This morning my friend Christopher was bitten by this dog, which broke his skin, so he had to go to hospital for a tetanus injection. He said he was just walking into the Post Office when the dog attacked him. Harry the shopkeeper came out with a brush to drive the dog away, and said it was not his dog, but one that belonged to a woman. It is not the first time that this dog has bitten somebody because there have been other children in my class who have also been bitten by this dog. So I am asking if you would be kind enough to do something about this before the dog bites somebody else and hurts them.

Yours faithfully,

Joanne Wild.

17 – 3 – 89

Dear Mr. Moxon,

I would like to thank you for letting me come to the Coliseum free to watch Godspell.

I enjoyed the play and thought the singers were very good. It was quite funny in parts. The costumes the actors were wearing were really nice. I liked the beginning of it best because the people were pretending to hit each other. I also liked the part when they were talking about their problems and the love tunnel. The lady with the red dress was funny, especially when she sat on that man's lap. Thank you for the wonderful play.

Yours faithfully,

Laura Buckley.

Dear Editor of the Oldham Chronicle,

Almost three weeks ago members of my class sent letters to the Parks Department explaining the situation of young saplings planted eighteen months ago in our school playground. Some of the trees they planted have been vandalised by people playing in the playground at night. Also, with the school having pupils of an age from four to six to them a tree is something to play around and they do not realise they are doing wrong. This all happened because members of the Parks Department came and took away the stakes which were helping the young trees to grow straight and nor to fall over. Now the trees are leaning sideways and some even lie flat on the ground. Members of our class are very disappointed that we did not receive a reply, and we feel that if you would publicise this we think it would result in a lot of action. Hoping to hear from you soon.

Yours faithfully,

Andrew Robinson.

- 3 – 88

Dear Sir

I am writing this letter to you to say how scruffy and disgusting our playground is when it's wet. Our playground slopes, so when it is really wet the water runs to a narrow passage which leads to the school entrance. It also takes mud with it and when the parents come to pick up their children a lot of them wait at the entrance so we get forced on to the mud, and with 200 or more infants and juniors coming in and out four times a day it makes the mud even worse. When we go inside we wipe our feet but there is still mud on our shoes. The flags in the playground are designed so that when the water flows down it just goes past the drain, so what is supposed to be grass is just mud and water. I would be pleased if you would come and look at just how disgusting it gets when it has rained heavily. On some occasions it rains so heavily that the water is so deep that we have to use the other entrance. The passage which leads to the entrance needs to be widened and the flags need to be levelled, so that when it does rain the water will go down the drains. I am sure everyone would be very grateful if you could do something about it.

Yours faithfully,

Kelly Ring.

5 – 10 – 88

Dear Sir,

Last Thursday I watched a programme called Wondermaths. I was disappointed in the programme as it was not suitable for Junior 4 pupils, it was more like an Infant programme. It was babyish the way they talked, and they were even more babyish when they argued over the cubes. They were talking to a silly computer and a robot. I couldn't understand some of the things the presenters were saying. They even went through that power cloud and when the power cut they acted frightened. I thought that was babyish. If you make another programme I hope you do better, then people might start writing to congratulate you instead of complaining.

Yours faithfully,

Nicola Hewitt.

Dear Sir,

Last week my class watched one of your programmes called Wondermaths. I was very disappointed in the way they were trying to teach us about maths. I think they were trying to make us laugh with their silly arguing and their baby ways. I would like to say that it didn't work on me and I don't think it worked on anybody else in the class either. I think it was a waste of twenty minutes.

Yours sincerely,

Nicola Hulme.

The last two letters were written to the BBC, and judging by the letter of reply from the Head of School Broadcasting, I must have sent a large envelope full of letters from virtually all the class following the programme. This is his reply.

4th November 1988

Dear Junior Four,

I was delighted to receive your letters but was naturally sorry that you found Wondermaths so disappointing. Part of the reason why you found the presenters so babyish is that you are obviously a very mature and intelligent class. I can tell that from your letters which were, I thought, exceptionally well written. Of course we have to make programmes to suit quite a range of children, including some younger than yourselves. I will show your letters to the producer (although not to the presenters because I know you would not want to hurt their feelings) and we will discuss what lessons we can learn from your opinions. Thank you very much for writing to me. It is very helpful to me to know what you felt about the programme. With best wishes,

Yours sincerely

Alan Rogers.

We then had further contact from the BBC which resulted in a visit to the school by two or three representatives, who spent an hour or so speaking to my class, and asking their opinions. The pupils were understandably delighted that their letters had been so successful. I was delighted, too, for throughout my years at Limehurst I had tried to take every appropriate opportunity to enable my pupils to write good letters, believing that when they later realised that progress can be made for their own, or others' benefit, they would know how to do something similar in their own personal circumstances. The letters I have included above are just some of those I must have decided not to throw away at the end of a school year, and probably indicate the flavour of what life in my classroom must have been.

Much though I always enjoyed encouraging my pupils to write such good letters, which probably began in my days at St. Joseph's, where I taught them to write their career application letters, what pleased me most of all was the high standard of creative and descriptive writing I tried to inspire my pupils to do. And although I never spent much time trying to teach them to write poetry, I certainly tried to motivate them to use poetic expressions. I would take my class outside to stand near a tree, or into a nearby field, appropriate for the occasion, to elicit ideas, images and pictures. In order to have a chance of being successful in so doing there has to be absolute attention based on strict and trusted discipline, to have the chance for ideas and expressions to be generated. My strict style of class control did much, I believe, to help my pupils to focus completely on trying to explore descriptive and imaginative expressions. Although I had taken my 6th form group outside the classroom during my time at North Chadderton, only at Limehurst did I develop the idea with a full class of pupils. My William Wordsworth theory, to which I made mention earlier, once again lay behind my decision to take them outside and I believe much of the good quality descriptive writing so many of my pupils achieved was inspired by the opportunity to absorb the atmosphere they were trying to describe. Over the years in which I took my classes outside I had an inner conviction that my style of teaching was successful, in that I believed their improved quality of writing and their enthusiasm to reach higher levels, was producing above average standards for pupils of their age. That is why at the end of some years I felt it worthwhile to save their writings that had been displayed on the classroom wall, just in case I could perhaps verify my beliefs at some future time.

But I never systematically saved their work, though I certainly wish I had. There were also years when the whole class's set of essay books were still in the classroom after the pupils had left, and I again must have randomly saved them. I have decided to include a selection from those I saved, to illustrate the standard that they achieved. I have tried to select a balance of examples by those written by pupils who had excellent literary skills, but also others written by pupils whose standard of writing at the beginning of the year had not been good, but who had enthusiastically striven to improve, confirming in my own mind that my style of teaching had succeeded. Whilst I was at Limehurst I felt sure that their standards were high, but had no way of knowing whether they were better than the work of pupils in other schools.

Attempting to accurately assess the standard that pupils in one school have achieved, however, can really only be done by comparing the standards in other schools, but how can a teacher do that? In mathematics a teacher can, in a discussion with a colleague, discover what stages a class has reached; but in a comparison of the levels of descriptive writing I could never bring myself to ask any other teachers to read my pupils' work, when the obvious inference being that I would be acting boastfully, or worse still, simply deluding myself. There had been many occasions when one of my colleagues would make favourable comments on having read the displayed writings, and perhaps a teacher from another school too, but I never pursued it further.

Long after my retirement however, once I had begun to write my life story, and read all the pupils' work that I had saved, I was still delighted at the high standard I felt they had achieved, over a decade later. So I approached Mrs Clare, who became head of the school following David Hindle's retirement, to ask what she thought of the collection I had retained. She said that she was very favourably impressed, but suggested that I seek the views of head teachers in schools that were not on council estates, where perhaps the standards were much higher. Mrs Angela McCormick and Mr Ray Garner, head teachers whom I had known when they were members of my Choral Speaking committee, were the first I thought of, so I went to ask their opinions, and both were full of praise for the writings. Ray's first words were "John, you should be proud of them," even after I had pleaded with him not to just be polite by telling me what he knew I would want to hear. Others have read them too, and have been favourably impressed. As I now include them in the following pages I do so in my belief that their work reflects the peak of my teaching career.

Jack Frost and the Sun

Jack Frost rides across Britain in his chariot of ice, spreading his white cloak everywhere he goes. The moon in the night sky could do nothing to stop him except tell the sun. The whole of Britain is an island of frost. Spreading over the land he freezes grass, leaves and other unprotected things. There is no force more powerful than this wretched master of crime except the sun, who will not rise for a long time yet. The sun's powers cannot be underestimated, and he rises earlier than expected to seek out the world's most hated villain. He creeps up on Jack and catches him red-handed. Jack swears to the sun that he will never terrorise Britain again so the sun lets him free. But the sun knew all along that he would try again. He then melted the ice prisons in which the grass was imprisoned, and promised that if Jack troubles them again he will be severely punished. The country is now safe from that winter hooligan, but not for long, I suppose.

Mark Howe

A Fine Autumn Day

It is a fine autumn day, berries and leaves glittering with winter frost. The atmosphere is cold and crisp, making the frost look like a big cloud of fog. A gull swoops down to perch on a branch and it settles down, but a few minutes later, with a flap of its wings, it's off like a shooting star, gliding across the sky. Suddenly it lands on the ground with a thud. The waddling gull walks right across the frosty landscape, leaving its footprints for the other moonwalker to follow. An aeroplane thunders by like a ski jumper going downhill, leaving its trail and continuing its journey. It is bleak and windy, making the trees tiptoe in the breeze. Suddenly the sun appears, rising up in the sky and beaming down a golden heat ray on the frost, trying to melt the silvery lake. Everything is silent except for a few birds chirping merrily.

Marina Turner

King Frost

During the night when everyone was asleep, all that was to be seen was the moon. Suddenly King Frost sprinkled his powers all over the grasslands. He tied all his prisoners together in chains and their arms were outstretched in agony. The sun began to build up strength, pushing itself gradually higher up from behind the clouds. Eventually it had done so and shot a huge beam of light at the guardsmen's faces, and they could not face the heat. They were sweltering and they fell to the ground. The sun had melted the chains and set them free.

Terry Evans

A Bright November Day

On this bright November day the sky is summer blue and cloudless. The sun blazes down, but it is still cold with frost. Minute jets leave their long forgotten trails to stray high above, whilst we look at the little aircraft as it glides across the sky to its destiny. Birds sing high in the treetops, their shrill notes like nightingales in top form. Gulls swerve in circles and swoop down like bullets to peck thrivingly into the soil at the worms, giving them no chance of freedom. They screech noisily like motor-bikes slamming their brakes, scaring off all the other timid birds. The long grass is frozen to the tip of the blades with the powdered frost. They stand out like knives pointing out of the ground ready for battle. It has been so cold that the insects have evacuated the place. The distant hills are covered with a sheet of mist like in a graveyard, and buildings on the hills look like silhouettes. Trees are trembling without protection. Now they have to survive the gale force blizzard in winter. Young saplings worry as winter draws near and the helpless roots have difficulty supporting the tree at war, the furious winter blast.

Gavin Haslam

Winter

Frosted pavements look as if sugar has been poured on to them. Snow gleams in the golden sunshine, half showing itself at the break of dawn. Tufts of grass stick up like the spikes on a hedgehog which has been disturbed and become frightened. Trees and berries are covered in snow until a blackbird comes to perch on the end of a branch, and he just sits there like a berry. Meanwhile the sparrow is searching for worms but never quite succeeds so he just hops about. At last the sun shows all its face and puts some colour into the sky. Trees look wonderful against the winter blue sky. The countryside is gorgeous in winter, like a white gown draped all over the houses. The view is breathtaking from the top of a hill, as if an artist had painted it during the night. It looks so unreal.

Jacqueline Cuff

Summer Holidays

Today is warm and still. All the fresh green grass is soft and tender and it smells of a lovely moisture. The sun smiles down upon every little bird as they form an orchestra and whistle out beautiful songs of nature. A tree looks like a tall statue with its long stretched out arms and its green twitching fingers. When the day is ending the tired sun climbs down a long rope of cloud and slowly goes to sleep.

Mark Wood

A Windy November Day

The wind howls, swaying the tree branches perilously, fluttering and flapping the few remaining leaves. The dark clouds overhead form a grey billowy eiderdown over the cold bleak moors. The wind blows the grass, making the field look like a seies of ripples on a lake, as each separate long stalk bends to the ground as if bowing their heads in church to pray. The trees shake as the wind weaves through their spiny forked hands, searching and seeking every frail leaf, snatching them away from the helpless twigs to send them scuttling and jumping across the wet marshy land. The bushes also seem afraid of the wind, and hide close to the ground, while a gull lands, the wind ruffling its feathers. It looks around for moment, wary now of the violent wind, then flies off again, obviously in search of shelter from the wind and the blasts of rain, the typical weather now that Autumn is in its midst.

Frances Turner

Spring Morning

This morning it was foggy, but as soon as the sun woke up he yawned and got ready to climb the long ladder to the sky. He broke the fog into little pieces and threw the bits away. He opened his heart to everything, and the flowers opened their buds, and blossomed with joy. The birds sang a song to wake up everyone. They sang a happy tune because spring was here again.

Bryn Parry

An Autumn Day

Today is a nice autumn day, with clouds looking like cotton wool balls. The weak and watery sun glows as it goes behind the clouds, trying to push through to brighten up the royal blue day, as it glistens in the distance. Look at the poor old tree reaching far into the sky with its tall thin fingers. The leaves twist and turn as they flutter down, making a carpet of colourful crisp leaves beneath the dying tree, standing there very lonely, waving its long thin arms about as though it was saying goodbye. The old tree stands shivering in the gentle breeze with no armour of clothing to wear, because its enemy the wind has blown them off. So the poor bare tree is standing there waiting for the long winter to end so that in spring it can be born once again.

Julie Bentley

A Spring Morning

It is a spring morning with signs of summer coming on. The mist has vanished and the sun has risen up into the sky like a burning ball. It is a delightful day; it is warm and has a calm breeze. The leaves are swaying as if they are saying thank you to the sun. The grass looks like a carpet with patterns of every colour. Each blade is pointing upwards enjoying the sunshine. The sky is clear blue and the few clouds are creamy white to blend with it. Birds are singing merrily, gliding through the air like darts. Butterflies are hovering above the flowers because they know they have produced pollen. Cherry Blossom trees are moving in the calm breeze, their luscious colours are appealing to see. Soon the sun will be going down for its good night sleep as the moon is awakening to take over from the sun to light up the world.

Paul Kelsall

A Spring Morning

Early this morning there was a gloomy mist, but as the sun rose into the blue yonder the mist gradually disappeared into the atmosphere. Now the cloudless sky looks like a calm blue lake, teeming with flying fish and boats. The sun is aloft and the day is warmer. The field looks embroidered with spring colours like a carpet. Leaves on the trees awake from a long winter's rest as they prance in the sunlight. The world seems to have come to life after a deep sleep. There is a fresh smell in the air of pink and white blossom as a calm breeze blows.

Nicholas Heap

A Wild Winter's Day

The trees are dancing to the wind's howling music, while the grass is swaying to and fro just like a ballet dancer, graceful and silent. The clouds are black and white, running wild across the sky like a zebra. The grass is squelchy and muddy, the roads wet and slippery. It is a bleak, cold wintry day, with no-one to be seen, as they are all inside where the icy wind can't get them. But the wind is crafty and sly, he is like a Viking warrior on horseback, riding round your house trying to get in, howling down the chimneys and tapping against the windows. Yesterday the wind invited the snow to come and stay. She spread open her coat and put a white sheet upon the houses, grass and trees, but the snow was not content and thought she would go to a colder, bleaker place than here. The sun showed one glimpse of herself today but as soon as she saw the cold world she went back to sleep again, and thought she wouldn't bother coming out. All the rubbish on the ground is being lifted in the air. It has been so cold the birds have not shown themselves today. But when the warmer weather comes the wind will be given its marching orders and will have to wait until winter comes back again.

Melanie Brown

A Bright Autumn Day

Today is bright and windy. The trees are moving with the wind as it blows, trying to shake the old and rusty leaves off the branches, but they keep clinging on with all their might. Just at that moment one leaf lets go of the branch and falls gently to the ground. Down below the blades of grass try to reach up to the sun to make them sparkle. Up above the bright blue sky holds the milky white clouds and bright beaming sun in its hands. The big bright ball of flame shines all through the day, then the flames die down and the day is over.

Gina Fox

Early Summer

It is summer and the light of the sun shines down on all that is below. The clouds look like scoops of whipped ice cream, melting in the heat of the sun. I sit and look up above me but the sun blocks my sight as it sends down its beams of light. Through the clouds shoots a silver dagger cutting through the silky blue sky to reach the heart of the sun. The leaves on the golden branches of the trees dance to the tune that the birds sing, with their enchanted whistles. The sun dies down but shoots back up again from behind the clouds and lightens our world with its wonderful glow.

Laura Buckley

A Fine Spring Morning

Today is a clear spring morning. The birds glide swiftly through the air as they take off and land. The sun looks like a roaring fire as it slowly climbs from the horizon. It brings new life to the flowers and the blades of grass shine brightly. The richly blossomed trees sway in the soft gentle breeze. It is a calm day as the leaves dance happily because spring has come.

David Davenport

A Lovely Summer's Morning

This morning is beautiful with no clouds in the sky. The gulls are packing their suitcases and getting ready to fly across the sea, but the trees stay where they are, lazily sunbathing. They are using their leaves as fans trying to keep themselves cool. The gentle breeze softly moves the grass which slowly moves to the side. The sky is a light blue colour in which an aeroplane looks like a silver bullet shooting through the air, leaving a trail of gunpowder behind it. The sun shines everywhere and the birds, trees, flowers and the breeze thank the sun for making their world like Paradise. When the night arrives the sun climbs down to the unknown, and everything goes to sleep.

Leanne Kerfoot

A Sunny Frosty Day

During the night the grass was taken prisoner by its enemy the frost. In the morning it was frozen and could not move an inch. The enemy was on guard duty, making sure that nobody could get through to the prisoners. But up rose the sun and shone its powerful golden light, knowing it would scare them away. The enemy was terrified knowing that they had lost the fight.

Samantha Howarth

A November Day

The sky is clear blue with not a cloud to be seen except above the hills. White feathered birds glide swiftly in the breeze and they scream like fire engines. The golden ball in the middle of the blue sky gleams on the thin layer of ice. The misty hills look like big white clouds falling down on Lego buildings and toy people below. The buildings are miserable and helpless in the frost, and their hollow chimneys spit out smoke.

Beverly Ashton

Spring Morning

The early morning mist has now disappeared. Now the sky is a lovely colour of blue and there is a soft breeze in the air. The burning sun is climbing up to the sky, where the birds are chirping happily and making a lovely sound. They swoop down and start pecking at the ground. The grass is glittering with dew. The trees that had died in the winter are now growing. Their lovely pink blossom looks beautiful, and smells lovely. The leaves on the trees look as if they are whispering to each other as they sway in the spring breeze. Below, the daises are like ballerinas with their frilly dresses on, as they dance to the birds' sweet music. They are stretching their heads and opening their eyes so that the sun can reach them, and they are glad that spring is here.

Tricia Dennett

A Bright Autumn Day

It is a bright, lively autumn day and there is a fresh breeze. The leaves on the trees are curling up, hiding from the wind and waiting, terrified that the next gust might come at any moment. They are drooping their heads, clinging on to the branches, trying not to be pulled off. The blades of grass are like little elves in green clothes, huddling together to keep warm as the strong wind blows. The sun shines on them and it is as if they are covered in glitter from head to foot. Above, the floating clouds look like white turtle doves, flying swiftly across a bright blue background. The sun seems like a torch being shone on the picture, making it become brighter.

Nicola Hewitt

A Bright Frosty Day

It is January, the middle of winter, and the sun is in battle with the frost and the cold wind. The frost has spread all around the field, trying to win the war of the two great features of nature. The sun is on our side trying hard to fight away the cold air and make us warm again. The frost is defeating the sun as the cold air freezes our fingertips and our toes, disabling us from the battle. The ice on the cold ground glimmers as the sun shines on to it, trying to melt it. The tree is asleep in hibernation, waiting for the time to come when the sun wins the war and spring is here again, when the tree can grow its leaves once more. The birds are chirping joyfully, because the sun is shining so bright on such a cold day. Soon, as the sun goes down, it will grow colder, but tomorrow the battle will commence once more until spring is here.

Sandra Lawless

A Cold November Day

The grey misty clouds drift further into the distance like cushions of dull smoke. The wind plays violent pranks, suddenly blowing the weak stems of grass to the boggy earth, and pushing the puddles further and further down the wet lonely lane. The trees seem to whistle as the wind passes by, vigorously blowing off their remaining leaves, which try desperately to cling on but the wind is too strong for them, as they quiver and tremble with bare cold. An old man trudges by, leaning wearily on an old walking stick, with his back bent and his head down. He is dressed in a dull mackintosh and an old grey cap, his face almost hidden from view, but you can just see his chapped lips and his crinkled cheeks. The birds are cosily snuggled up in their warm nests. Maybe a solitary gull will come and peck for worms in a field, but who knows? They may all stay in on this cold, wet and windy day.

Tracey Smith

The Snowflakes

The dizzy snowflakes twist and twirl as they tumble down to earth. They slip silently down, some alighting on bare twigs or branches, and others landing on windowsills to form drifts. The heavens seem full of it, and so do the trees, their boughs weighed down with crisp, soft snow. Suddenly the fall quickens its pace, blown on by an icy wind, as many more billowy, feathery flakes come, drifting swiftly down to a white snowy grave on the ground, now totally disguised by a white eiderdown. The exquisite flakes fall, veiling the snow capped hills in a grey mist, over which an eerie silence remains, only to be broken by the noise of a traveller returning to his warm home.

Frances Turner

The scene From The Castleshaw Hilltop

The clouds hover above as if on a string. Down below the reservoir glittered in the sun. Leaves fluttered in the breeze. Upon the hill the stone walls make it look like a jigsaw, whilst a plane cuts through the air like a knife through butter. A farmer's dog barked at the lazy sheep nibbling the grass, whilst the birds chirped like little penny whistles. Shadows of the clouds masked the hills, where the sheep, like cushions, lazed on the pastures. At the top of the hill people looked like dolls, and trees just stood there in the calm atmosphere. From the hilltop it was beautiful.

Mark Murray

Captured in the Night

During the night the frost crept down to capture the field and to command the city of grass. The King ordered his soldiers to put the people in an ice chamber. They tried to escape but there were too many to fight them. In the early morning when the King and his soldiers were asleep the grass looked up to the flame in the sky. Seeing the cruelty in grass city the flame took one deep breath and blew his heat on the city of ice and destroyed it. The soldiers promised not to conquer the city of grass, but the sun knew they would come back.

Shane Doyle

A Bright Spring Day

As the early morning sun rises from its sleep the mist slowly evaporates into thin air, and nature comes to life to find spring once again. The birds in the light blue sky fly swiftly through the air, singing gracefully and peacefully as if saying thank you for the spring once again. The leaves on the trees are glad to be alive and have a new green coat. The field is bursting with joy for the loveliness of its flowers and the freshness of its grass, on which the dew is shimmering. The flowers look up to the sun as though they are trying to reach it. Spring is here and brings joy to people and nature.

Marcelle Buckley

A Frosty Morning

The frost has taken command over a whole grass army. Each minute blade is kept prisoner in the desolate surroundings, huddling together wondering if they would ever be set free. Gradually a big bright light came from behind the clouds, and the sun sent lots of heat rays to destroy the white cloak. The ice man began to retreat from the ball of fire. He melts and disappears, so the whole grass army is free again.

Vicky Fraser

A Bright Autumn Day

It's a lovely breezy day. The clouds look like islands in a sky blue sea. It's another world up there, where God's home is. The sun is a person who hides his body behind the clouds. He reaches out his arms and gives the crown of the trees a golden touch. Some branches sway to keep the tree's balance, while the wind drags the dying leaves away as if it is picking berries. The leaves hold tight and cry "Help", because they do not want to leave their mother. Suddenly a leaf's hand slips and it lands on the grass, and begins to rot away. When the day ends and all is quiet the sun switches off its lights. Until they switch on again in the morning – blackness is above us.

Rina Patel

A Late Summer's Day

Today the sun is like a beaming torch, and the clouds are like fluffy balls of wool floating lazily across the sky, which is like the sea with speedboats zooming across, leaving waves behind them. Birds look like fish, lazing about, happily enjoying the sun while they can. Trees sway gently in the breeze, as if they are happy because the sun is out and they can feel its warmth. The grass is a velvet carpet patched out all over the world. Flowers sway, dancing in the sunshine, as if the sun was never going to come out again.

Kelly Ring

Spring

As the old ageing winter fades away, goodness in life rises. Trees no longer wither and rot, for they are capable of growing strong and healthy, ready for the next winter when it comes, with help of the lush natural beauty of spring. Up in the tree-tops the delicate whistle of

216

new born birds can be heard, whimpering for food while their parents merrily chirp to their hearts' content, saying "Thank you" for the beauty and happiness all around them. The frisk humming of an observant bee breaks the peace, whilst the silent fluttering of a playful butterfly cannot be heard. The grass sways about, at ease in the relaxing sunshine, but the new blades clutch together, feeling frightened, looking at things in this new strange world.

Gavin Haslam

Autumn

The weak sun creeps across the almost cloudless sky. It's tired of playing hide and seek behind the clouds. My armour of leaves were protecting me until my enemy, the wind, blew it away. Now my bony fingers can feel the pain of the cold. Soon the winter will come and I shall sleep. Then spring will come and I will awaken and have a new coat.

Jonathon Scholes

Spring

In the air there is a fragrant smell, telling us that spring is here. The flowers begin to bloom and the animals are waking up from hibernation. The birds are warbling sweetly in the glistening sunshine, and the buds struggle vigorously to see spring again. Young birds peep out of their nests, getting a glimpse of the world outside. Grass begins to germinate after its long cold spell under the snow and is becoming verdant. The flowers sway in the soft breeze as if they are ballet dancers. The sky is vivid blue, with white clouds looking like patches of foam. At last spring has come.

Joanne Moore

The Frost

During the night the frost invaded grassland, but because the sun was not awake, he got away with it, Meanwhile he was having fun by freezing things and putting frost on everything he could find. But when the sun saw what harm he was doing to his country and his people he took action. With the first beam of his laser he set free his people, with the second beam he disintegrated frost, with the third he killed frost's army, and with the fourth he unfroze everything that was frozen. Once more grassland was safe from frost and his army.

Kaye Carrigan

A Lovely Morning

It is a lovely summer's morning. The sky looks like the sea. Little speedboats dart across it leaving a trail of splashing waves behind. The sun shines like a burning desert in the middle of the sea. The trees are dancing in the cool breeze. They are showing off their camouflaged suits. Daisies put on their frilly dresses and sit down on the fresh green grass. Bit soon the sun will drift back to the unknown, leaving everything behind asleep.

Vicky Weiss

Grange Cottage

Grange Cottage used to be a place of shelter. Now it is like an abandoned site. Stones are decaying and falling out of place, slates are falling off the roof, and the sun and rain are eating their way through the stones into the house. Weeds go slyly through the house as if they are trespassing. If the owner came back to see it now, I think he would be upset. Inside are smells of condensation and rotting wood. There is an old chair in the house, which must be about 200 years old. The chimneys are bent and crumbling. Some of the walls have holes driven through them. I wouldn't like to go inside because it looks spooky and dark, but it still stands up to storms and lightning as it is not afraid.

Scott Flynn

A Spring Day

It is a hazy spring morning as the sun slowly climbs into the sky from over yonder hills. Birds glide gracefully in the cool fresh breeze. The sky is a lovely blue, with beautiful cotton clouds. The green fields are woven with patterns of flowers, all fighting for a place in the sun. Trees sway gently in the calm breeze, they seem to be stretching to touch the clear blue sky. The birds fly swiftly from the trees on to the sweet smelling grass, each blade happy because spring has come. The blossom on the trees is lovely to look at and beautiful to smell. So spring is here at last, giving new life to animals and flowers, and most of all giving joy to us.

Craige Swindells

A Spring Morning

It is a very lovely Spring morning. The sun has dispersed the dull mist, to light up the world. The sun is like a beaming torch, shining over the trees and grass. The sky is like a sea, with clouds like gentle tides, splashing softly on the shore. Birds are enjoying the heat of the sun, and when they feel too hot they dive in search of shade. Down below the leaves are happy on the branches, swaying from side to side, enjoying the gentle breeze. As the day goes on the sun moves back to the horizon, where it came from. The grass and trees are sad because the sun is going down to rest, having given us a lovely day to remember.

Scott Richards

All the descriptive pieces I have included are exactly how the pupils had written them, having corrected any mistakes they may have made, by themselves, before being displayed on the wall. My original intention was to include just a few pieces which my pupils wrote, but as I read and re-read the many excellent efforts, it convinced me that my William Wordsworth philosophy had been far more successful than I had ever believed. As I have already explained there were more years after which the pupils' writings were not saved that when it was, so the examples I have included can in no way be described as the very best of my fourteen years at Limehurst. What they do, I believe, is show how pupils, when given the opportunity to write in the very atmosphere they are trying to describe, can benefit greatly from the experience. This is also enhanced when they have the opportunity to listen to how others in the class had described the scene, and then become even more motivated to think of their own imaginative expressions.

At the beginning of each new school year, once the class had settled into my routine, and had adapted to my insistence of silence whilst they were doing their work, I would take them outside for the first time. During my preparatory talk I would explain what we were going to do, give them the title, such as A Fine Autumn Day, after which they would take their notepad and pen and walk to a corner of the playing field. They would spread themselves out so that they were ten yards or so apart, which helped to ensure the necessary silence, and they then stood, leaned or sat down, according to how it suited them, as they looked at the nearby trees, green fields, distant hills, with the sun or clouds above them. For perhaps fifteen minutes everyone, myself included, would be writing away, with not a word spoken. Then, when it seemed the right moment, judging by their demeanour, I would gather them together then ask some of them to read out what they had written. This being the first time they had taken part in an exercise of this kind, many of their writings would be fairly ordinary, but I never made any critical comments, simply moved from one to another, often detecting those who seemed eager to be asked. Soon there would be phrases such as a 'lonely' tree, leaves 'glittering,' or an aircraft 'gliding' across the sky. After a pupil had read such a piece I invited comments from the class. Invariably they would say they liked such good phrases, and I would then add my words of praise, and explain that such expressions were not to be copied. They had to try to find their own descriptive phrases.

After a few more readings, including mine, sometimes, they would spread out again, perhaps moving to a different part of the field, and inspired by the ideas that the readings had generated, they began again, and for another fifteen minutes, during which I could often detect a greater sense of enthusiasm in their mannerisms as they began to realise how an autumn day could be imaginatively described, and as they strove to think of their own images and expressions. Another gathering together usually lead to many more poetic efforts, and each such phrase, praised as it was, led to feelings of pride and self confidence, and increasingly motivating everyone to create their own good descriptions of an autumn day. Their final effort was made in the classroom where they opened their essay books and began again. In their minds would be the feelings they had experienced outside, the sounds of birds singing, the wind howling, aircraft flying across the sky, insects, trees, the sun and shadows, and with all the images that others had described, this was their opportunity to be as creative as possible. Once I had read and marked their efforts, again with some being read aloud, I would ask the writers of the best ones to copy them out perfectly before being displayed on the corridor wall.

Having had their eyes opened, as it were, by their first experience of writing outside, they began much more eagerly when they next went out, perhaps a month later, with an appropriately different title. Whilst the brightest pupils would normally produce the best efforts, I was always pleased to see the delight in the eyes of the pupils of lower ability when their classmates acknowledged their good descriptions and ideas, bringing back memories of Barry Jones, all those years before. My main aim was to convince all the class, especially the less talented ones, that they could write at higher levels, give them encouragement, and during the year I would see how that self confidence and determination to improve resulted in some of the pieces I have included earlier. As each school year progressed the pupils increasingly adjusted to the new ways of writing and, I believe, it often improved their confidence in their approach to learning other subjects.

The basis for much of their success in my classroom was that I taught in what I believe was a sensibly disciplined atmosphere. Discipline requires the ability to be enforced. If it cannot, for legal reasons, then it cannot, and does not, exist. The chances of my being able to do today what I did in the 1970's and 80's are slim. Teachers should be encouraged to develop their own theories and methods. I always appreciated the trust that David Hindle placed in me as he saw me doing things my way, never at any time trying to restrict my unorthodox methods of motivation. But the longer I remained in the teaching profession the more I felt frustrated by the strengthening influence of the trendy education officers and college lecturers. Schools were becoming increasingly pressurised to adopt the modern theories on how to teach, ostracising anyone who disagreed with them. Career progress was virtually blocked for any teacher who resisted change, as schools with traditional classrooms with doors that could be closed were being replaced by wide open areas of mayhem. I have always been in favour of change because that is how progress is made – but why throw the baby out with the bathwater? Pupils need the quiet atmosphere in which to think, concentrate, study, calculate, read and write. For this, silence is a necessity. But what did the innovative crackpots insist on? Circular tables, so that half the pupils have their backs to the teacher. They could not see the blackboard, so get rid of it! Pupils allegedly learn better when they help each other. Utter nonsense!

The most important person in the classroom is the teacher, who must motivate the pupils to the best of his or her ability, using a wide range of teaching skills in a recognisably disciplined environment. A teacher can distinguish between the clever and the less able pupil, the shy and the confident, the polite and rude, the hard working and lazy, and needs to enforce the necessary authority in order bring the best out of them. Nothing gave me greater pleasure than to see a pupil who believed he was a total failure, suddenly realising he could understand something and get it right.

All at once he felt confident and eager to try the next challenge. As I referred to earlier, children are candles to be lit, not cans to be filled, but they cannot learn how to do everything by themselves, and need the teacher to explain things, and in these situations there is a need for silence and concentration, with no distractions that the trendy idiots insist on, such as the wide open spaces which prevent a teacher from practising the basic classroom skills.

One to one is appropriate and necessary on and off throughout the school day, but so is whole class instruction, explanation, and question and answer, with the teacher making the most efficient use of the time available. The trendy modernisers condemned traditionalists such as myself as being too strict, not allowing pupils to develop, allegedly cramping their individuality by the stern disciplined control. Nothing could be further from the truth. How could so many of my pupils ever have written such excellent imaginative pieces if the atmosphere in the classroom had been one of fear?

It has always been my conviction that the training of teachers is fundamentally flawed. When I had my first experience of the student in the year ahead of me being my tutor in my second year, despite having no classroom experience himself, I thought it was probably an exception to the norm. Soon, however, as I became aware of 'academics' applying for research assistants posts which would lead them up the tutorial ladder, I became more cynical and unhappy with the system, but as I was getting on with my career it seemed simply a background matter. Eventually, though, the newer theorists stampeded their weird and crazy theories into the school system, especially at Primary level.

Where I believe the training of teachers is flawed is in the lack of experience in the classroom of the college lecturers. A far better way for preparing students to train as teachers would be for the lecturers to have spent the first half of their careers in the classroom themselves before becoming tutors, thus having the perfect background of experience on which to base their tutorial skills. Otherwise I would close the colleges down and devise a system whereby students go to a range of schools during their training, acting as classroom assistants with increasing opportunities to take lessons, learning throughout that period from the very people who are doing the job, at the coal face. Academic studies could be programmed at colleges or universities during appropriate parts of each training year. Doubtless my controversial views on this subject will be rejected out of hand, but if a census was taken of the number of years college lecturers had spent actually teaching before they embarked on their training college careers I would lay strong odds on the average number of years being fewer than the fingers on one hand, which is ridiculous.

12 Choral Speaking Festivals

Teaching my pupils to write poetry may never have been on my timetable, but encouraging them to enjoy it, to learn and recite it, certainly was. My Limehurst classes enjoyed reciting poems, but it was thanks to an amazing coincidence that I had the idea to initiate and organise the largest poetry festival of its kind in the country in 1985, one which gave me immense pride and satisfaction – the best idea I ever had during my career. The spark ignited on the evening when I had attended the Rochdale Youth Festival of Music and Speech, to watch my daughter Sarah's recital in 1984. Having been delighted by her successful recital, I was merely awaiting the performance to be concluded when a whole class group came on the stage to recite two poems, followed by two more school groups. This immediately reminded me of our concerts at Limehurst, where my classes similarly presented poems each Christmas. My pupils would learn a poem by heart, then after much practice in the classroom, recite it with precision and imagination, for the enjoyment of the large parental audience, as well as the delight they felt as it was successfully completed.

As I sat in the theatre that evening my mind began to explore the possibilities of presenting poetry on a wider scale. I had seen for myself how much my own pupils had benefited from their accomplishment in firstly memorising the many verses, then everyone reciting them in absolute unison, and finally undergoing the nervous phase of presenting the poems before an audience. The sheer joy and pride they felt when the recital had been completed had to be seen to be believed. Always it was a whole class performance, not one that was partaken only by the more talented pupils. Indeed it was of special benefit to the less able pupils, who were delighted and proud to have been equally contributive to the recital's success, giving the whole class a sense of fulfilment. As I returned home that night, still delighted at Sarah's own recital, my mind began to buzz with the thought that I should take my idea forwards.

First of all I contacted Mrs Owens, Headteacher of one of the partaking schools, and became acquainted with the Rochdale arrangements, and within a few days I decided that my best way forward would be through Oldham Metro Rotary Club, of which I was a member. My view was that a poetry festival would be an appropriate activity for the club to be associated with, not organise, but to offer sponsorship and assistance. I was a member of the club's Vocational Service sub-committee, which was chaired by Roy Teague who, very conveniently, was an Education Officer. I outlined my ideas at the meeting, and ultimately it was unanimously agreed that the club would be willing to sponsor a festival of poetry. Roy Teague arranged to speak to Education Officer for English, Ian Middlebrough, who soon came along to Limehurst to discuss my ideas. He was in favour of such a festival and soon publicised the idea, calling a meeting for any teachers who might wish to get involved. The inaugural meeting took place in November 1984 with fifteen teachers present, and Ian asked me to outline my ideas and the support that the Rotary Club would provide, and the benefits such a festival would have for the pupils who took part.

All the teachers were excited at the prospects and believed it would work, and I was elected as chairman of a committee which was formed that night to arrange and promote a Choral Speaking Festival. None of the teachers was more enthusiastic about the idea than Mrs Jackie Matthews, who became the secretary, and what a crucially good appointment that was, for she did outstanding work for the Association for the following twelve years. At all our committee meetings I tried to ensure that every member had the opportunity to express opinions, not simply rubber stamping my ideas, which had been the basis of our formation, and there developed a mutual trust and respect as we worked towards our first festival, held in March 1985.

All the work, preparation and meetings took place during after–school hours, of course, but inevitably it was Jackie and I who had the largest share of the work to do. Having received some initial advice from Mrs Owens, we now consulted with Mrs Audrey Carter who had agreed to become our adjudicator at our first festival. She had many years of officiating at poetry competitions in different parts of the country and was happy to pass on her advice. She in turn understood and appreciated that our festival would be our creation, a festival, but not a competition, an event where children would recite poetry to their highest standard and for enjoyment, and in no way to be branded losers or failures if their class had not been announced as winners. Mrs Carter would go on stage to review the recitals at the end of each session, would offer advice, recognise the standards each group had achieved, but in no way place them in order.

So it was, on the first day of spring 1985, at the Grange Arts Centre, with enough entries for three different categories, infant, lower junior and upper junior, and with a total of 24 school groups participating in four different sessions, a total of 750 pupils went home delighted to have been applauded off the stage. Everyone involved was relieved that everything had gone to plan, and the pupils, their teachers, who had all volunteered to enter their classes, and the members of the organising committee, felt a sense of achievement, following the many hours of hard work and preparation. The Rotary Club had donated a rose bowl to be presented to the school achieving the highest standard in each age group. No announcement of this was made at the festival, but the three schools were contacted the following day, and Jackie Matthews and I accompanied the club president Philip Hibbert to each school later in the week to make the presentations. Everyone regarded our first festival to have been an unqualified success, and we were soon to be making even more progress.

The 1986 festival was held at The Coliseum Theatre, thus enabling us to invite parents to attend, and the seats in the Circle and Gallery were virtually full each session, whilst seven or eight school groups, totalling 250 pupils, filled the Stalls. The number of groups taking part had grown to 40, the festival spread over two days. In his programme notes Ian Middlebrough, who had been very supportive throughout, wrote, "The festival was the brainchild of John Cleary" and he thanked all the members of the committee for "their hard work and organisation." The rules were simple at every festival. All school groups being entered must be whole class groups, not an elite group drawn from different classes, nor only the best from any one class. We were thus ensuring that the benefits of partaking in the festival were enjoyed by children of all abilities, as had been my policy at Limehurst. Schools were invited to present two contrasting poems, and most teachers probably encouraged their classes to share with them in deciding which poems to recite. There is a wide range of poems recited at every festival, but one characteristic has been consistent throughout them all – humour. 'Dog in the Playground,' 'Dad, the Cat and the Tree,' 'Colonel Fazackerly' and 'Night Mail' are just some of those very popular poems that the pupils enjoyed reciting, and were equally enjoyed by the pupils in the other groups, listening attentively and appreciatively.

Every festival has been available to any class group from Reception to top Junior and, significantly, to pupils of Special Schools. When the classes from Park Dean and Foxdenton schools took their places on stage the applause expressed at the completion of their recitals was very moving, as everyone in the audience, children and parents, realised how difficult it must have been for them to have recited their poems so successfully. For those of us on the founding committee in 1984 this was a development we had not foreseen, but we were all thrilled to see them taking part. A huge amount of credit is due to the teachers who prepared their pupils so meticulously for the festivals, the amount of hard work required to train them not just to memorise their poems but to overcome their nervousness as they stepped on to the Coliseum Theatre stage. Without the teachers' dedication there would have been no festivals. I

227

am convinced that all the pupils who have taken part in a festival will have acquired a love of poetry for the rest of their lives, which has made all those involved in arranging the festivals very rewarding.

In 1987 the festival grew to 50 groups, lasting two and a half days, with more than 1500 pupils taking part. By now the Education Authority provided supply teachers for the schools whose members of staff needed to be at the festival, and members of the Rotary club were still helping out selling programmes and guiding the school groups to their seats. Our committee met at various times of each year, always remaining open to new ideas. Committee changes did take place, mostly as a consequence of a teacher moving to a new post. Thankfully there were always teachers happy to join the committee. Those who served the lengthier periods of time were Ray Garner, who would follow me as chairman, Jo Hadfield, Jenny Lee and Angela McCormick. I did my best to divide the various responsibilities equally, but it was inevitable that Jackie Matthews and I continued to bear the brunt of the work.

By 1989 and 1990 the numbers of participating schools continued to grow, and our festival had become recognised as unique. And thanks to the Coliseum management, who allowed us to use their facilities free of charge, many hundreds of pupils were able to present their poems to enthralled audiences, all of whom would cherish their moments on the Coliseum stage for many years to come. There were 60 participating groups in each of my final two years as chairman, bringing the total number of pupils to have taken part over the six years to 10,000.

When one has an idea, and sees it turn into a successful reality, it inevitably leads to a feeling of satisfaction and pride. That is exactly what I felt, and still do, as the festival continues to thrive, thanks to members of the Rotary club, who now organise it. I have enjoyed attending the festival every year, which on occasions brings back the feeling of sadness I had felt as I stood on the stage at the conclusion of the 1990 festival, knowing that I would no longer be involved in what had been my most memorable achievement. Since 1985 more than 30,000 pupils will have had their day on stage, and acquired a love of poetry for the rest of their lives, something I feel proud of.

I was pleased to receive a letter from Oldham's Director of Education, Dr W.R. Kneen, apologising for having been unable to attend the festival, but saying how delighted he was that it had been a great success, and adding, "I was very sorry to hear that you intend to resign as Chairman. Thank you for all your excellent work for Oldham." I was even more pleased when I received a letter from the Education Officer, Ian Middlebrough, who had supported my idea of arranging a poetry festival in 1984, and who had been helpful throughout the next six years.

Dear John,

I felt that I must write to thank you for the tremendous effort and dedication which you have brought to the choral speaking enterprise. What you have given to the children of Oldham is incalculable and I think that the pupils and teachers of the town have every reason to be grateful to you. I can think of no other undertaking which has been as successful in my time in Oldham, and it is due entirely to the vision and organisational flair which you have shown during the last five years. I am sure that everyone has already wished you well in your retirement; may I add my sincere good wishes and grateful thanks.

Yours sincerely,

Ian Middlebrough.

This was another of the letters I had totally forgotten about until I recently came across it. There could be no better way of rounding off my proud memories of the best idea I ever had.

13 Good Days and Sad Days

By the early 1980's Richard, Lucy and Sarah were growing up fast, getting ready to enter the big wide world. They had loved what they had seen of it across the Atlantic, of course, and soon their school days would be over, and they would be making their career choices. Richard was the first, when in 1982, having done well in his 'A' levels, was awarded a place at Huddersfield Polytechnic to study law. I would never have believed it possible before it happened, but on the morning he was about to go across the Pennines, as I was taking the dog for a walk, I had tears in my eyes, feeling emotional, as most parents surely do, when a son or daughter 'flees the nest'. Lucy, a year later, would be leaving Loretto to begin her career at Sun Alliance, and Sarah would soon be starting her first job at Barclays Bank.

Going to Abersoch was once again something they looked forward to and enjoyed, especially with the bigger and faster speedboat. Sometimes we went as a family, then gradually they began to take their friends, but always left it clean and tidy for the families hiring it the following week. Not that I hired it out much in those days, following the completion of the repayment of the initial loan, but lettings did help to finance improvements to the chalet, including replacing some of the original furniture which had been of modest quality. The annual site fees had risen sharply too, so a few lettings balanced the books, enabling me to keep it attractive, both for ourselves and for those who hired it. Of those who did hire it two had been goalkeepers for Bolton Wanderers – Ken Grieves, perhaps known even better for his cricketing career, and his family; and Eddie Hopkinson, one of my schoolboy and cricket teammates, and his family. Another was the owner of the then famous Talk Of The North night club in Eccles, who, having hired it twice, invited Susan and I, along with Richard and Judith Murphy, to his club when the great Tommy Cooper topped the bill, our table being on the edge of the stage. What a funny man he was! Another who hired the chalet was a rugby league prop forward for Swinton, a player I disliked for his dirty play against my team, Oldham, causing injuries. When I realised who he was when he and his wife came to collect the keys the week before their holiday I kept my thoughts to myself, rather than risk being injured myself by such a huge chap, and he might have left the chalet in a mess too, of course! Not that we ever had trouble like that, thankfully, as virtually every family who hired it left it in good order. By the early 1980's the price of a new chalet was roughly ten times the amount I had paid in 1969, so it made even more sense for me to keep improving my DIY skills to keep the chalet attractive.

I was also beginning to learn a little of the world of finance, thanks to becoming one of a dozen or so who formed an investment club, mostly, but not entirely, made up of former Round Table members. We met every month, discussed various company shares, and once our monthly subscriptions had grown, we began to dabble in the stock market. We all came from different walks of life, but tips or inside information, sometimes accurate, but sometimes – indeed often – inaccurate, led to our various investments. Mike Lindley, a man in the banking world, was one of those who helped to set up the club, along with Keith Chadwick. Another member was Ron Wolf, a Rochdale Round Table member with whom I had become good friends, thanks to his wife, Anne, and Susan having been close friends since their schooldays. As our portfolio grew, our meetings became increasingly exciting, discussing when or whether to buy or sell. Our aim was to learn something about the stock market and to try to make some money. There were about twelve members, all of us paying £10 per month. We took out a subscription with the Penny Share magazine, which tempted us to some very high risk deals. One of these was Central Pacific Minerals, a company which had a formula for changing shale into oil. It was, we all believed, going to make us a small fortune, so we dived in at £5.45 a share. Two or three years later we ended up selling them for 30 pence each. It had not been our best investment! We did have some successes, though, and when our shares were rising we all enjoyed our meetings, and a few pints we would normally drink afterwards, even more. We also enjoyed our Christmas night out, which we always spent in a Chinatown restaurant, when there would be more spent, out of our funds, of course, on the drinks than on the meal we had eaten. After five or six years, at the time when two of our members were due to move away from the area, we decided to wind the club up, which our treasurer Mike Lindley oversaw. It had been a very pleasurable experience. Our monthly subscription had only been modest, and therefore affordable, but it made me reach the conclusion that I would never risk a sizeable sum of my own money, even if I had any, on shares.

Another club I became a founder member of in 1982 was Oldham Metro Rotary Club, and it was in the same year that I once again became actively involved at the place of all my boyhood dreams, Royton Cricket Club. I had watched the occasional Sunday game, including the one at Castleton Moor on 1980 when Royton won the League Title, but with my six-day working week cricket had been on the fringe of my life. My re-involvement began thanks to David Shannon, then club captain and a member of the cricket committee which had begun to arrange Sportsman's Dinners in the clubhouse. I attended the first of these, when David Lloyd was the guest speaker, and the following year David Shannon invited me to speak about my own cricket memories whilst formally proposing a vote of thanks to the main speaker, John Hampshire. Anxious not to make a mess of things I prepared my speech carefully, often reciting it to myself as I drove my car, and on the night it went down very well. My uncle Frank even came up to me afterwards, patted me on the back proudly, telling me that my speech had been better than John Hampshire's. As for myself I was just delighted to have seen the smiles on their faces, many of whom I did not know, newer members who had joined the club since I had ceased to be actively involved some fifteen years earlier.

I was now back in the swim of things and was later asked if I would be willing to organise the single wicket competition once again, the one I had started in 1965. I accepted, and now that I was also going into the club for a drink on Friday evenings, I managed to form a large group of members who were willing to help. One or two preliminary meetings were held, and I suggested that we re-jig the whole thing. So this time we would have a double–wicket competition, which would be preceded by a schools' event. The outcome was a huge success, with hundreds of families attending on the Sunday afternoon, enjoying countless fund raising competitions and stalls arranged by members on the tennis courts, bowling green and all over the car park, whilst on the cricket field twelve or more primary schools took part in a variety of friendly competitions, such as egg and spoon, sack racing, tug of war penalty shooting, all over the ground. We had invited some Oldham Athletic players to come along, and the children were thrilled to be introduced to them, and for two hours or so there was terrific excitement as the schools competed in the friendly environment. Then the cricket began, which lasted until about 7pm, with well known professionals and amateurs taking part, and the club made over £3000, thanks to the efforts of so many members. I felt relieved that everything had gone to plan, and the fact that I had co-ordinated the whole event meant that I had become involved with members old and new, and that my fifteen years away from any participation seemed to have vanished. I felt I had never been away.

Life at home was also changing. Thanks to the busy and exciting times during my Round Table days, when our social calendar grew year by year, there seemed no reason to think that it would slow down very much following my retirement in 1978, because of the many good friends we had made, and whose company we enjoyed. But it did. For quite some time arguments between Susan and myself had been taking longer to resolve, and were recurring ever more frequently, and far too often the atmosphere at home was strained. We had a number of discussions as to why we were arguing so much, but never agreed why. There was no third party involved, but we were reaching a deadlock. When a marriage is in trouble the innocent victims are the children, and for their sakes alone I was desperate to find a solution, as I am sure Susan was, but we could not. The arguments continued. Eventually, out of despair, perhaps, I decided that the only way to try to make any progress whenever we were alone in each other's company, was to stay silent. That way there would be no more arguments. Our family situation did not change much, though. We continued to spend time at Abersoch, usually went out for a meal on most, if not every, Sunday, and had various days out. One of the best of these was at Wimbledon. Lucy and Sarah had often said how good it must be to watch the tennis there, so as a surprise for them I followed up an advert in a newspaper and bought four Centre Court tickets, at £55 each. Richard was studying at Huddersfield that year, so he missed out. Thankfully it was a lovely day, which we thoroughly enjoyed, including the traditional strawberries and cream. I never mentioned what I had paid for the tickets, which had originally been £8!

Days like that one were special, but rare, and life at home was very different when the children were not there. Having decided that there would be no more arguments meant that our social lives came to a gradual standstill. No more arguments led to increasing silence. The days became weeks, and then months, and ultimately, years, until, in 1985, the end came, followed by divorce proceedings. It was during those silent worryingly stressful years that Lena Martell first sang 'One Day At A Time', a song which totally summed up my life then, and as I played the tape when driving my car it helped to give me the strength to keep going. Thankfully I managed to, and thankfully too, despite what Richard, Lucy and Sarah must have emotionally suffered during those bitter times, I believe they came through more or less unscathed. Perhaps the fact that they were entering the world of work had helped to take their minds off the atmosphere at home, and during most of this time they were still coming to the market with me on Saturdays.

14 My Final Years in the Classroom

Congleton had been part of my life for the past eleven years, but, amazingly, still no-one at Limehurst was aware of it. As I have previously explained, when I had first arrived at the school I was anxious to be perceived by my colleagues as a dedicated teacher, and believed that if they were to know that I had a business sideline they might have concluded that I was not fully committed to my role of deputy head, so, as had been the case at Werneth, I kept quiet about it, hoping they would not find out. After such a long time however, all such thoughts had vanished. Now it was more a matter of wry amusement that they still did not know, even though for the past few years I had been selling them slippers in the run-up to Christmas, telling them that it was a friend of mine who was in the footwear business. Then finally, after twelve years, they found out, after a teaching assistant and her husband had been caravanning in the Congleton area, and had visited the market where she spotted me on my stall, but had been so shocked at seeing me she felt unsure as whether to let on, and decided not to. The first I knew about it was on the Monday morning at break time in the staff room when an infant teacher Beryl Buckley said, "You look very well John. Was it sunny in Congleton on Saturday?" She couldn't have put it better, and I smiled as I replied, delighted that they had at last found out, pretending that I had thought they had known about it for years. They were even more surprised to learn that I had not just had my Saturday stall, but that for four years had been driving to Congleton on Tuesdays too, right under their noses, as it were.

Perhaps they should not have been surprised at all, because they had always regarded me as a 'spiv,' after hearing me on the telephone negotiating for bargain prices when I was arranging the school visits every year. Not that I was arranging quite as many by that time, because of changes in legislation which ridiculously entitled parents who could not, or would not, pay for their child to take part in such a visit, to insist that their child went free of charge. At Limehurst we felt we dare not take the risk, for it was essential to book hotel rooms, theatre and admission tickets months in advance, so, thanks to Kenneth Baker, the Education Minister, a long tradition came to an end. I did manage two trips of a different kind, however, the first being a huge success, the second an absolute disaster. David Hindle and the school governors were trying to raise money for improvements to be made in the school, and I was asked if I would like to organise a train to Stratford-upon-Avon and Warwick Castle, on which pupils from primary schools throughout the town could take part. I wrote letters to every school in Oldham and in no time every carriage had been booked, thus guaranteeing a handsome profit for Limehurst, and the pupils and staff who took part feeling that they had enjoyed a wonderful day for a fair price.

That experience gave me the idea of organising a similar trip in 1988, the 400th anniversary of the Spanish Armada, of which there was a special exhibition at the National Maritime Museum in London. The success of our first train visit no doubt prompted the quick response to my letters, and soon every seat had been sold. On the morning of the trip I went to Derker Station, where the train was due to begin its journey, calling at Mumps, Oldham Central, Werneth and finally Hollinwood, collecting school parties at every station. The train carriages were to be prominently listed from A to K, enabling every school group to be positioned on the platforms accordingly. As I waited on the Derker platform I was told by the driver of another train that ours would be late. It was – by an hour! To make matters worse, it came into the station back to front, the carriages showing K to A. With the train an hour late, I felt we could not waste more time by trying to change the carriage letters, hoping that we could solve the problems whilst we were on the move. Utter chaos is the only way to describe the situation as the train finally moved out of Hollinwood station, where the largest contingent of pupils, parents and teachers boarded the train. In some carriages it was impossible to move, while others were empty.

Eventually, many miles down the line, we got everyone seated, and I felt utterly exhausted as I moved from front to back countless times contacting the school groups to get everything sorted out. Our one hour's delay then began to increase as we travelled, because our train had to give precedence to mainline trains, so the hour became an hour and a half, and all the school parties now having their planned day seriously curtailed. Thankfully everyone on the train knew it was British Rail's fault, not mine, but as it was my task to resolve the problems it was a stressful experience that I had never anticipated. Once the train had arrived in London each school party was swiftly on its way, according to its schedule. In virtually every case one or more planned visit had to be cancelled, but in some cases, where a coach had been booked at a specific time, especially if it was to be at the time of our planned arrival time, then even more problems loomed. Our Limehurst party made the most of the day, and I made sure we did not waste any time when we had to walk from one venue to another, always hurrying them along, so much so that one or two elderly school governors who were taking part in the visit, could hardly keep up, but I regarded that as their problem, and kept up the fast pace at the front. All the pupils enjoyed each visit we made, especially at the National Maritime Museum, and by 6.30pm we were back with all the other school groups at Euston Station for our return journey. By this time I had put the morning's stressful experience behind me, and had a relaxing journey home.

The following morning, however, I began to seek appropriate compensation for the time lost in London. First of all I telephoned the British Rail staff with whom I had made all the original arrangements, and all I was given in reply was a list of excuses – not even an apology.

Then I wrote to the Area Manager, detailing every aspect of the day, only to receive more lame excuses, and an offer of another train to London at a reduced price. So then I decided to contact Sir Robert Reid, British Rail's top man. It worked, as the following correspondence indicates.

Dear Sir Robert Reid,

I know that you have received letters from colleagues of mine who were dismayed and disappointed that the Oldham Schools' Charter Train to London on May 17th was one and a half hours late on arriving at Kensington Olympia, on its way to Maze Hill. As the organiser of the train on behalf of the Oldham schools, however, I am writing to you now because I am dissatisfied not only by the original lateness, a full account of which is detailed in my enclosed letter, but particularly by the absence of any initial response by British Rail, and the totally inappropriate and unacceptable offer when it was eventually made. My purpose in writing to you now is to ask if you would intervene, and do the only fair and reasonable thing which would go towards recompensing the pupils whose day was partly spoiled, and at the same time restoring the reputation of British Rail, by providing another train, not necessarily to London, and getting the times right, at no cost whatsoever.

I am appalled at the apparent indifference of British Rail toward a train's lateness. Not a word of explanation or regret was forthcoming from anyone until, in a telephone conversation with Mr. Kay on May 26th, I drew attention to that fact, and that even nine days after our trip, no-one had had the courtesy to apologise for the delay or inconvenience, whereupon he made a belated apology. Lateness, he inferred, was a frequent occurrence and then he made mention of the new timetables, a fact that seemed to provide a convenient excuse to hide behind. I would like to make only one further point. When I as a teacher complain about your unsatisfactory service, I do so not on my own behalf. If I want to go to London I do so at my own convenience. But when I take a party of pupils and collect money for an organised day for which a good deal of educational preparation is made, I do so on behalf of young pupils for whom the whole day was to be the highlight of the school year, and in some cases the most thrilling single day of their lives. Many of those children, especially those from disadvantaged areas such as where many of the pupils taking part in this visit live, have never been on a train in their lives, and have certainly never been to London.

In taking the trouble to courteously outline our difficulties I hoped to elicit from Mr. Burrill a generous response. I did not demand a refund, as a private person would perhaps be expected to do. That would not be appropriate in my opinion. But for British Rail to offer another train at £4,000 indicates that they have failed to appreciate the essence of our dissatisfaction. The children had been paying £1. weekly since February, so to make an offer of this kind is entirely meaningless. In order to take advantage of such an 'offer' schools would have to attempt to persuade all the same pupils to pay for another trip, which, in view of the special occasion of the May 17th Armada-centred visit was, would simply not be feasible, taking into account also the additional costs to be incurred on such a day. If you are to offer to run a train in recompense then I suggest that it has to be one in which all the very same pupils who went on the Armada excursion can take part. This might be perhaps best achieved by offering to put on an excursion say, to York, at no cost, so that every pupil can take part, the only requirement being spending money and a minimal amount being necessary for visits to places of interest according to the schools' own preferences.

That is what I think would restore the reputation of British Rail, be well received by the Oldham schools, and realistically enable the poorer children to be recompensed for their curtailed day on the 17th of May. In my conversation with Mr. Kay at Manchester, and Mr. Check at Birmingham I have felt that they are blatantly refusing to make the offer of a replacement train on the quite indefensible grounds that it would set a precedent for other such situations. May I appeal to you to make a quick intervention and instruct Mr. Burrill to provide a train for the whole party as soon as possible, because this is a crowded summer term, and many of the pupils involved leave their primary schools in July.

Yours sincerely,

John Cleary.

Two weeks later I received a letter from British Rail's Customer Services Manager.

Dear Mr. Cleary,

Sir Robert Reid has asked me to reply to your letter of June 7. I would like to add my own apologies to those already offered to you and I am disappointed not only by the original circumstances of the journey but also that we have been unable to resolve the matter subsequently in a way which is satisfactory to you. I have good news on the second count. I know that Masie Cairns at Manchester Piccadilly has been speaking to you about what we might be able to do and we are now confident we will be in a position to run a charter train to York for you, free, in mid July. She will be in touch about the details. I trust that this is a satisfactory alternative to the offer of a reduction in price for a future charter train to London which, I appreciate, would be difficult to repeat for the pupils directly affected. We are running the train to York in view of the particular problems experienced on May 17. May I wish you well on the day and I hope it will leave the children with a rather different impression of British Rail from that they received in May.

Yours sincerely,

Jeremy Cobb.

So the very first 'free' British Rail train arrived on time, and made its way to York on the penultimate week of the summer term, which was a very appropriate way for many of the pupils to look back on their Junior school years as they were preparing for life in Comprehensive schools after the holidays. All the schools groups enjoyed their day in a city full of attractive places of interest, including, of course, its historic Minster, and city wall. There were no snags, but there would have been if one school had had not pulled out because of other arrangements that had already been made. The train which took us to York was filled to capacity, but if Mills Hill School had been able to take part it would have been chaos again, because they had filled two and a half carriages on the London train. I would, no doubt, have had another stressful day. Luckily, no, and at the end of the return journey it seemed as if the driver was under the strictest of instructions to be absolutely on time. During the final mile we seemed to be about to arrive at Hollinwood Station slightly earlier than scheduled, but the train slowed, and gently crawled its way to arrive exactly to the minute. My letter of thanks to Sir Robert Reid was despatched the following day!

Whilst visits to London, York, Stratford-upon-Avon or the West Country are valuable experiences for children, so are visits to appropriate places much nearer home. Sometimes it can be done without involving much expense, by travelling on a bus, rather than hiring a coach. I took classes to Tandle Hill Park in Royton, where I once made arrangements for the Reverend Cannon Shaw, a well respected horticulturist, to guide us round the large country park, and he captured the pupils' attention so brilliantly by details he explained so imaginatively. I also took classes to Greenfield, from where we walked to Dovestones Reservoir, along the craggy footpaths by the fast flowing stream, ending up near the foot of Indian's Head, a very well known local landmark. So long as everyone behaves well, and no-one, perhaps excitedly, acts recklessly, then accidents are easily avoidable. But that brings me back to my unshakeable belief that strict discipline is the essential ingredient in order to achieve this when crossing roads, climbing stiles, walking near water or doing anything out of the normal classroom routine. At the end of every such visit I arranged I could see the unmistakeable look of appreciation on the pupils' faces, indicating how much they had enjoyed, and learned from, the experience.

I also found that I could easily take pupils into other parts of the world too, thanks to David Attenborough. His many wonderful wild life TV programmes in the 1980's were simply outstanding. I realised that virtually none of my pupils' homes would anything remotely educational be watched, especially in those days when there was only ever one television in a house, so I taped them at home every week, and let the class watch it the next day in the classroom. There were no distractions, there was no work they had to do afterwards, simply watch the programmes, and become fascinated by the world of Nature. Their eyes said it all, as they sat there, mesmerised by what they watched. I could not attempt to quantify how many of my pupils might have gone on to study any of the subjects that the programmes or school visits covered, but I am convinced that as they grew older if they experienced similar opportunities they would be eager to follow them up. All a teacher can do is plant the seed, and hope that it takes root, then flowers in later life.

Another TV programme that some pupils will still remember with affection was that of the final day of the Headingly Test Match in 1981, 'Botham's Test'. It was the Tuesday of the last week of the school year, and pupils from all the classes were moving in and out of the main hall, practising in the choir or other such activities in the final rehearsals for the end of term concert. Having seen the end of Botham's unbelievable innings at the end of Monday's play, hoping, as was every cricket enthusiast in the country, that there would be miraculous ending to the game, I decided to take my class into the TV room, along with pupils from any other class who wanted to watch it. I also decided not to mention my idea to David Hindle during the morning break, just in case he disapproved, and anyway, the rest is history. Some of the pupils continued to watch it after the midday bell had rung, and almost missed their lunch in the dining room, so exciting was the play, and thanks to Bob Willis that day, the miracle took place.

There were times during those years when I felt I needed a miracle myself, but by the late 1980's my life at home had comfortably readjusted. Richard, having left Huddersfield University after the first year, had succeeded in his application for a post at finance company in Manchester, but after a few months decided that it was not what he wanted to do, and to my great surprise, and unease, he decided that having enjoyed his days helping me at Congleton, he would become a footwear trader too. He worked various markets, and at one of these, Macclesfield, he met and would go on to settle down with Veronica, and in July 1989, she gave birth to my grandson John. Lucy's career at Sun Alliance was blossoming, and she became an inspector. She was still living at home with me, and would help me out if I needed her at Congleton, especially on the busier pre-Christmas Saturdays. Sarah had remained with the Barclays Bank, and was for a while based in London.

My mum and Tom had sold their bungalow in Kirby Avenue, and moved a few streets away into a warden-controlled bungalow owned by the council. So it was to St. George's Square where I called for my lunch after paying my 'Slippertime' cheques into the nearby Nat West Bank every Monday, and on Saturday evenings on my way home from Congleton, with a Pink Final, the football paper, for Tom. During 1989, though, after settling in well in their new home, my mum still seeing the many friends she had made in the twenty eight years she had lived in the area, had begun to feel unwell for a number of weeks, and her doctor, unable to diagnose the problem, referred her to a specialist, who assured her that it was not a life threatening problem, and that an X-ray or two would help to resolve it. For this she had to go into Royal Oldham Hospital, and I would call after school to see her, then go back later in the evening. They were still not sure what the problem was, so arrangements were made for her to go to a Manchester specialist unit, and on that afternoon, as I entered the hospital ward, one of the nurses took me to one side.

My mum, she said, was still asleep, but the results of her tests were now known. It was cancer of the pancreas, with a life expectancy of a few months. I was devastated. One can never assume a 78 year old person is going to go on for ever, but the assurances that she had previously been given had led us all to think, and hope, that her condition would be treatable. The nurse went on to tell me that the hospital had a policy of being truthful with their patients, and that once my mum woke up, if she were to ask a nurse about the results of the X-rays, she would be given an honest reply. Within seconds I realised that when my mum did wake up, it would be for me, sitting by her side, to break the bad news. The hospital policy was undoubtedly the correct one. Attempted deception must lead to innumerable problems between the patient and members of the family, but no such thoughts were in my mind as I, feeling utterly distraught, not only at having been told that she was dying, but that any moment now I would have to tell her. Slowly she began to show signs of waking up, bringing the dreadful moment closer. She opened her eyes, was pleased to see me and told me that she had been in an ambulance to Manchester for her X-rays. I listened, and, hopefully at the right moment, quietly told her that the nurse had asked to speak to me as I was coming into the ward, told me that the results had been received, paused, and tremblingly whispered, "It's cancer." We just hugged each other and wept. There was little either of us could say. I stayed by her bed much longer than on earlier afternoons, and close that we had always been, as surely all mothers and sons are, that day we seemed to be re-living our lives as never before.

There were more tears flowing when I arrived home and told Lucy the bad news. Lucy, who had been particularly close to my mum, was inconsolable, as was Sarah. I then went to see Tom, and spent an hour with him before going back to the hospital. Every night the routine was the same. Tom would have been with her during the day, I would call after school, then Lucy and Sarah would follow me, after which I would go back until nine or ten o'clock. As the weeks went by the painkillers increased, and Christmas was not so easy to celebrate. In January she was placed in a private room where, on Sunday the 28th, as Tom, his son Norman, and I were sitting by her bed, she passed away. Sad that the moment was, at least her suffering had come to an end, and I am sure that all families who have watched a loved one undergoing pain, have experienced the same anguish and helplessness as they sit by the bed, their minds in emotional turmoil. That is how I felt. I had been her first born child. She had never known her own mother or father, and I meant so much to her, as she always has to me.

Within two months of my months of my mum's death I was saying goodbye to my teaching career. I had always enjoyed my time in the classroom, still getting the same feelings of satisfaction when my pupils made progress as I had done when I had first entered the profession, but times were changing. One particular change, though, was going to make a crucial difference as to when I made my final classroom decision – when to retire. I had never seriously contemplated taking early retirement, simply moving on from one year to the next, whilst becoming increasingly aware or the risks of being suspended when in a position like mine, in charge of school discipline. But it was the introduction of LMS, Local Management of Schools, due to come into effect at Easter 1990, which persuaded me, and many more teachers in their middle fifties, to retire. It was understood that after that date any teachers who retired before the age of 60 would not be eligible to receive their pensions until their 60th birthday.

It was, therefore, a simple choice for me to make, either to go at Easter or to wait for another six and a half years. There was no way I could have committed myself for so long, so I applied for retirement, on what would be a reduced pension, of course, but knowing that as I already had a Saturday income and would be able to find a stall on another day too, my pension shortfall would be compensated for by "Slippertime" earnings. As Easter approached I spent the penultimate week of my career at the Coliseum Theatre, chairing my sixth and final Festival of Poetry, which was when the feeling of sadness at my career coming to its end reached its climax. Similar nostalgic feelings flooded back during my final few days as I began to tidy up my classroom, which was full of paperwork I had accumulated and stored, and it was then that I realised how many of the displayed creative and descriptive essays I had saved. There was no way I was going to bin any of those, so I put them in cardboard boxes, took them home, where they remained untouched for another fourteen years.

Everyone, in whatever occupation, who looks back with pride on what he or she has done, must feel emotional in those final career days, and I certainly did as the retirement cards and expressions of good wishes bombarded me from pupils and parents. My colleagues presented me with two gifts, carefully selected to reflect my interests, a painting of a cricket scene and a lovely chess set and board, and as the final bell rang I stepped out into my retirement world with thirty years of lively, challenging, innovative, inspiring – and risky – classroom years to cherish. I had done it my way.

15 Back to the Wicket

I had been doing a few things my way at Royton Cricket Club too. The Double-Wicket Carnivals, which I had first organised in 1984, had become a popular annual event. They were the club's biggest fund raisers, enabling improvements to be made to cricket, bowling, tennis and clubhouse facilities. Members put in countless hours of work, and in so doing, many personal friendships, both old and new, were cemented by the feeling of success we were experiencing. I was delighted that my return to becoming involved at the club had helped to trigger such a popular annual event. At the clubhouse dinners I had been asked by David Shannon to become the M.C., so for the next four or five years I was on the top table when Mike Cowan, Geoff Cope, Colin Milburn and Fred Trueman were our guest speakers. At all these dinners Paul Booth was the first speaker, and in his humorous style helping to create a good atmosphere as he welcomed the guests, and I performed my role to the best of my ability from the start of the evening until the end, when I was ready for a strong drink, or two. I must have done reasonably well because one of our guests, David Shepherd, the CLL chairman, invited me to become the M.C. at the league dinner. Cricket had definitely become a big part of my life once again. For five or six years I was on the top table at the annual dinners and was later invited to play a leading role in the organising of the CLL Centenary Dinner in 1992.

The principal speaker was Sir Colin Cowdrey, the entertainer Kevin Connelly, and the MC – me! The league officials insisted that I fulfilled that role, and the dinner was held at Royton Assembly Hall, with all sixteen clubs each filling two tables of ten, and with players past and present, club members and guests, all delighted at what was a reunion celebration evening, one which I was thankful it was so successful. It was my role during the dinner to introduce each club, one by one, naming the members who had contributed to their clubs over the years, on and off the field. Everyone in the room applauded many of the great players who had enhanced the league but perhaps the loudest applause of all was when I introduced Cec Pepper, on one of the Rochdale tables, sitting with my old friend Peter Greene, the club president. It was an evening enabling players to renew their acquaintance with their friends and rivals, creating the perfect preamble to the excellent speech by Sir Colin, and the unbeatable impressionist, Kevin Connelly. I felt honoured to have played a part in the evening's success.

Helping to arrange the Centenary Dinner had taken quite a bit of my time, but that was nothing to the amount of time my role at Royton had been taking since the carnivals had got under way. For some time I had been expecting someone to try to persuade me to put my name forward for election to the general committee, but I was totally unprepared for what Fred Rawstron had to say when he approached me at the club one day. Mine was the name of the person who had been nominated to become his successor as president. Would I do it? I was stunned. I had only been back in action, as it were, for three or four years, and at 50 years old I felt too young for the honour, believing it should go to an older and more experienced club member. I assured Fred that I very much appreciated the offer but felt it right to decline it. Fred suggested that I give it some thought and we could perhaps have another talk about it. It was a confidential matter, of course, but I did have one or two discreet conversations with members whose opinions I respected. It was such a great honour to be asked, and after speaking to Roy Lees, a long time friend who was a former president himself, and Fred Rawstron once again, I decided to accept the nomination. I also felt that if I had declined it I might have gone on to regret it, so I was determined that if I were to actually become the president at the 1987 A.G.M. I would give it my best shot. And indeed I did.

No-one was more delighted that I was about to become president than my mum, who had, along with my dad, so many years before, bought me my first membership card for my eighth birthday. She arranged for a tankard to be engraved with my name on it to commemorate my presidency, and every pint of beer I drank at the club during my two years as president was out of my tankard, which had its own special place of honour behind the bar. It now stands prominently in my lounge at home. During those two years I tried to follow in the best traditions of my predecessors, Fred Rawstron, Roy Lees and Stan Boyes, all of whom were active members, figuring strongly on the bowling green. Now that I was president I became a familiar face on the bowling green, and on the tennis courts too, not playing, of course, but attending their competitions and supporting their teams in various finals and vital matches, and happy to buy a round of drinks for the members taking part, just as I did for the cricket team in their cup matches.

But the biggest challenge I took on was very early in my presidency at a committee meeting when it became clear that the club might lose its bar licence if it did not replace its electric wiring, before the next Fire Brigade inspection at the end of the year. The cost involved would be about £2,000. I offered to take on the responsibility for raising the money, seeing it as my opportunity to express my thanks for the honour of my presidency. Within weeks I had the fund raising plans drawn up. John Murray, who was the first team wicket keeper, would chair a group of members to organise a concert at Royton Conservative Club, and Roy Kerr and Neil Crompton would, along with me, arrange a sportsman's dinner at Royton Assembly Hall. All three had been enthusiastically involved in the carnivals, and were happy to take on these new challenges – successfully too. John Murray's group arranged an excellent concert, which raised over £300, a large sum for such an event, and the sportsman's dinner, for which we were committed to selling nearly 200 tickets in order to cover the costs of the speakers, the meals and the hire of the hall, made over £1600, so the two evenings funded the club's rewiring. For me, though, what had begun as a one-off opportunity to help the club in a time of financial hardship, would grow into much more.

The idea that our dinner would become an annual event had never entered my head. Indeed from the moment the decision had been taken to book the hall and the guest speakers I seemed to be wholly preoccupied with trying to ensure that we sold enough tickets to make the evening a success. I knew that most of the seventy or so of those members who attended the clubhouse dinners would buy tickets, but we needed more than three times that number, and most of these would be non-members. Virtually every time I met up with friends and acquaintances I brought the dinner into the conversation, I contacted many former Royton players, and approached people in the business world, such as some of those in the Rotary club, and gradually the numbers climbed to about 225. I had booked Peter Parfitt and Goldie Goldsmith to be guest speakers, with Neil Midgely as the M.C. and as the evening approached I began to feel a little edgy. Will the speakers turn up? Will the meal be OK? Will there be some guests who have had too much to drink and spoil the night? These and other worries are bound to cross an organiser's mind, especially before the first dinner. When the evening is a success, though, as ours was, there is an inner glow of relief and delight.

Both our speakers had been excellent, and Neil Midgley, with whom I became very friendly over the next fifteen years, did a superb job, and with a fair bit of mickey-taking, mostly at my expense. At the end of the evening so many of the guests came up to congratulate us, and asking about the next dinner, many promising to bring their friends too. We had never given a second dinner the slightest thought, but our success that night almost automatically bounced us into the next. Roy Kerr had put oceans of ideas and thoughts into the planning, and overall we felt we had created our own individual style, rather than one of the bland characterless dinners that some were. Over the ensuing years our reputation grew, and so much of the jovial atmosphere during those evenings was created by Neil Midgley, who became closely associated with our club. The numbers of tickets sold grew, as did the profit we made, and soon there were 350 people filling the Assembly Hall, happy to take part in the fund raising raffles, pick-a-team, stand-up-bingo, and auctions of various memorabilia at the end of the evening. Our guests knew that all the funds we raised were going towards making improvements in the club's facilities, and were generous in their support. We always enjoyed a five course meal, the roast beef speciality of our caterer Trevor Anderton. Companies began to sponsor individual tables, and the main sponsors and their guests would be introduced to, and be photographed with, our celebrity guest speakers in the hospitality room before the dinner.

The speakers in the fifteen dinners I helped to arrange included Tommy Docherty, Jack Charlton, John Conteh, David Lloyd, Denis Law (twice), George Best, Jimmy Greaves, Alan Ball, Paul Fletcher and others from the sporting world. Peter Brackley, David Gunson, Chris O'Dell, Kevin Connelly, Roger De Courcy (three times), Bernard Manning, Dr. Kevin Jones and Mike King, who also filled the M.C. role four times, provided outstanding entertainment for our guests. The most outstanding celebrity I was ever privileged to meet, however, to have sat next to on the top table, and had the honour to stand up and thank, on behalf of the audience, was the great Brian Johnston, CBE. By 1989 I had completed my second year as club president, and John Holder had been elected as my successor, and during the 1990 season I asked him to approach 'Johnners' at one of the Test Matches John was umpiring, to ask him if he was willing to be our guest speaker. Brian's reply was more or less, "Thanks, but no thanks". He explained that at the age of 78 he spoke only at functions in the London area, with no overnight stays involved. However, when I met up with Brian, along with John, at Old Trafford, he happily agreed to be our guest speaker, knowing that John was our club president. I arranged to telephone him after the Test Match to finalise the arrangements, and in that conversation when I had mentioned that I was going to Australia that winter he said, "Oh, I'll see you in Adelaide then". What a lovely, relaxed, genuine and jovial character he was, and very generous too. After one or two discussions, first in Adelaide then at his hotel in Perth, he offered to come to speak at our dinner for no fee, but for a gift that we would present to him on the night, plus his expenses, of course. Having discussed it with his wife Pauline he rang me to say that he would like an answer phone – and definitely nothing else.

Monday March 18th 1991 was the night of the most memorable dinner of them all. Tickets had been sold out within days, and everyone was eagerly looking forward to hearing him speak, and for the fortunate few, including the main sponsors and their guests, the privilege of meeting him in the hospitality room beforehand, where he was an absolute gentleman. He greeted people warmly, and took a genuine interest in the club and what we were doing to improve it. It was an honour for me to sit next to him throughout the evening. When he was on his feet he had the audience in raptures, and after forty five minutes or so he sat down to a standing ovation. I then stood up to thank him, and to announce to the audience that Brian had generously been our guest speaker without charging a fee, but as a gesture of friendship to John Holder. Once again the audience stood to applaud him. Neil Crompton, the newly elected president following John's two years in office, then presented Brian with the best answer phone we could find, and I passed the microphone to John, who then presented Brian with a special cut glass decanter and a bottle of vintage port wine, a surprise gift which he was delighted to accept.

The evening itself raised nearly £7000, and is remembered with affection by everyone who attended. The following morning I collected him from his hotel in Oldham and drove him to Piccadilly Station – the most famous man ever to sit in my car. What a wonderful man! During the following months we began to transform what had been something of an eye-sore spectator area into an attractive one, with special seating and lawned bankings, which is commemorated by a plaque acknowledging Brian Johnston's contribution to our ground development. I sent him photographs of the ground, before and after, and if there had been a free Sunday during the Old Trafford Test Match in 1993 he would have come along to officially open the spectator area, so his colleague in the commentary box at the time, David Lloyd, who was to be our guest speaker later in the year, officially opened it on Brian's behalf, paying tribute to him for that wonderful evening in 1991.

That was also the year when I rejoined the club's general committee. Having retired from teaching I felt I had more time available, and as the club chairman was about to step down at the AGM in February I was approached by a number of members asking me to put my name forward. I agreed to, as did a number of others who were being nominated for the first time, and when the newly elected committee first met I was elected as the club chairman, a role I would play for the next six years. Being chairman of a sporting club such as Royton involves a good deal more than turning up every first Thursday in the month for a meeting. At that time there were many members who felt that the club needed a shot in the arm, because it seemed to be drifting instead of being driven. All members' clubs, however, are totally dependent on volunteers who give their time free of charge, so it would be unfair to point critical fingers at those who had been serving previously, but as our 1991 committee settled down, the more ambitious views expressed by some of the newly elected members began to gain support, and we began to reshape the club.

We totally refurbished the main lounge areas, a very expensive exercise funded by a bank loan, but thanks to Nick Hopwood, the finance chairman, with whom I had almost daily contact and whose judgement I trusted, we switched our brewery links so that instead of making 33% profit on the bar takings we were now making over 50%, enabling us to repay the loan. With the newly refurbished club now much more attractive, members and their guests used it far more frequently, thus increasing the overall profits. Providing and maintaining sporting facilities is expensive, and it needs shrewd business skills to manage such clubs' finances, and I always appreciated Nick's policy of keeping a watchful eye on every penny we spent. I spent a good deal of my time keeping in contact with each committee member, offering support if they needed it, whatever their responsibility, and making sure that they knew I was always available if a problem cropped up. By now I was on Congleton

Market every Saturday and Tuesday, and Sandbach on Thursday, so with the various ambitious projects at the club I was involved with, my life seemed to be as busy as it had been when I taught.

It was to get even busier when we began to plan for our biggest project, the clubhouse extension. This had been talked about for many years, as the eighty year old wooden 'tea hut', which had done great service for the club, was now well short of the hygienic standards required, and needed to be replaced. The previous committee had considered plans to build a single story extension to the clubhouse, but had backed off at the last minute, but members felt it was essential that we re-open the matter. The original plans were re-designed, and having received various quotations, the committee put forward the final project to the members at a special EGM. Fund raising was a necessity, of course, the first of which would be the 'Paddockline' weekly draw, and the club members voted to support the proposals. The new extension would incorporate a kitchen, dining room and toilets downstairs, and a lounge upstairs, where members, match sponsors and guests could wine and dine, and watch cricket through the front windows, and crown green bowls through the back. £56,000 was the initial sum we had to raise in order to complete the project, and I submitted a detailed application for a grant to the Council for Sport and the Arts, in those days before the National Lottery. As the months went by I made further contact with them, aware the recent introduction of the Lottery had cut their fundings, and my persistence finally paid off when we eventually succeeded. We had applied for the maximum, i.e. 50% of the cost, £28,000 and were offered £20,000 which we gladly accepted.

Meanwhile the Paddockline was up and running, and thanks to members and friends it also raised £20,000. We had also been receiving donations from members and companies who generously did so to help our efforts to improve the club, knowing that the planned new facilities would benefit a wide range of the people of Royton. The most generous donor was Olive Jones, an elderly lady, a lifelong supporter who watched every match, home and away, and was full of good humour, sharp, and popular with everyone, and her total contribution also reached £20,000. By this time the plans for the extension had grown, and some of the interior designs improved, especially upstairs which would have a bar and be well furnished. The target became £80,000, and that was achieved by £20,000 raised and donated by the Past Presidents' Association, the name I had given to our group of members after that initial 'one-off' dinner in 1987. Thanks to the efforts of many members the work was completed, and the club's facilities are now regarded as excellent, and when former members, perhaps those who have moved away from the area, come to the club and see how many changes and improvements have been made, not only to the clubhouse but on the playing and spectator areas too, they seem amazed.

Much that fund raising had occupied my time during my six years as chairman, there were countless other club matters that I also felt ultimately responsible for, and had become involved in, which took up a lot of my time. I took on the role as cricket section chairman for two or three years, and continued to give as much support as I could to the bowling and tennis sections, having enjoyed my links with them during my term as president. There were times, though, when I felt that I was not enjoying my time in office quite so much, and after six very intensive and busy years I decided not to put my name forward for re-election at the 1997 AGM, feeling totally drained by the various responsibilities I had been undertaking to drive the club forward. A common misconception that many people have is that a club chairman has authority. He does not. In a members' club a chairman has influence, and can only persuade, not order, his fellow members to become actively involved for the benefit of the club. I had used mine to the best of my ability throughout my years of fund raising, before I took on my official roles, but looked forward to a more relaxed time after standing down.

Our sportsman's dinners were by now widely regarded as one of, if not the, best in the area, and the money they raised had helped to fund many of the projects I have described. But not only had I set up the Royton dinners, but the Rotary club's too. A friend and fellow Rotarian, Garvin Crabtree, impressed by our first two dinners, suggested that we should arrange one for the Rotary club, and soon, with Garvin, Stuart Mellor and Keith Wood becoming involved, the first was held in February 1990 at the Queen Elizabeth Hall, Oldham. I had booked Goldie Goldsmith, who had excelled at Royton's first dinner, and asked him who he thought was the best sportsman speaker on the circuit. "Jack Charlton," he said, so along with Neil Midgley, the trio made an ideal line-up for the inaugural dinner. Jack was superb, so much so that on the night I booked him for the Royton dinner later that year. He is a real character, a very genuine and dependable man, and the only speaker I ever booked who insisted on being paid by cheque, plus VAT. That first Rotary dinner was attended by 450 guests, and raised £7,900 for local charities, thanks to the generosity of those attending in being supportive of the fund raising on the night. Their generosity continued throughout the five dinners I was involved with, raising a total of £35,000 for local charities, when I handed over to Garvin after the 1994 dinner, at which Roger De Courcey was outstandingly funny. We had been well entertained each year, Neil Midgley being the superb MC in all of them, creating a great atmosphere right from the moment we walked on stage; in 1991 by Billy Beaumont and Stan Taylor who were both very good; in '92 by the brilliant impressionist Kevin Connelly followed the equally superb Denis Law; and in '93 the Air Traffic Controller David Gunson shared the bill with the brilliant Peter Brackley, but the most nervous after dinner speaker I have ever met. Roger De Courcey did not show any signs of nerves, however, and he followed in Neil Midgley's footsteps in using me as the butt for some of his jokes, and his witty comments about my white socks are still alluded to at dinners I attend more than decade later. He was so good that I booked him for the Royton dinner later in the year, a dinner that people still remember, not so much for him, even though he rescued the night for us, but for the most talented footballer I ever saw, George Best.

At our Royton dinners in the Assembly Hall we had also had many talented and entertaining speakers. Whereas our first dinner had attracted 225 guests our numbers had grown and from the 1990 dinner when Jack Charlton and David Gunson topped the bill, our dinners were virtually all sell-outs. Denis Law with Chris O'Dell, then David Lloyd with Kevin

Connelly, dinners which followed the unforgettable 'Jonners' night in 1991, put us in an "How do you follow that?" situation, so we decided to book George, even though there were increasing stories of his failure to turn up. That was why we felt we needed Roger De Courcey – just in case. George's partner at the time was Mary Shatila, who had succeeded, for a while, in restraining his wilder drinking and gambling lifestyle, and she was arranging his speaking engagements. I spoke to her during the summer and she assured me that there would be no problems, and gave me her word that she would come up to Manchester with him. On the morning of the dinner, however, she phoned me to say that George would soon be on his way, but that as George was flying to Ireland the following day she would not be coming with him. She went on to suggest that I tell George that the white wine was not very cold, and to put plenty of ice in his glass. Was there an ominous a message there? In a few hours' time we would find out, and during the afternoon I must admit to feeling apprehensive. The moment I met George, however, all such feelings vanished. What a charming man he was. Virtually all our guest speakers, before and after, have been very friendly – with one obnoxious exception – but none has been as fulsome in the warmth he radiated in the hospitality room when being introduced to the sponsors and guests, and then having photographs taken with them.

The evening could not have got off to a better start, and with Neil Midgley on top form, at George's expense rather than mine, the audience buzzed with anticipation. All my six months of uncertainty had surely been unnecessary – or had they? I had put plenty of ice in his glass, and placed the bottle to my right, out of his reach, and during the meal he never asked for a refill. During the meal he was relaxed and chatty, and with Neil Midgely sitting to my right also enjoying meeting up with George, things could not have been better. They could, though, after the meal when George asked me where the toilets were, and off he went. A few minutes later Neil asked me where George was. I checked the toilets, but they were empty, and soon we knew why. He came back to the table and began to talk to the president, his voice slurred. He was obviously drunk. What we only found out much later was that he had gone to the bar, ordered a pint of white wine, and within five minutes he had downed it. I cannot describe my feelings at that moment when, after being on cloud nine during the last two hours, with all worries out of the window, suddenly it had all gone pear shaped.

None of the audience could have been aware of the situation, of course, but they were a few minutes later when Neil Midgley introduced him and he stood up to speak. The atmosphere in the hall visibly changed. Their smiles had become looks of sad disbelief as his slurred voice betrayed the intoxicated state he was in. He managed to tell his famous "Where did it all go wrong?" story, and one or two more, but after about ten minutes he stopped, and offered to answer any questions the audience might wish to ask. Neil Midgley then had the problem of inviting various people with their hands raised to ask a question, but he was unable to prevent some stupid ones being asked, and things were becoming chaotic, so the questioning came to a halt. Thanks to Roger De Courcey the faces in the room were soon smiling again, and roaring with laughter as he stayed on his feet even longer than his normal forty minutes, doing exactly what I had booked him for, ending the evening on a high note. Whether it ended on a high note for George, though, I do not know, but after he had signed countless autographs I shook his hand, saw him into his taxi, but instead of going back to the Midland Hotel he went to the casino, according to the taxi driver who came back for more fares. I was later told by Neil Midgley that George had lost virtually all the £1,500 I had handed him, in the casino.

That night, remembered for all the wrong reasons, could have been even worse, as I realised a few weeks later, when I read a report in the Macclesfield local newspaper. George had been the guest speaker at a dinner in the town, and at the end of the meal had asked to be directed to the toilets. A few minutes later when the organisers went to look for him they found the toilet window open and George had vanished, with the money in his pocket! As I read the story it reminded me of my conversation with Mary on the afternoon of our dinner, when she had asked me to pay him as he arrived at the hall. I did explain to her that we always paid our speakers as the dinner ended, but she said that on many occasions there were so many people wanting George's autograph that he sometimes had difficulty finding the organiser to collect his money. I agreed to do so, but when I met George he was so lively and friendly I simply forgot about it. But what if I had not forgotten? Would he still have gone to the bar for his pint of wine, or climbed through the window and vanished? Perhaps we had not been so unlucky after all. Many people, especially after his death a decade later, said that they believed that there were really two George Bests; we definitely saw them both at our dinner.

We had no problems a year later when Jimmy Greaves and Mike King entertained us, just a few with Dermot Reeve, who I managed to outwit, by ensuring that he did not arrange for the caterer to put an extra place setting on the top table for his girl friend, as he had apparently done at some dinners. We never had the slightest problem with our super star Roger De Courcey, in 1996, nor in the extra dinner in the following March, the only time available Bernard Manning had, with his busy autumn schedules. Bernard generously agreed to charge us only two-thirds of his normal fee because of my friendship with his brother Frank during our St. Bede's days, and he was superb. Later in the year we were sublimely entertained by the heart surgeon from Bury Hospital, Dr. Kevin Jones, who followed in Roger De Courcey's footsteps in rescuing us from another disastrous start when a former county cricketer and umpire spoke for exactly eighteen minutes without putting a look of interest or smile on one of the 350 faces in the room. Dr. Kevin Jones certainly did, as did Mike King, our MC that night. Roger was back again, with Mike King as MC, in 1998 when Alan Ball surprised many of our guests by the superb speech he delivered, and everyone spontaneously stood to applaud him.

As we began to make arrangements for our 1999 dinner I decided that it would be my final one. I had begun to enjoy the freedom from responsibilities at the club now that I was no longer the chairman, and it seemed to be an appropriate time to relieve myself of the pressures that came with organising the dinners. Not that I expected to have any in this one, with Denis Law once again topping the bill. Denis had been so friendly and relaxed at the Royton and Rotary dinners when I had sat alongside him, and I was looking forward to meeting him once again. So with Mike Craig as comedian and Neil Midgley returning for his tenth dinner as our MC, all the tickets were soon sold out, and as the evening drew near I felt totally relaxed, but once again the unexpected happened. It began on the evening before the dinner when I telephoned Denis to be sure that he had received my recent letter confirming the arrangements, and that he would be arriving by 7pm to meet our main sponsors. He reassured me, and said he was looking forward to the evening, but went on to say that he would like to leave early in order to turn up at his mother-in-law's 90th birthday party.

Only after our conversation ended, however, did I begin to realise that he might intend to leave immediately after his speech, not something that helps the atmosphere, and especially when many so many of those attending would find themselves unable to obtain his autograph. As I told Tony Spence, Trevor Lewis and Alan Taylor, my fellow organisers, what Denis had said, as we met at the Assembly Hall the following morning, our suspicion was that this might be merely an excuse to leave early. It was also puzzling that a 90th birthday party would be being held so late, an event more likely to be celebrated at midday rather than nearly midnight. Denis had, apparently, recently left another dinner early, so we would all be turning up feeling a little uneasy. When we did turn up we found we had a different problem. The M62 Motorway was jammed near the Trafford Centre, and some of our main sponsor's guests were stuck in it. So too was Denis, as I discovered when I took a call from Denis's daughter, who explained to me that he had telephoned to ask her to contact me at the hall to apologise for his late arrival, and to reassure me that he would be arriving as soon as he could. I appreciated that he had taken the trouble. Neil Midgley announced why the proceedings would be delayed, and during that next half an hour or so I assumed that as he was arriving late, he would surely not now be leaving early, and that there was no longer any need for us to worry about it. I had also been reassured by Neil that there was no way Denis could be going early.

Once things got underway every thing seemed to be going swimmingly. Neil was in top form and on our table the conversations were jovial and relaxed. Suddenly, however, towards the end of the meal, I overheard Denis saying to our president that he would be leaving early because of his mother-in-law's birthday. I couldn't believe it. I knew I now had to do my best to persuade him not to leave early, so I carefully and quietly said to him that during the day, when I had explained to my friends that he might be leaving early, they thought that if he did leave early it would spoil the atmosphere and disappoint the guests. As I was explaining this, as calmly as I could, Neil Midgley, aware of our conversation, said, "Are you OK Denis?" His loud and slow reply was, "I'm going. I'm going – NOW!" The look in his eyes was fierce, and he rose slowly to his feet. Neil tried to calm him down, and was doing his utmost to help. I was almost numb. I had made sure I had not told Denis that these had been my thoughts, but those that had been expressed to me, but his reaction had floored me.

"I'm going to think about it," he said, and walked towards the hospitality room at the end of the stage. I got on to my feet and followed him, and apologised to him if what I had said had offended him, assured him that I had not intended to, and ended by pleading with him not to leave, saying that if he did it would ruin my life. I should have used the word 'reputation,' but before I could say any more Denis shouted, "Ruin your life? A death in the family ruins your life, nor a dinner!" "I know," I said, and fumbled about trying to explain my feelings, when Neil Midgley came in, and said, "John, have a sit down. Leave it with me," so I returned to the table, sat down, simply staring into oblivion, wondering what would happen next. My head was in a whirl. This was to be my last dinner. No doubt about it. It was definitely my last. Strangely, as I sat there, looking around the room, I realised that everything seemed normal, as the guests were finishing their meals, none of them remotely aware of the events that had been happening on the stage. Then suddenly it all changed again!

"I'm staying, John. I'll stay." Denis stood on the edge of the stage, with a big smile on his face, alongside Neil, and they came back to the table. I felt as if I'd won the Lottery. Neil had assured Denis that I was a genuine bloke who would not have intended to offend him, and had obviously talked him round. Certainly, without Neil that night, I am sure Denis would have walked out. Thankfully he did not. Neil went on to announce to the audience that for personal reasons Denis would not be able to stay until the end of the evening, and that for those who wished to get his autograph, Denis would sign them now. Denis went down to the front of the top table, and as charmingly as ever, signed for them all in the long queue they had formed. More than once he looked up at me, seeing me still sitting there blank faced, and called, "Smile, John. Smile." I did, and began to regain my senses.

But if I felt much better as normality returned, I felt exceptionally better a few minutes later once Denis had returned to his seat, when suddenly, to my total surprise, Neil announced that as I would be stepping down from my role in organising the dinners, my fellow organisers would like to mark the occasion by presenting me with a cut glass decanter and brandy glass and a bottle of special brandy, the bronze plaque on the presentation tray expressing recognition and thanks for my contribution to the success of our dinners, which had raised £66,000. It was a special moment for me, and I appreciated their gesture very much, and that of all the guests who loudly applauded as I received my farewell gift. If I had a smile on my face as photographs were taken of the presentation, there were smiles on everyone's as Denis gave his speech, making it, especially for me, a night to remember. Later I walked to the car park with Denis, where we shook hands as sincerely as if the moment of madness had never taken place.

That was my final night on the top table, and I feel privileged to have enjoyed the company of so many genuinely friendly celebrity speakers, and appreciate the contributions made by my fellow members to ensure the success of our dinners, which over the years also included John Holder, Nick Hopwood, Bert Ward and Barry Woodward, following Roy Kerr and Neil Crompton, when we started them in 1987. Since then I have enjoyed attending the Royton dinners without a care in the world, sitting at a table where there was no work to do, speeches to make, or any responsibilities at all. I was no longer on the committee either, so when I turned up at the club, be it winter or summer, if there was a problem it was not mine. Very relaxing indeed. And then came Howard Dronsfield and his shock to my system when he told me that I had been nominated to become the CLL president. I have thoroughly enjoyed my three years in such an honoured role, and hope that I have fulfilled my responsibilities as successfully as all my predecessors did. Whereas my cricketing life was becoming comfortably lazy, enjoying a pint, watching the matches, in the company of my fellow members and friends, now I am attending meetings galore, visiting all the clubs in the league, and appreciating the warm welcome I receive everywhere. I have had the microphone in my hand too, at the end of both seasons, making various presentations of trophies, cups and medals, and one or two speeches too. I have also bought some new shirts, jackets and trousers, something else I never expected to do.

16 Johnny Slipper

Becoming accustomed to life as a trader on an outside market was as big a culture shock to me as the one I had experienced when I began to run my dad's business in the cotton world a decade earlier. First of all I had to learn a new language. A market is a "gaff"; the market officer who collects the rents is the "toby"; and the customers are "punters." When I arrived at Congleton the "toby" offered me a "pitch," which is a space, not a stall. What I did with my "pitch" was up to me – put my own stall there, put all my "gear" on the floor, or whatever. Fortunately it was a dry day so I put my "gear" on the trestle table I had strapped to my Austin Cambridge roofrack, and sold my first slippers. Within weeks I had bought metal bars, boards, plastic sheeting and metal clips, so that I could set up my own stall, and began to adjust to the problems that all outdoor traders have in the wind and rain. Standing next to and across from other traders helped me to become familiar with the way the market operated, and to get to know other stallholders. It was years, though, before I knew what their names were. Nor did they know mine. In Congleton I would become Johnny Slipper, and become friendly with Eric Pots, Ron the Vac, Terry Shirt, Toffee Bob, Johnny Cheese, Café Ron, Chris the Fish, Reg the Veg, Rick the Bag, Catalogue John, Greg Socks, China Terry, Towel Rick, Butch Phil, Pictures John, Arthur Flowers, and many more, as everyone knew each other, as did the punters.

Never having been behind a counter before, apart from a few occasions as a young lad behind my Grandma's toffee shop at Shaw Road End, and then mainly to scrounge a few toffees, which were still on rations, I slowly learned how some punters do their shopping. "Have you got this in a size 5, duck?" In the Congleton area the ladies always say "duck" or "duckie," which was another surprise for me. If my answer was "Yes" then I usually made a sale, but there are some who are notorious for saying such as "Oh, right, I'll tell her then. Bye," or "You'll be here next week, won't you?" or "I'll think about it," and walk on. It was also in those first few weeks that I realised how early in the day an outdoor market starts. Some traders arrive before 6 o'clock. Unloading large vans and setting up the displays can take two hours and more, and as other traders arrive everywhere is crowded. It needs a good deal of co-operation between them so that the vans can be driven off, enabling others to drive on. Similarly at the end of the afternoon when it is time to load up, there has to be a lot of goodwill to ensure that every trader can park up next to his or her own stall. Thankfully the selfish traders who totally ignore everyone else's situation were very few in the years I spent at Congleton and Sandbach, and were regarded with contempt by the vast majority, who were always happy to help each other out.

This also happens when any unexpected problem occurs. Vehicles break down, keys get lost, tyres flatten, stalls can be blown over in strong winds, and so on, but everyone helps each other out. There is a great trust between traders. A full day on a market is very demanding, and all traders need moments away to do an errand, go to the toilet, and get something to eat, so there is always a need to "keep an eye" on each other's stall while a trader is away, including making sales, with no suspicion that the cash received would go in the wrong pocket. There were, sadly, one or two, but only one or two, traders who no-one trusted, and we all knew who they were, and people really did "keep an eye" on them.

I didn't often need to ask other traders to "keep an eye" for me during my early years at Congleton, because I always had at least one of the children with me. Richard was ten years old when he came with me on that first day in 1974, and gradually, over the next few years, Lucy began to work some Saturdays, as did Sarah. Taking it in turn suited them, enabling them to enjoy most of their Saturdays. They also enjoyed their time on the "gaff," at least once they had adjusted to climbing out of bed before six o'clock! They also enjoyed being paid their wages, and especially the moment we reached Alderly Edge on the way home. There we would go into a sweet shop, have an ice cream each, and I always let them buy a £1 of whatever toffees or chocolate they wanted. In those days that meant a large bagfull, and they shared them equally as we arrived home. Meanwhile, if it had been a good day, I would buy a bottle of wine, quite a luxury for Susan and I in the 1970's. The best market day of the year for the children, though, was on Christmas Eve. All three of them would come, crowded into my Volvo Estate, with which I towed my trailer, or in the van I hired once or twice. As we arrived home I paid them double wages for that day, and a £1 bonus for every Saturday they had worked for me during the year. They must have felt like millionaires as they went out on Christmas Eve! By the late 1970's I was selling more than just slippers, which were good sellers all the year round because the local shops only stocked them in the run-up to Christmas. Pumps and football boots sold well, especially at the start of every school term, and then trainers, which were growing in popularity, became my most lucrative line. This is apparent when reading some of the weekly advertisements I used to place in the Miscellaneous Sales section of the Congleton Chronicle, some of which I illustrated earlier.

BIGGEST selection in Training Shoes. Leather, Suede, Canvas, Vinyl. Strong, sensible and stylish. Swish,smart, special, superlative – see for yourself. No fancy prices. Why pay more? Slippers galore. Visit the specialist. Congleton Slipperama.

ASK ANYBODY. Superb Trainers display. Trendy styles. Leather, nylon, suede, vinyl. See for yourself. Save money. Be amazed. Join the satisfied thousands – at Slipperama

ABSOLUTELY Unrivalled trainers display. Superb new styles this Saturday. Everybody's sizes. Concorde Quality at Skytrain prices. Fly direct to Johnny's Trainers Stall. Congleton Market.

ABOUT a million Back To School bargains. White pumps £1.30. £1.45. £1.75. Suede Trainers £4.99. £5.99. Soccer boots £2.99. Yes £2.99. Leather screw-ins £4.99. £5.99. Everything price labelled. Ask anybody. They travel miles to Johnny's Slipperama.

BEAT the Soccer Boot Stampede to Johnny's Soccerama. Keenest prices. Superb quality super-subs. Try before you buy. 1000's must be right! Johnny's Slipperama.

ANOTHER thousand Soccer Boot Bargains from £2.99. Join the Lads' and Dads' stampede to Soccerama. No rubbish. No gimmicks. Everything labelled. See for yourself. Trainers. Pumps. Autumn slippers galore. Save ££'s. Congleton Slipperama

They must have had a positive impact, trying, as I always was, when I wrote them, to arouse interest and amusement. I was amused myself one Saturday when a gentleman came to my stall to tell me how much he enjoyed opening my weekly letter to the Congleton Chronicle. He was the editor, John Condliffe, and I felt flattered that he had taken the trouble to come to the market to tell me that he was always amused as he read my advertisements. I am sure the next one amused him, too.

ADVANCE to Congleton Market. Go directly to Slipperama. Collect your Christmas slipper and trainer bargains. Seize your chance on Saturday. Monopolistic selection. Bond Street quality at Old Kent Road prices!

ABSOLUTELY unbeatable slippers display. Prices to suit everyone. Exchanges after Christmas. No rubbish. Everybody knows my successful policy – I cut my profits and double my sales. We're all happy! Make it a Slipperama Christmas.

ABSOLUTELY Express Trainers display. Fast-moving good trainers. Inter-City quality at Away-Day prices. Remember! This is the age – of the Trainer! Take the Saturday excursion to Congleton Market. Be on the right lines.

I think I probably was on the right lines myself in the late 1970's when open markets were busy, and I had comfortably established myself with all the other traders, with whom I got on very well, even though they did not know that I was a teacher. It seemed better to keep quiet about being a Saturday only trader, having got the impression that they were frowned upon for preventing full time traders get a stall on the best trading day of the week. I was still setting up my own stall on the same "pitch" I had been given in 1974, but that changed in 1981 when the market was switched to a different site and I was allocated a stall. Loading and unloading became a quicker process, which was especially handy for me on the new Tuesday market, when I drove to Congleton twice a day, with every minute precious so that I would not be late for school in the morning, nor in the late afternoon to load up the boxes that Alice would have already packed. Life was beginning to seem as hectic as in my Junction Flyer days. I would normally drive "up the valley" to do my buying on Fridays, and even though I was trading on two days each week I usually only bought one box of any line of gear I fancied. Hence I became known as "One Box John," a name given me by Shaun Cosgrave, one of the wholesalers.

"Blusher" was the name I would later give to Stuart, a trader with whom I got on very well with in my early days at Congleton, but before I did so he should really have been known as Gambler Stuart, because of his involvement in greyhounds and his daily visits to the bookies. He was the one who, in 1986, tempted me back into my teenage betting habits. He and I would have a bet on a football match, especially one involving Stoke City, his local team, and the 'Latics, or Manchester United, mine. At first the loser bought the cakes and coffee, but we once had a £10 bet, which I won, and the banter between us after that rapidly increased. It lightened up our market days no end. The "crack" was fierce. I loved it. I loved it a few weeks later when we had another bet, and we both won. Stuart had been at one of his regular greyhound tracks when "this bloke" standing next to him told him that a particular dog in the next race looked to be a good bet. Stuart's reply was to tell him not to back it because it wouldn't win. "This bloke" listened, weighed up the rest of the field, and then came back to Stuart to insist that this was the best one to back. Stuart then said. "Don't back that one. It's my dog. I know it won't win. Try that one." After which "this bloke" put his money on the winner, and came back to thank Stuart, and gave him a tip too. "I have a horse called Water Canon which is going to win the race it won last year." He would not say any more, so Stuart would have to look in the racing columns every day to find when it was due to run. No doubt if Stuart had known when and where Water Canon was running the word might have got round and the odds shortened. The owner, to whom Stuart had been talking that night, was none other than Francis Lee, of football fame, and a good cricketer too, some years before. For weeks Stuart and I looked out for Water Canon, and we began to think it might not be running, but on a Saturday morning he spotted it in the paper. Having won my £10 off Stuart I decided to put it all on Water Canon, and I came home with £100. Almost all the traders must have backed it too, and the local bookies were even threatening not to accept any more bets from Stuart in future.

But the £100 was to go a step further. He got another tip a few weeks later – well, not one, but two. His Fridays were then spent on Prestatyn market, to where some of the stable lads from Milton Keynes would come and hand him money to put on for them, it being illegal for them to place bets themselves, apparently. Shortly after the Water Canon bet Stuart told me that they would be giving him the names of two horses down to run at Aintree on Grand National day. I had to promise not to tell anyone. I promised. Nor had I to place my bet in Congleton, so I made arrangements for Lucy to put my money on somewhere in Oldham. Stuart had also said that I could tell Richard, who worked Macclesfield Market on Saturdays, so we had to make arrangements for telephone calls to be made once I had arrived at Congleton and found the names of the horses. I phoned Lucy, and also my mum, to whom I had been talking the day before, when calling to see her and Tom at lunch time. I asked her how much they were going to bet, and when she said £20 I asked her to put another £20 on for me, too. So I had £120 going on a win double, not an each way bet. It was all or nothing. I had convinced myself that whatever happened I couldn't lose, because I was it was my winnings from my earlier bets I was gambling with.

Our horses were running in the first and last races at Aintree, and I still remember the excitement I felt our first horse won at 5 to 1. So I now had £700 going on the last race, and it felt like a long afternoon. We all began to load up our gear at 4 o'clock, and with my car radio switched on I was able to listen for the result as I did so. Once the Grand National was over, though, most of the coverage was on football. Suddenly I heard the broadcaster say he had the result of the last race, but there was no mention of our horse. I felt rather numb as I got into my car, to begin the one-hour journey home, calling first, as I always did, at my mum's, with Manchester Pink Final for Tom. All the way home I felt mixed emotions. One half of me was telling me not to be disappointed, because the bet had not cost me anything, as it had been my previous winnings that I had gambled on this ambitious bet. But the other half was having a greater effect. I was just so despondent that we had got so close, and then nothing!

As I reached my mum's house I could see Tom standing at the window, looking rather glum, I thought, but as I stepped into the kitchen I was simply overcome with what happened next. I said to Tom, "Well, at least we got one winner, didn't we?" to which he said "Eh?" seeming puzzled, when I caught sight of my mum standing up in the lounge, holding up a large envelope, shaking ten pound notes all over the carpet. "Just look," she said. "We've got a thousand pounds here!" I could have had a heart attack. I had jumped from despondency to ecstasy in seconds, and couldn't believe it. Obviously the result of the last race I had heard on the radio had been at a different racecourse, and the torment of my sad journey home had vanished, and all I could do was to sit down, slowly let it all sink in, knowing that I had won over £3000. Both Lucy and Richard, each of them knowing that by this time I would be at my mum's house, telephoned excitedly, and I enjoyed the whisky my mum poured me to celebrate our win. It certainly had been a day to remember – thanks to Stuart. Richard had won about £1500, but Lucy had not risked much, never having gambled before. Once I had collected my winnings from the two bookies on the following Monday, and watching my back as I came out through the doors, in case there were people lurking around awaiting the big winner to step outside, I was relieved to get into my car safely and bring the cash home. I gave Lucy £500 for her part in the day, and Sarah £500 because she had not been part of the secret build up. Everybody was happy.

We were not very happy a year later, though, when Stuart gave me another tip. This was for one of the big races at the Cheltenham Festival, where a horse called Nudge Nudge was being carefully and secretly prepared to win. That was the story, and Stuart gave me the tip when the horse was priced at 33-1. He told me that the owners had backed it at 66-1, and that he himself had got 50-1. I immediately put £40 on it to win, and told my friends about it. The festival was still two weeks away, so there was time for the word to spread. I told my Limehurst teaching colleagues, friends at the cricket club, in my local pub, The Horton Arms, at the Rotary Club, and the Investment Club, where insider tips were always welcome! The word spread, and into the finance community in Manchester, and the odds shortened alarmingly. Then, on the day before the race, Nudge Nudge was "balloted out." Apparently if there are too many horses entered for that race the officials have to limit the number of runners. The rules, however, are clear; that the horses with inferior records must be withdrawn first. In this instance, as was widely reported, Nudge Nudge had been taken out despite having a better record than others that were allowed to run. In a newspaper the following day it stated that Nudge Nudge had been heavily backed in the North West. That must have been my fault, I'm afraid, but I was totally unaware of this kind of thing happening. Obviously the link between bookmakers and horseracing officials is very close. Enough said! At least we were given our money back.

The link in greyhound racing seems equally close, after an experience I had, also with Stuart, at the Blackpool dog track, some years later. He had told me about a dog that he and some of his friends near his home in the Potteries had been preparing to win at the Blackpool track, where its odds would be good because it was being entered under a different name. So for the first time in my life I went to a dog track, ready to put £100 on their dog. I found the atmosphere fascinating as the bookies, standing inside their little cabins, all in a row, kept changing the odds which they chalked on the tiny blackboards. Once Stuart, walking round with his mates, had given me the nod to put my money on trap five in the next race, I watched the odds on the boards changing and had gambled £80 when suddenly every one of the six bookies wiped the trap five dog off the boards. Stuart and his mates had, each at the same moment, placed a big bet with every bookie, thus ensuring that none of them had any warning of the big money any of the others had received. I watched this with surprise, but I had another one a moment later, when the traps opened and the dogs were off. I strained to see where 5 was but as they raced round the final bend nearer to where I was standing, all I could see at the front were other numbers. What a waste of time it had been, after all. Having driven all the way to Blackpool, and gambled £80, the dog that couldn't lose had not even finished in the first three. Suddenly there was an announcement. "Ladies and Gentlemen. The race has been abandoned. Trap 5 failed to open. All bets will be repaid." I wonder why the trap failed to open? Could it have been the close link between the bookies and clerk of the course? I had learned a lot more about greyhounds that night, just as I had about horse racing on the Nudge Nudge day.

Over the years Stuart has told me about various tricks of the trade, so much that when I watched an investigative TV programme a few years ago, revealing some of the dubious, undercover and corrupt practices involved in the racing world, I didn't learn a thing – I had already been made aware of it by Stuart. Thankfully my being a good friend of Stuart never tempted me back to my teenage habit, but whenever he has given me a tip I have usually backed it. Some have won, others have lost, and it has made life interesting, too. It was certainly interesting when we both had a bet one Saturday, when the race was being broadcast as we loaded up, and our horse, which had been nudged into the rails on the final straight, and had finished second, was declared the winner following a steward's enquiry. A week later, after Stuart had been in touch with the man who had given him the tip, he told me what was said to have happened. Before the race jockey A had been told that he would receive £10,000 if his horse won, and jockey B was told that he would receive £5,000 for not winning. Jockey B demanded the same amount as jockey A, and in an angry moment was told that he would be getting nothing. Hence jockey B did his best to get his revenge on the man with the money, but failed. I won about £300 on that race. As regards betting generally I take the view that if it is just spending money that is being gambled, then OK, but one shouldn't put one's mortgage on it.

I had gambled in 1969, when I spent that £405 as a deposit on the chalet in Abersoch, and which turned out to be another winner, thanks to my having successfully hired it out to help to repay the loan. Following my retirement from teaching, my life felt quite leisurely. I had begun to work Sandbach Market on Thursday, and would do my buying on Friday, work Congleton on Saturday, before driving down to Abersoch for two or three days. That I continued to do until, in 1994, as the new season opened, I realised that the roof had been leaking and the damage would have been too costly to have done, especially since a chalet of twenty five years old would have been in one of its final years on the site, anyway. So it was with sadness that I said farewell to the friends I had made during my many very happy years on the Warren and drove home, cherishing the many happy times I had spent there. All three of my children have their own happy memories too, because K24 was their second home. With new ones then costing between £75,000 and £150,000, according to their size and location, I did not have a difficult decision to make. Amazingly, in 2007, the newspapers printed photographs of a chalet that was available on the Warren for £500,000. And to think that when I bought mine in 1969, £3,000 seemed a fortune.

That leisurely start to my retirement years had begun to quicken when in 1991 I became Royton Cricket Club chairman, and in 1992 when Richard gave up his markets as he set up his wholesale business, I thought it best for me to work the Tuesday market at Congleton, which he had taken over from me in 1985. For the next eight years or so I would work three days each week, and began to notice how shopping habits had been changing over the years. Whereas I had been fortunate to have been offered my first pitch in 1974, because extra space had just become available, on virtually every other market that was worth trading on in those days there would simply no vacancies. Twenty years later a "casual," as a new trader is known, was rarely turned away. Competition had become fiercer, not so much from other traders but the increasing number of shopping malls, and the preference that the younger generation had for driving out of town to visit them. Also, in the same way that supermarkets had killed off a large number of the traditional town centre and local shops, the bulk buying of many high street companies had enabled them to sell at very competitive prices. No longer could a market trader, by working on a smaller profit margin, undercut the big stores. The average shopper would always expect to pay less for the same item on a market than in a shop, and if the price was the same many customers would often put their trust in the high street.

The one-day per week markets have the best chance of remaining successful, as they provide a weekly shopping routine for relatives and friends to meet up each week, and enjoy also seeing other friends and acquaintances as they meander round the market. During the 1990's many traders struggled to make a living, with increased rents, wages and tansport to pay, out of declining sales. Whereas in the 1980's virtually every stall had two or more people running it, in the 90's the majority of stalls were run single-handedly. I experienced it myself. I had always had one of the children to help me during the early years, but as they started their own careers I began to employ local girls, with the market swarming with punters. Jane was the first to work for me, and later Debbie Cooke, who became an excellent assistant, and worked for me a number of years, becoming known as my "manageress". She also came along to help me years later, after she had started her own career, on the busy December Saturdays, during the Christmas slipper stampede.

That was the only time of the year, in the 1990's, when I needed an assistant. But once I had switched from my stall to the prime pitch which Richard had worked on his Tuesday market, I needed the physical help of a fourteen or fifteen year old lad to help me put the bars in place, climb the ladder, clip the plastic sheeting into place, carry the boards and boxes, and unload my car and trailer. That was a Saturday and Tuesday routine which Michael, who had worked for Richard, was the first lad to do for me, until he was eighteen and on his way to University. He would probably work an hour and a half, then come back in the late afternoon to help me tidy the gear away, load up the trailer, then dismantle the bars, boards and sheets. On the occasional days when he was unable to help me I would be utterly exhausted as I set off on my journey home. Other lads worked for me during the final five or six years. One, Chris, was a cheerful, reliable and dependable lad, as was "Anorexic" Dave, as I mischievously christened him, my final assistant. The help I received from all those who worked for me I very much appreciated, and I think that the experience they had, in finding out what work was like, whilst so young, was probably helpful to them too.

Selling slippers might seem a simple operation, but not quite so in those early 90's when so many changes were taking place in the footwear industry. Travelling "up the valley," as I did every week, I could see how so many manufacturers had been forced to close down, having been undercut by the goods imported from China and India, where labour is cheap, and from Spain, which received bigger EU grants than the UK. What has happened in the footwear industry has also taken place in many other trades, as other stallholders have complained about whilst trying hard to keep their businesses afloat. I was fortunate trading mainly in Congleton, where I never had to compete against any of the cut-price merchants who went on some markets and charged such low prices that a regular trader simply could not survive, and either switched markets or went out of business. It also took me a few years to realise that the bigger the buyer, the cheaper he pays, enabling him to undercut the "One box Johns" such as me. In some cases, though, I was also fortunate to be given the chance to buy at the lower price the various wholesalers charged the bigger buyers.

In the wholesaler's showrooms the price of each item would be displayed, but it was only in the 1990's, once I had begun to do my buying during the day rather than late afternoon, that I met up with and enjoyed the company of other traders who worked different markets, and who explained to me how the system worked. Whereas a shoe or trainer might be priced at £4.50, +VAT, therefore being retailed on the gaff at £7.99, a big buyer would pay £4.+ VAT, and retail it at £6.99. It suited the wholesaler when the buyer bought enough gear to fill his large van, and might even buy every box of a particular line. One such trader, Alan Capper, was one of the five or six shoemen on Sandbach market, where I worked for ten years, and he had people working for him on markets all over the country. I was thankful that he never came to Congleton, because I could not have survived on that smaller market, against his prices. Amazingly, though, I was often able to buy at the lower price myself. I always seemed to get on well with all the wholesalers, some of whom began to do me a favour when they realised that I was trading at Sandbach against Alan Capper. As 'One box John' I always knew I had no clout, but I often managed to come home with some bargains, which I always appreciated. I also appreciated their support in sponsoring tables at many of the sportsmen's dinners too, especially as the dinners were taking place fifteen miles away from Rossendale, and it often involved their hiring a mini-bus, and providing overnight accommodation for some of their guests who had travelled from other parts of the country. Shaun Cosgrave had taken ten guests to our first dinner in 1987, and the Hargreaves brothers, Richard and John, Tony Livesy, Shaun Morley, and David Wilkinson, of Slippers Direct, who had been main sponsors of the George Best dinner, all sponsored tables over the next twelve years. I must have been doing something right for such a small buyer to be given such support. I think that not being a full time trader, I came across to them, so I was told, as different from your typical market man. No doubt my lifetime in the classroom made me that way.

I was not your typical market man at Congleton, either, of course, but they did not know that until later. There were a few things I didn't know, as well. Having been a Saturday trader for sixteen years I had not realised how different the midweek shopping habits are. Saturdays are mainly family days, when parents buy their children trainers, pumps, football boots or slippers, all of which can be tried on at the stall. Many husbands and wives do their shopping together, but not many women buy their shoes then. They may look at the display, even try a pair on, but walk away, sometimes with a knowing look on their faces, indicating to me that they will be back very soon to buy them. It was only after I had widened my range of footwear as I worked the midweek markets that noticed it, especially after I had begun to sell the M+S "footgloves" at about half the price the store charged, and casual shoes and sandals. "I'll have a pair of these in size 5 please. I bought a pair from M+S last week. I haven't worn them yet, and I've still got the receipt, so I'll get my money back." So said one lady, and similar comments were often made. Some ladies told me that they had tried on a pair in the store, knew exactly what size they required, then bought them from me. Invariably all such incidents took place on the midweek market days, with their husbands having no idea what their wives had bought.

That is when many ladies do their shopping in twos. It can be helpful when a potential customer is perhaps a little uncertain about what style or colour to buy, and the other lady offers advice and encouragement. This happens frequently when the ladies are related, such as mother and daughter, on their weekly get-together. When the two ladies are merely friends it is not always so straightforward. Most of them are genuinely helpful to each other, and each benefits from the other's opinions. Some, however, do not. A lady would be trying on a pair of shoes or sandals, and saying that they felt comfortable, when her friend might say, "Do they feel big? They certainly look too big for you," or "That colour doesn't suit you." Remarks such as those usually dissuade a customer from buying them, and the pair walk away. On many occasions the lady would come back to the stall on her own, buy them, with her facial expression saying it all, as she carefully placed her shoes out of sight before rejoining her 'friend.' Thankfully instances such as this did not happen every day, but other traders talked about experiencing similar situations, but as the saying goes "There's now't so queer as folk."

I always found the people who shopped on the market very friendly, and the longer I traded at Congleton the more I felt part of the local community, even though my broad Lancashire accent made it obvious that I was not. Shoppers enjoy having conversations with stallholders they know, and the whole market atmosphere and environment is so much more personal than the anonymity of the supermarkets. I have now come to believe, after those earlier declining times, that markets will survive the fierce competition from the big stores, especially the centre of town one or two days a week markets. Markets are popular for those who visit a town too. I was surprised that some of my 'punters' lived many miles from Congleton. My traditional final words of thanks as I gave them their change, usually a penny, were, "I hope you are pleased with them." They would invariably make a friendly reply, indicating that they usually were happy with my 'gear,' but some would say, "Thank you. I always buy my slippers from you when I come to Congleton," and go on to say that they lived in far away places, such as Scotland, Banbury and Hayling Island, being three of those I can remember who came three or four times each year, presumably to visit relatives in the area. I am sure that all traders have, and continue to, enjoy the pleasure one feels when a customer expresses appreciation in such a way. It may seem strange for me to be writing this but in some ways the satisfaction a trader gets from pleasing a customer is not dissimilar to that a teacher feels when getting the best out of a pupil, and motivating a class to do well. As one who has experienced life in the classroom and behind a stall, I recognise the similarities that not many people might imagine exist. Motivation and salesmanship are not far from being one and the same thing, and for me, in my double life, perhaps one helped the other. No doubt the good deals I negotiated when making arrangements for the many school trips I organised resulted from my experiences of buying footwear up the valley. I referred earlier to the trust and goodwill that exists between traders, with virtually everyone willing to help each other out when difficulties occur. I became aware of this very early on, and over the years became increasingly impressed by their sincerity. During my life I have been closely involved in the teaching profession, the Round Table and Rotary movements, and the cricketing world; meeting, working alongside, and becoming friendly with so many. I rank market traders as amongst the very best of the people with whom I have been acquainted and friendly. They are the salt of the earth.

17 Life in the Wider World

Having taken the decision to retire in 1990 I was able to spend more time in Abersoch, and during the following two or three years, especially in the summer months, I would regularly drive down on Saturday nights, and come back on Tuesday or Wednesday. However, during those same years I began to travel much further than North Wales, and enjoyed some splendid holidays. The first one was to Adelaide and Perth, after three nights in Singapore, to see the 4th and 5th Test Matches in 1991. I found Adelaide to be a very attractive city, famous for its many churches, and with many parklands too. There was only one spare day before the Test Match began so I decided to take a coach tour of the area surrounding Adelaide, including the Barossa Valley, a Wildlife Reserve where koala bears seemed to be everywhere, and a winery where we sampled quite a few famous red wines. It was an excellent ten-hour tour, and the friendliness of the people of the state of South Australia was clearly visible. The next five days I spent at the Adelaide Oval, and was sitting in my seat in the stand, along with most of the other English supporters, when, on the first morning, a very controversial incident took place, involving David Gower.

During the days prior to the Test Match the England team had played an up-country game during which David Gower, not playing in the match, had flown a light aircraft over the ground, flying extremely low, back and forth, as a prank. His sense of humour was not enjoyed or appreciated by the tour management, who fined him £5.000, with no right of appeal. Gower was reported to be very angry at being punished for his escapade, and what happened on the field as he came out to bat aroused suspicions of most, if not all, the English supporters in our stand, from where we had a perfect view of the controversial incident. He came out to bat to face the first ball of the last over before lunch, bowled by McDermott, who placed a fielder on the mid-wicket boundary, right below our seats. His first ball bounced short, and Gower lofted it high in the air towards the mid-wicket fielder, but thankfully, for all of us watching in the stand, the ball fell short of the fielder, and the batsmen, Gower and Gooch, took a single. As they did so the sound of disbelief in our stand was clearly audible, with everyone puzzled why such a talented and elegant batsman had played such a risky shot on the first ball of his innings.

But worse was to come. Gooch played three dot balls, then took a single, leaving the last ball of the session for Gower to face. The fielder came back to his spot on the mid-wicket boundary, McDermott again bowled a short ball, and once again Gower hooked it high in the air, this time higher and further, before being caught by the fielder. The groans from our supporters were twice as loud, and Gower turned, then walked off by himself, with Graham Gooch, the captain, standing motionless at the bowler's end, looking shocked and furious at the manner of Gower's dismissal, before slowly making his way back to the dressing room, in which I imagine there must have been many angry words exchanged. All the English supporters in our stand at that moment believed that Gower had deliberately given away his wicket, in response to the fine he had received. The fact that McDermott bowled two short balls with a mid-wicket fielder in place also added to the suspicions that the dismissal had been carefully planned in advance. England were set back by Gower's dismissal, but even though they trailed there always seemed an outside chance of a victory, but it never came.

There were only two days between the Adelaide and Perth Tests, and I spent most of that time on one of the world's famous train journeys, across the Nullarbor Plain. Six of the English supporters in the same tour party as me were also booked on the train, and during our time in Adelaide we had all got on well together, so that made the journey even better to look forward to. The train seemed to be almost a mile long, as it entered the station from Sydney. The front two carriages were our first class ones, next were two lounges, one with a piano, and then the dining compartment. Beyond that were the back-packers and goods carriages, all locked out from our superb luxury accommodation. Hour after hour we were looking at what 90% of what Australia really is, flat, parched land, mainly sand, a few small trees and the occasional kangaroo, mile after mile. We had set off at 5pm. on Wednesday to begin this forty-hour journey, and the train made only one stop before we reached the town with the most isolated post office in the world, Cook. There we were encouraged to walk around, post our cards, see the one-man prison, before setting off towards Kalgoorlie, the gold mining town, where, at about 9pm. we had a coach tour arranged for us, with the driver explaining the significance of everything we passed during the half hour, including his interesting comments about the ladies sitting outside their well-lit houses in the famous red light district. Our coach moved very slowly through this part of town, but it did not stop, before we returned to the station. Everyone was eager to get back on board, because the temperature was extremely high, and though we had enjoyed the tour we were glad to step into our air-conditioned carriages.

That evening a number of us were sitting in the piano lounge, and someone noticed that there were sheets of music in the piano stool. No-one else admitted to being able to play, so for half an hour or more I played one popular tune after another, with a choir of cricket supporters standing behind me singing their heads off. It took me back to my childhood days when my mum and dad would be singing Galway Bay, my mum's favourite. If only she could have known what a lovely evening on the train across the Nullabor that my keyboard skills provided, just a year, almost to the day, after she had passed away. She would have loved it. At the end of the evening we spent our second night in our cabins, and by 8am, we had arrived in Perth, with only three hours to go for us to take our bags to our hotel, then make our way to the WACCA. Our hotel was in sight of the ground, and we were comfortably in our seats before play started.

Once again our seats were in a section of the stand which was more or less reserved for the English touring groups, but, as had happened at Adelaide, when we walked round the ground, we came into contact with many Australians, and I enjoyed the banter with them, remembering from the Cec Pepper days how an Aussie will roll a weakling over, but be happy to buy a pint for a 'pom' who gives as good as he gets. Here in Perth I had two things to do as well as watching the cricket and having a drink. The first was to contact Brian Johnston at the Sheraton Hotel to finalise our arrangements for his forthcoming visit to speak at our Royton dinner. The second was to contact Alec Stewart, at the same hotel, to ask him to arrange for the members of both Test teams to sign the cricket bat I had brought with me, which we would auction at the forthcoming sportsman's dinner. John Holder had been in touch with Alec, who unfortunately was not in the hotel when I called, so Angus Fraser offered to get both teams to sign it for me. However, it did not turn out to be quite so straightforward, as I discovered two days later when I walked round the ground towards the dressing room area, hoping to collect the signed bat. Angus Fraser, who was not playing in the match, was sitting in the stand and must have seen me as I walked by, came down to tell me that all the England players had signed it, and that it was now in the Australian dressing room along with more than fifty other bats, none of which had been signed.

I thanked him, then began to think of how I might solve the problem. Eventually I took a chance, approached a steward and told him that my friend John Holder, a Test Match umpire, had asked me to have a word with Terry Alderman, the opening bowler, who would at that moment be in the dressing room as the Aussies were batting. The steward popped inside, and a moment or two later waved me in and introduced me to Terry himself. I explained to him that John and I were members of Royton Cricket Club, and that John had asked me to pass on his good wishes, and to ask him if he would arrange for all the Australian team to sign our bat. With a smile on his face he said that yes he would, "because John might not give me any LBWs if I don't." He told me to find the bat amongst what must have been a hundred still waiting to be signed, and I came back at the close of play to collect it. At the Brian Johnston dinner in March the bat raised £250, the highest price any auction item had raised at our dinners.

One more off-the-field moment of interest during the game was when, during the England innings, only moments after David Gower had been dismissed, a light aircraft flew directly over the ground trailing a banner with the words GOWER IS INNOCENT. It seemed apparent that Gower had tried to make arrangements for the aircraft to make its flight whilst he was at the wicket, and that the timing had gone slightly wrong. My view of the Adelaide incident has never changed. Meanwhile, on the field the cricket had been good on all five days, but the Aussies had the edge and won the series. There was a week in which we could now do as we wished, and a group of us spent two of them watching cricket at North Perth, where Tom Moody was playing, before he came over to play for Worcestershire. We also enjoyed a day at Freemantle, where many old boats were on display, but probably not the one that Keith Miller and Cec Pepper had boarded when Don Bradman made his crucial phone call! We all enjoyed our time in Perth itself, strolling by the Swan River, and all the members of our tour group got on well, also often meeting up with people in other groups, helping to make it a superb holiday. We even had an extra day too, because there was so much snow in Luton that our plane could not take off for 24 hours. Richard and Lucy had planned to collect me at Luton on the Monday we should have returned, but as neither of them could do so on the Tuesday, I cadged a lift with Ernie and Ken, with whom I had become very friendly, and they dropped me off on their way back to Accrington.

The three weeks had been excellent. The time spent in and around both Adelaide and Perth had been very enjoyable, as it had been to follow the Test team, even though we did not win, but as much as anything was the fact that throughout the holiday everyone had been so friendly. It had been my first experience of going on holiday on my own, and any doubts I had had in the weeks before the tour started simply evaporated. One year later I would be off again, this time for a 7-day visit to Egypt, beginning with four nights on a cruise boat, then three in Luxor, where the cruise up the Nile had begun. We visited some spectacular ancient Egyptian sites, especially The Valley of the Kings, where, amongst others, we went into Tutankamun's burial chamber, and the Temple of Queen Hatchepsut, the only ever woman pharaoh. The historical significance of every site we visited was well explained and interpreted by our guide, and it was awe inspiring to see how so much of ancient Egypt had been so well preserved. We discovered the Egypt of the Ptolemies when we visited the imposing and extremely well preserved Temple of Horus, begun in 237 BC. Our final visit was to Abu Simbel, where the towering figures of gods and pharaohs adorn the façade of the Temple of Rameses 11. Amazingly every stone had been taken down and rebuilt on this higher ground before the Aswan High Damn was constructed in 1960, or it would have lost under water for evermore. Its reconstruction has been described as a 'modern-day miracle.' Later that day we drove to Luxor, and stayed in the New Winter Palace Hotel. Once again everyone on the tour had got on well, especially as there had been so much to talk about and enjoy in the many ancient temples and tombs we had visited.

In Luxor we had no guide, and could relax or go sightseeing as we wished. I found Luxor Temple well worth a visit, but Karnak Temple was much more impressive. It is said to be large enough to contain ten cathedrals. Its 134 huge stone pillars rise very, very high into the sky. The whole site is mind-boggling. Karnak was the final visit I made, but in Luxor I found great pleasure in visiting the bazaars where millions of souvenirs are being touted. Throughout the week we had been approached many times by locals trying to sell various artefacts, and the skill is to barter with them to buy it from them as cheaply as possible. I regarded this as a challenge, and soon learned to play them at their own game. I let them tell me how much they wanted, never make an offer myself but kept them interested by saying I liked the object, and once the asking price had halved I might make an offer about half of that. Finally, as they could see I was going to walk away, knowing it was my final offer, they invariably accepted it. They would not have done so if they were losing money on it, so a deal was a deal. If I did my bartering when I was with others in the group, some commented that I had been rather cruel, but, amusingly, others suggested that I might barter on their behalf and get them some bargains. I regarded it as having been a big part of the week for me, one which I had enjoyed for another, even more important reason. Throughout the week I had not drunk anything from a bottle if I had not been sure it was sealed before being opened in my presence, I did not eat food that had not been boiled, never used ice cubes, and ate fruit only if I had peeled it myself. Hence, I did not suffer the 'runs' that some did, and helped me to enjoy my second holiday.

After this whole experience, both in seeing parts of the ancient world, and realising how easy it had been for someone travelling on his own to get on well with the others on guided tour holidays, I decided to try another one, two years later, to China. Once again it was a well-organised holiday, a group of fourteen escorted by an excellent guide. We began with three days in Bejing, where we strolled around the then peaceful Tian'anman Square, visited The Forbidden City, which is said to be the Grandest Palatial Complex of The World, The Temple of Heaven, and many other parts of the city. As we did so, usually in our mini-coach, it amazed me to see how many cyclists there were all over Bejing, often taking up more space on the roads than cars did. There were none on the famous Great Wall, though, and it was something special to walk along it, and climb the many steps as the wall rose to a hilltop, and appreciate the what an achievement constructing it so many years ago must have been. From there we flew to Xian, China's ancient capital, where many visits had been arranged, the most memorable being the one where we saw the awe inspiring Terracotta Warriors which, having been buried for over two thousand years, were discovered in 1974, and were still being excavated. Unfortunately we were not allowed to take any photographs of them. I was tempted to sneak the odd one or two, but I thought better of it, with all the risks involved. Our third city to visit was Guilin, the highlight of which was the cruise down the River Li, passing through stunning mountain scenery at the water's edge, and seeing the many rounded mountain tops, known as 'Tors'.

We left mainland China and flew to Hong Kong, to enjoy another well organised three days, including going to Victoria Peak, the view from which is phenomenal, looking down on to what seemed to be almost a million skyscrapers. Among the places we visited were one or two of probably the more respectable sweat shops, where employees busily sewed away. In the time we had to ourselves I managed to find shopping areas with secretly located rooms where copy watches were available. The skill there is not so much the bartering, but in making sure that what a person actually agrees to buy is what is actually placed on the bag or box the trader wraps it in, usually behind the counter or in another room. The ones I decided to buy I made sure I kept hold of them myself, and let the trader pass me the bag. Once again, throughout the twelve days, I did not buy any of the food on offer in the streets, but did enjoy the various Chinese dishes in both hotels and restaurants we visited. Again the general friendliness in our group helped to make the holiday even better, but the most surprising thing about it was that I never heard anyone asking what my, or anyone else's occupation was, throughout the tour. Such a question is probably asked simply to make conversation, and if the reply is of the 'Company Director' level, not many questions follow, but if it is 'Market Trader', then the questions never stop. Being ready for the question I had a reply ready, but it was not required, until a later holiday.

As I have described earlier I was now working three market days, was busy in my role as club chairman, and organising sportsman's dinners for Royton and the Rotary Club, so a holiday was something I now looked forward to for a rest. I booked a place on the1994-5 tour to Australia, but this time I was not going to be a total stranger on the trip. I discovered just before I set off that Royton's scorer for the past twenty five years, David Hughes, was also on the same tour, and although we were on different flights to Sydney, we met up at the airport on our arrival in Melbourne, before the first day's play, which began on Christmas Eve, not on the traditional Boxing Day. Two things surprised me on that opening day. The first was how big the MCG is. As I sat in the stand facing the pavilion I noticed that two or three upper layers of stands were empty and my first reaction was to assume that it was not a big crowd. Then I realised that the ground held 90,000 people – and now it holds even more. That day there were over 50,000 spectators, far more than any English ground could accommodate. The other surprise was that whilst I had been seated in the shade all day, I had become sunburned – by the sun's reflections off the plastic seats in front of us. There were not many pleasant surprises for England on the field, though, as two or three doubtful umpiring decisions went against us, and the game was virtually over by the end of the fourth day's play.

I decided that as we were to fly to Sydney on the morning after the final day's play, I would give it a miss and go on coach tour of the Great Ocean Road, described as the finest scenic coastal drive in the world. The tour lasted about ten hours, with the driver throughout the day explaining every significant feature of the places we visited, and excellent though the whole day was, and the places we visited, nothing was as spectacular as the breathtaking coastline. For us this began at Port Campbell, described as the jewel in the Great Ocean Road's crown. The rugged limestone cliffs surround the inlet, near to the famous Twelve Apostles, those mesmerisingly attractive rocks which stand there bravely in the fierce ocean, on a coastline where more than a hundred and fifty ships lie wrecked between Port Philip Head and the South Australian border, so powerful are the waves. We saw the famous London Bridge, which in 1990 had ceased to be a bridge, when the ocean had pounded it away. We were able to make our careful way across the rocky coastline to see the different vantage points, and what impressed everyone was the sheer power of the ocean when, even on a lovely summer's day, the waves were constantly smashing against the rocks and rising high, well above the tall cliffs. It was spectacular. Our cameras never stopped clicking. It had been the best way to spend the final day of the Test Match, which was over by lunchtime, with Shane Warne having taken a hat trick. I had first recognised his talent when I was at Old Trafford to see him bowl the 'ball of the century' to dismiss the bewildered Mike Gatting, but I had no regrets about missing his hat-trick when I came back to our hotel that evening, having enjoyed a wonderful day, a tour I would recommend to anyone.

286

Melbourne, in the State of Victoria, is indeed Victorian itself in some ways, with quite a few old buildings and where trams still travel up and down every main road. It is very different from Sydney, with its famous Opera House and the Harbour Bridge dominating the skyline. The harbour itself is much larger than I had thought, as I realised when we took a cruise, providing some splendid views of the winding coastline. We enjoyed the traditional firework display on New Year's Eve as we sat with hundreds more on Circular Quay, and after our two days of exploring the famous city we were in our seats at the SCG for the next five. It was fiercely contested match, which could have gone either way, and I thought England were unlucky not to have won it. Darren Gough had what was perhaps his finest Test Match, with both bat and ball, deserving the standing ovations he received. The only sad moment of the match came when Graham Hick, under pressure from his skipper to reach his century by the time he had made his mind up to declare, and being prevented from getting his crucial two runs by the determined Australian defensive tactics, Atherton declared the innings closed, with a day and a half to go, and Hick on 98.

One of my best memories of the match is of the afternoon when rain had stopped play, and I decided to go to the shop to buy an SCG tie. Unfortunately the shop was in the area reserved for members only, so no visitors were permitted to pass the spot where the steward stood, at the end of our stand. Apparently during the 1992 tour of England none of the Sydney members had been allowed to enter the pavilion area at Lord's, and this was the Australians' retaliatory action. I could well understand the reason for the decision, and was surprised when the steward, to whom I had been taking for quite a few minutes, suddenly told me that he would let me through. I found my way to the shop, then enjoyed wandering round the museum, and finally came outside to find I was close to the pavilion itself. I walked towards it, stood by the nearest entrance, merely looking at the ground and stadium from a different angle. At the foot of the steps was a steward, and we chatted for a while, and then he looked at his watch and said that it was time for him to take a break, and said "Cheerio." I thought this was too good to miss, so I walked up the members' steps, then into the pavilion, itself without anyone saying a word. The huge room was full of players, past players, countless celebrities, though not many of them MCC members. I enjoyed looking at the memorabilia on the walls, sampling a pint or two, then decided to make my way back to my seat, profusely thanking the steward who had allowed me to go through in order to purchase my tie, which I was now wearing. Play had still not restarted when I joined my friends, but before I could get to my seat David Hughes spotted my tie, and said that he, too, wanted to buy one.

So off we went, approached the friendly steward who waved us through, and after David had purchased his tie we strolled towards the famous pavilion. As we reached the gate there was no-one around, so we began to make our way up the steps, where we then saw a steward. He had obviously assumed that I was a member, having seen my tie, and waved me, and my guest, as I had described David, through the door. David was as thrilled as I had been to step inside the pavilion, and when he realised how many famous cricketing celebrities there were he said that he would like to get some autographs. Having no paper with him he decided that his white sun hat would do, and I helped him to persuade ever so many to sign it, including all the England team as they came out of the changing room. It was the only time I can remember enjoying being at a cricket match when it rained, and I doubt if David has ever worn his sun hat since that day.

There was still a week of the holiday left after the match ended, and for the next four days I was one of a group who had booked to fly to Cairns, staying at the Colonial Club. Not much of our time was spent in Cairns, however, as we went on some exciting visits. Our first was to Kuranda, an historic journey on the Cairns Kuranda Railway, constructed in the late 19th century, through the Barron Valley. It is said to have been an engineering feat of great magnitude, with 15 tunnels, 93 curves, dozens of difficult bridges mounted many meters above ravines and waterfalls, all of which was constructed without any modern equipment, but with "strategy, fortitude, hand tools, dynamite, buckets and bare hands." Another visit we enjoyed was when David and I went with Tony and

Colin in a hired car, and drove up the coast as far as Cape Tribulation, enjoying the views, of land and sea, every mile of the way. The most memorable visit of them all, of course, was the one we had signed up to travel to Cairns to experience – The Great Barrier Reef.

We travelled by coach to Port Douglas where we boarded a Quicksilver catamaran, which took us on a two-hour journey to the magnificent Agincourt Reef, on the Outer Barrier Reef, one of the furthest from the coast. Once on the reef I was soon climbing into the underwater observatory boat, which moved slowly, enabling us to see so many unbelievably beautiful fish. There are, apparently, more than a thousand species of multi-coloured reef fish, and more than two hundred species of corals in what can only be described as an underwater wonderland. We also enjoyed a helicopter trip, an optional extra which was well worth the money, allowing us to see so much more of the reef, flying low so that we could see thousands of spectacularly coloured fish through the glass floor. I took another underwater boat trip before it was time to begin our Quicksilver sail back to Port Douglas, for our final night at the Colonial Club. Once we had returned to Sydney we still had three days left, one of which we spent in the Blue Mountains, with Tony and Colin once again doing the driving, whilst David and I relaxed in the back seats. We went on the Katoomba Scenic Railway, drove to Sublime Point, Anvil Rock, Burra Moko Head, saw the Three Sisters and Echo Point, Katoomba, and many others. We took a trip on the Scenic Skyway, which crosses a gorge 350 meters above Cook's Crossing, where the views are indescribable, as was the whole day, thanks to our two chauffeurs! We made the most of our remaining time to see as much of Sydney as we could, and spent our final evening having a meal outside on Circular Quay, where David and I had watched the firework display a fortnight earlier. After a 24-hour flight we were back in the cold climes. It was great to have been to the MCG and the SCG, where I had once again enjoyed the banter and friendly rivalry with so many Aussie fans. It had also been a holiday in which I had seen some wonderful and picturesque scenery, and I still treasure the moments I spent at Cairns, the Barrier Reef, The Blue Mountains, and The Great Ocean Road.

Holidays now seemed to be on my agenda, and it was not long before I was being asked where I would be going the following year, but the decision was made for me when I received the invitation to a wedding in San Francisco. Nicholas, the elder son of my step-brother Norman, was to marry Kendra, on October 12th 1996, and the prospect of returning to my favourite city excited me. So, after visits to my travel agent, I decided to take the Canadian route to California. I flew to Calgary, and spent a day on my own exploring the city before the coach tour began. It was to be a week of spectacular views, some of them from the coach, with its high windows, enabling everyone to see the mountain ranges on either side. Our first night was spent at Banff, where we took the Gondola Ride over 2000 meters to the top of Sulphur Mountain, with incredible views of the mountain ranges. At a much lower level was the beautiful Lake Louise, across from which a glacier rises beyond the blue water. An artist could not paint a more attractive picture. I was one of the lucky members of the group who had a room at Chateaux Lake Louise, and enjoyed every moment there. The following day, on our way to Jasper, we visited the Athabarca Glacier, where we stepped on to the Ice Explorer, which took us to a flat part of the glacier, and we walked on the frozen snow, perhaps gingerly, on a sunny but freezingly cold day, so there were no complaints when we were asked to step on to the Explorer to return to dry land. Having seen much wild life from our coach and on the various brief visits we had made during the tour, as we arrived at Jasper we now saw it on the streets, where the elk roamed around in groups. We were advised that it was not a good idea to try to get too close to them, and seeing the size of their horns, I kept well away.

We had seen millions of trees on the mountain ranges we had driven through, but during the next two days we would see almost a million times more, once we had boarded the Rocky Mountaineer for "The Most Spectacular Train Trip in the World." We were told that the scenery would be 'dramatic' and indeed it was. No-one read any newspapers or played cards. Everyone gazed through the windows, thrilled to see the breathtaking scenery throughout the journey to Kamloops, during which we saw the highest peak in the Canadian Rockies, Mount Robson; the river valleys of the Monashee and Cariboo Mountains; Pyramid Falls; and the climb over Yellowhead Pass alongside the North Thompson River. Overnight we stayed in Kamloops, and on the second day on the Mountaineer we saw the Cascade Mountains; the steep slopes along the Thompson River; the lush green fields of the Fraser River Valley; the rushing waters of Hell's Gate in Fraser Canyon, before we reached Vancouver. The two days had been memorable, and once again all the others in the group, people from virtually all over the world, were excellent company. I felt sorry to be saying goodbye to them before taxiing my way to the airport.

Arriving in San Francisco brought back the happy memories of our 1979 holiday, and I was particularly eager to make my way to Market Street in order to experience my first ride on a cable car, up and over the steep hills, down towards Pier 45. At last I had made it! I made it to Alcatraz too, and to other parts of the lovely city in the two days before Norman and Pat arrived, along with the other guests they had invited to the wedding, all of us booked in at the splendid Sheraton Hotel – almost as luxurious as the hotel in New York where we ended our 1981 holiday! It was good to meet up with Norman and Pat, and, of course, their sons Nicholas and Christopher, who had spent a week with us at our chalet at Abersoch about eight years earlier, when they had been staying with my mum and their granddad Tom during their summer holidays. Before the wedding we were all invited to Kendra's, by her parents, whose lovely house was on the hill near the Golden Gate Bridge, overlooking San Francisco Bay, a most stunning location. Everything went perfectly, the wedding could not have been orchestrated better, and those few days in the city where Tony Bennett left his heart, brought another happy holiday to a close.

I had Michael Palin to thank for what would be the last of six great holidays. His 'Round the World' TV programmes I found interesting, but the Peru episode mesmerised me, and in 1997 I booked the holiday of a lifetime. It began in Lima. Our visits included those to the Plaza de Armos; the Government Palace and Cathedral; the 17th century San Francisco Monastery; and the Gold Museum, where we saw gold artefacts of the Inca and pre-Inca civilisations. One of the strangest features of the city we saw as we travelled on our coach, passing houses which were two stories high but with no roofs on them, were second floors with four walls. Their occupants were mainly the poorer people. Apparently it never rains in Lima, despite the many cloudy days when rain seems imminent, and all the locals know that anyone carrying an umbrella must be a foreigner.

From there we flew to Cusco, for three nights at the Hotel Liberator, where we were advised to go to bed, and rest for the whole day, in order to adjust to the high altitude. Special tea was available in the hotel lounge to help visitors to acclimatise. By the early afternoon I had left my room and felt fine, so I stepped outside. I decided to have a look around and take a short walk down the main street, but not to go too far in this strange city on my own. Having reached a major crossing I began to make my way back up the slight incline, but after only twenty yards or so I had to stop. I was breathless – my first high altitude experience. After that I walked more slowly. Our guide appeared later in the day, and our visits began the following morning, the best of which was to the ruins at Sacsayhuaman. It is one of the most outstanding megalithic structures of the ancient world, where huge stones, some as large as twelve feet high, ten feet wide and eight feet thick, all different shapes and sizes, have stood there for centuries with not a razor blade of space between them, so tightly were they built. Cusco itself is a picturesque city, with its maze of narrow streets, colonial architecture and Inca remains. It has an ancient cathedral, museums, an artisans' quarter with plenty of galleries, and many shops selling an array of souvenirs. It was certainly a fascinating city to explore, with a visit to an even more fascinating city to come.

We set off towards Machu Picchu by coach, to first visit Pisac, with its famous Indian market, then the Inca fortress of Ollantayambo, and a tour of the Sacred Valley. After an overnight stop we were up very early for the train ride to the 'Lost City of the Incas,' discovered in 1911 by Hiram Bingham. It is described as one of the world's most spectacular train journeys, through the narrow Urubamba River gorge. There was not an empty seat as we travelled alongside the river, winding our way beneath the precipitous sides of the gorge which rose to dizzy heights, with our excellent guide pointing out the many attractive features we were passing, including parts of the Inca Trail itself, where we could see some of those making their four-day trek. It took us about two hours, and having stepped off the train we then had another journey to make, by bus, up the zig-zagging steep road with its twenty one hairpin bends to the top.

Most visitors to this ancient city have about four hours to see the breathtaking remains of the only Inca city never to have been found by the Conquistadors, and it is understandably quite crowded as the many tourists explore the wonderful features that are explained by the guides. Our group was one of the fortunate few who were staying overnight in the only hotel on the site, which has about thirty rooms, and after three o'clock we had the ancient city to ourselves, as the people made their way back to the train. Everyone knows how unique Machu Picchu is, and many will have seen it on TV, but throughout the time I was there I was simply overawed by its historic character. Long before I had set off this was to be the highlight of the holiday, and it more than lived up to my high expectations. I explored virtually every inch of the site, which seemed to be even more awesome during the afternoon as it became silent, and without groups of people everywhere. All the many photographs I took still bring back to life that memorable day, even a decade later.

Once again there was a very good relationship between everyone in our group, but on this holiday, while we were at Machu Picchu, I was asked what my occupation was. My reply was that because of the Official Secrets act I was not permitted to tell anyone. It worked. I did intend, on perhaps the last day of the holiday, to tell them that I had misled them, and to see if they could guess what my occupation was. Unfortunately we were split up into different areas on that day, so I was not able to see the outcome of my kidology, because I am sure I would have found it amusing. I had been amused to see the puzzled looks on their faces when I answered the question, but was never to find out what they actually thought. I knew what they thought about their holiday, though, and as we travelled back to Cusco for one final day we were all looking forward to the next part, The Galapagos Islands. First we flew to Quito, the capital city of Ecuador, for one night, before flying to San Cristobal, possibly the only Galapagos island inhabited by humans. We were soon boarding our cruise boat where we spent the next four nights, and visited six islands, two each day, superbly escorted by our guide, as we saw the fascinating wildlife and flora that is unique to these islands. No wonder Charles Darwin went there to discover vital evidence for his theory of evolution. To see turtles, sea lions, reptiles and birds that exist nowhere else on earth, was a marvellous experience. We spent about three hours on each island, all of which had its own unique collection of wild life. It was camera time for everyone, and as none of the creatures, especially the birds, were afraid of humans, they simply never moved as we walked by, or stood watching them.

Thankfully all my rolls of film were processed successfully, and along with the Machu Picchu ones they are a unique collection of photographs of that memorable holiday, thanks to Michael Palin! We had our final day in Quito where I stood on the equator, with one foot in the north, one foot in the south. The following day brought to an end the last of my seven very enjoyable holidays since my retirement from the classroom, which had also enabled me to do a few more things that I had not been able to do during my teaching career.

The first of these was to watch more cricket, and while it was not until I had retired from my market stall that I became a Lancashire member, I was, in the 1990s, able to see many NatWest Trophy games, which were usually played on Wednesdays, and I spent many enjoyable days at Old Trafford, where I also watched some Test matches. I can still see the expression of total disbelief on Mike Gatting's face as he walked towards the pavilion, having been bowled by Shane Warne's first ball in a Test match – the 'ball of the century'. Another rare occasion in any Test Match is a hat-trick, and when Dominic Cork got his against the West Indies in 1995 in the first over of the day the whole crowd stood to applaud him, but there were hundreds who missed it by not arriving at the ground early enough. I also stood to applaud David Gower when he overtook Graham Gooch's total of Test Match runs, even though the memory of his suspicious dismissal at the Adelaide Oval was still vivid.

The most memorable matches I watched in the early 1990's, though, were on the football field, when Oldham Athletic were enjoying the best days anyone could remember. Joe Royle had built up a good squad of players during the eight years he had managed the club, and the 1989/90 season was unbelievable. I had hardly ever been able to watch a match since I had been market trading, but in that season there were so many cup-tie replays being played in the evenings I seemed to have become a regular supporter again. Back in the great days of the Jack Rowley and Bobby Johnstone era, whenever there had been a cup match against a top side, such as Liverpool in 1962, with a crowd of 41,000, or Wolves in 1967, when we conceded a two-goal lead in the last five minutes before losing the replay, the Latics never won. In both cup competitions in the 89/90 season, though, things were very different. In the Littlewoods Cup they had beaten Leeds United both home and away, to progress to the third round, then with Frankie Bunn's six-goal record enabling them to beat Scarborough 7-0, their fourth round opponents were Division One leaders, Arsenal. This was the game which thousands of Latics' fans had been waiting for all their lives, to beat a top team. Thanks to goals by Andy Ritchie (2) and Nick Henry, and brilliant goalkeeping by Andy Rhodes, they won 3-1, but there was more to come. They beat another First Division club, Southampton, in the fifth round, and in the semi-final beat yet another top side, West Ham United, 6-3 on aggregate, having slaughtered them 6-0 in the first leg at Boundary Park.

In the FA Cup, having progressed to the fifth round, they had been drawn at home to Everton, so I was able to watch the replay at Goodison Park, also a draw, before they won the second replay. Their fixture list was so crowded that the sixth round match against Aston Villa could not take place on the scheduled Saturday, so I was able to watch the brilliant 3-0 defeat of the club then top of Division One, the following Wednesday. They were now in the FA Cup semi-final for the first time since 1913, and were drawn against Manchester United at Maine Road, to be played, thankfully, on a Sunday, so it was another game I could watch. It was a thrilling game, ending 3-3 with the Latics every bit as good as United. Sadly we lost the replay, as indeed we lost at Wembley a fortnight later, 1-0 to Nottingham Forest, in the Littlewoods Cup Final. I was at Wembley along with 30,000 other Latics fans, some of whom had travelled from as far as Australia to see their team play for the first time at the famous stadium. In big matches a team from a lower division needs a little stroke of luck to beat a top team, and though Brian Clough's side had employed tactics to prevent the Latics having enough possession, there were two very close near-misses, which, on another day, might have sprung a surprise against the favourites. As we came away, with everyone looking back on what had been an amazing season, the very best anyone could remember, even though we were disappointed that we had not won the cup, everyone recognised what a wonderful achievement it had been for Joe Royle and his team, to the delight of the thousands of fans who had enjoyed such a memorable year.

All the cup matches and replays must have taken so much out of the players that their hopes of gaining promotion gradually faded, but they were reignited in the following season when they beat Sheffield Wednesday in the last game of the season to become Second Division champions. I hardly saw any of the games in that season, but I saw two or three in their first season in the First Division for 68 years. A friend of mine from my local pub, Roger Meanock, sponsored a number of Latics' games in the name of his company, Motor Bodies Oldham Ltd, and he invited me as one of his guests. He also agreed to become Royton Cricket Club's main sponsor, too, for three years. Meanwhile Joe Royle's team had adjusted successfully to playing in the top flight, and in 1992 they became founder members of the Premier League. Had they not achieved a miraculous end to the season, beating Aston Villa, away, then Liverpool and Southampton at home in the final eight days, to rise above Crystal Palace on goal difference, they would have been relegated, but that winning streak ensured their third season in the top flight. In the 1993/94 season though, they were only a whisker away from a glorious success when they were once again drawn to play Manchester United in the FA Cup semi-final, this time at Wembley.

I booked four seats on a luxury coach, on which meals and wine were served, with all passengers, as in a first class train carriage, seated in tables of four, a most relaxing way to make the long journey. Richard, who had watched some of the big games too, came along, as did my brother-in-law Sim, and David Wilkinson, my slipper manufacturer friend from the 'valley'. Both Sim and David were United fans, and thought it sensible to keep quiet about it on our Latics' supporters coach. They were up on their feet cheering though, when Mark Hughes scored for United to make the score 1-1, after a game in which the Latics had played well, and deserved to have won. Sadly we lost the replay, this time at Maine Road, and United went on to beat Crystal Palace on the day that could well have been the crowning glory day for the Latics. Instead they were relegated. The glory days were over.

I did not watch much football during the next four years, but I did so in the 1999/2000 season, thanks to David Wilkinson. He told me that he had been offered the option to buy two Manchester United season tickets, but because of his business commitments he was declining them. I suggested that we shared them, and the outcome was that for

My Grandson John at Old Trafford on the day United won The Premiership in 1999.

the next three seasons we had tickets for every United home game, on an alternate basis. The seats were in the Salford Suite, five rows from the front in the third tier of the North Stand, superb seats almost on the half way line. When it was my turn, and if the game was on a Saturday, I gave the two seats to Richard, Lucy or Sarah, but on Sunday games I took my grandson John, then ten years old, and a United fanatic. We would arrive at the ground two hours before the kick-off, enjoy a leisurely meal, watch the pre-match TV programmes, before strolling to our seats as the players came on to the field. At half-time we went back inside,

My Granddaughter Emily at
Hadrian's Wall

drank our cups of coffee, returned for the second half, after which we relaxed, again watching all the highlights and other football reports, for at least an hour, while the thousands were squeezing their way from the ground. It was great to spend time with John, and of the many games we saw at Old Trafford the one we were particularly thrilled to have watched was the final game of the season when Dwight Yorke's goal against Tottenham Hotspur secured the Premiership for United, the first of the famous 1999 Treble.

As John lived in Macclesfield, I did not have the chance to spend as much time with him as I did with my granddaughter Emily, Sarah's daughter, who lived locally. For a number of years I had collected her from school once each week, and call at a pub with a play area, when she was young, sometimes with one of her friends, and have a snack. As she grew older a Big Mac was her favourite snack. I took her to Martin Mere Fowl Trust and we had a day visiting Hadrian's Wall, and as she was approaching her examination year, when I had been reading Shakespearian plays with her, I booked tickets to see Julius Caesar at Stratford-upon-Avon. Emily, her friend Chloe, and I, travelled by train and we saw a superb performance. Both girls loved it. Emily is now hoping to gain a university place very soon, and John has just completed his first year at Derby. As John and Emily are looking ahead to their adult lives and careers, I am delighted that Richard, Lucy and Sarah are all happy and successful in theirs, and hope that I have given them the same love and support that my parents gave me.

Finally, having spent much of the last five years looking back on how my life unfolded, I have become increasingly aware of how fortunate I am to have made so many friends during my hectic life. All this began, of course while we lived in Queen Street, and my lifelong involvement at Royton Cricket Club; then my membership of High Moor Motor Club, Royton and Chadderton Round Table and Oldham Metro Rotary Club, and the many colleagues at the five schools in which I taught, and the teachers in other schools whilst involved in after-school activities such as football, cricket, chess, and especially the Choral Speaking Association. Add to these the market traders, and the many punters from the Congleton area for nearly thirty years, and the many more I friends I have made at the 'Jim the Dog' luncheon club, which has gone from strength to strength over the past eight years, and the many more I have made during my three years as president of the Central Lancashire League, and those from different walks of life I met during my involvement in organising the Sportsman's Dinners. I have many friendly neighbours, and enjoyed the company of countless friends in the various pubs I have frequented over the years, especially The Horton Arms and Church Inn, my two 'locals' for the past forty years. I feel privileged to have remained friends with so many, some of whom, of course, as life moves on, I see only rarely. I am also sure that there are also a number of people, thanks to my John Keats philosophy "Beauty is truth; truth beauty", whom I may have upset over the years. I'm hardly likely to change now, but I do genuinely appreciate the friendship I have, and continue to enjoy, with hundreds of people. I also hope that the hundreds of pupils I taught feel that I helped them to progress. I certainly did my best to do so.

18 And Finally ...

Finally, definitely finally, having been a member of Saddleworth Writers group for a number of years, and having attended some creative writing courses during the past six years, I have decided to bring my lifestory to a conclusion by including some of the poems I have recently written.

MY ATTRACTIVE VISITOR

A great spotted woodpecker zooms through the sky
To land on the trunk of my tree,
His pecking begins at such rhythmical speed
Making compulsive viewing for me.

Almost faster than light he keeps pecking away,
Enjoying his head butting fight,
His colours, so rich, they sparkle and shine,
I just stare, so amazed, at the sight.

He leaps to the feeder that hangs from a branch,
Now he's nutpecking fiercely and fast.
He will pause for a second the hammer again
Enjoying his feast while it lasts.

He listens and looks as he's pecking away,
Such a sensitive creature he seems.
A noise or a movement and he's gone in a flash,
But he'll be back tonight – in my dreams!

SEASIDE MEMORIES

A day trip to Blackpool was every lad's dream
When I was just ten years of age,
It was too much to ask though, for most mums and dads
Who needed far more in their wage.

But my dad cleaned windows all over the town
And worked very hard for his brass,
So he took us one day on a charabanc trip
After going to eight o'clock Mass.

We got to the seaside, then ran to the beach,
A memorable moment indeed,
We saw Blackpool Tower, the trams and the piers,
Then went up the street for a feed.

I rode on a donkey but not very fast
And watched Punch and Judy act daft.
We went on a tram for the very first time
And oh how we chuckled and laughed.

We made our sand castles and paddled in't sea,
Then an ice cream and big piece of rock,
What a wonderful treat this had turned out to be,
When my dad said "Hey, look at the clock!"

Time to go home now and climb on the 'chara'
To drive all the way back to Oldham,
What a marvellous day we had spent by the sea,
My pals would be green when I told them.

But how things have altered in sixty-odd years,
As the coach has been swopped for the 'plane,
Now it's Benidorm, Tenerife, Disneyland too,
Or Paris from London by train.

The world is much smaller than in those old days,
And children can go far and wide.
All changed from the times when a thrill for young kids
Was to get on a bus for a ride.

BOYHOOD MEMORIES

When I was just a lad we lived in Royton
Its little quiet streets all built in lines.
Two-up two-down, a front room and a kichen,
Was everybody's castle in those times.

Our back yard too was equally essential,
When growing up and living through the war,
The way we always left the house or entered,
Past the 'lavvy' and the 'coal hole' near the door.

We never went outside much in the dark, though,
No gas lamps shone whilst bombers crossed the sky,
Our torches led us to our air raid shelters,
Protection from the bombs being dropped from high.

Life just went on as normal in the day time,
With people working hard as busy bees.
As chimneys spewed their smoke across the skyline,
We queued for what seemed hours for chips and peas.

There weren't so many people owning cars then,
The doctor was the only one I knew,
He saved the lives of patients nearly dying,
With scarlet fever, measles or the 'flu.

Our cobbled streets were noisy every morning,
As workers clogged their irons to the mills,
The milkman's horse and cart was even louder,
Bringing milk from all his cows on nearby hills.

The best day of the week was always Thursday,
We all made sure we did not come home late,
It was the meal we'd waited every day for,
As mum served up rag puddings on the plate.

The hero of the country then was Winston,
His inspiration led us through the war,
Our servicemen were bravely fighting battles,
On land and sea, with bombing from afar.

Then just as good times were returning,
As the lamps on our streets all burned bright,
We suffered a bleak winter of snowdrifts,
Which froze up the pipes overnight.

Then at last came the spring and the summer,
And our football and cricket returned,
Our lives were now happy and peaceful,
With buckets of coal to be burned.

A FULL MOON

Waiting for nightfall
All afternoon
Aching to witness
An autumn full moon.

Stroll through the garden
Stare at the sky
Not long to go now
Time passing by.

Look through the window
Pace round the room
Cannot be long now
Oncoming gloom.

All so romantic
To see its bright face
Lighting the night
For the whole human race.

To think man has been there
That step for mankind
Such memorable moments
Still fresh in my mind.

Then came the eclipse
Yet another great day
When midnight-like darkness
Stunned an August midday.

Such great recollections
Re-lived in my mind
Do much to relax me
And help me unwind

I sit by my window
Through which I just gaze
Awaiting the moonlight
To burst through the haze.

Content and relaxed now
Curled up in a heap
Can't think how it happened
I dozed off to sleep!

MY SELECTED OBJECT

Through the glass
I strain my eyes. Have doubts.
Peer at the moist misty scene.
Up above, all smooth and bright.
Below, a swirl of cloud. I wait.

A chink of hope.
Rich colour slowly emerging,
Like golden sun rays, providing warmth.
So calming, reassuring.
Quickly rising, soon settled.

I grasp it with both hands.
Raise it carefully,
Savour the moment.
"Same again, please".
What a good pint!

MY MENTAL MOTORWAY MADNESS

A crazy thought occurred the other day,
My mind is like a human motorway.
The way to go, the speed of thought,
But not too fast, I might be caught.
Foot on the pedal, eyes on the road,
Watching for hazards like drivers who goad.
Speeding past lorries, enjoying the space,
Like an elegant 'roller', gliding with grace.

That's the perception, the hope, the ideal,
But is it quite so in the world that is real?
My mind's slowing down now, striving for speed,
The engine's worn out too, losing the lead.
Life's empty roads are all bottlenecks now,
Struggling to move up the gears anyhow.
The brain's getting gridlocked, few gears to engage,
No speed left to summon, all gone at my age.

Crawling along in the slowest of lanes,
My motor's lost power, as energy wanes.
Is it my age? I just wonder each day,
As most of my journeys take longer I'd say.
Drifting so slowly, one hand on the brake,
Windows wide open to keep me awake.
This is the picture I see in my mind,
Though the image is blurring each day, so I find.

It's time for a bypass, for my brain not the town!
To miss all the jams as I drive up and down.
Time for a by-plane to soar in the sky,
Gliding to freedom as life passes by.
The world looks so lovely when seen from above,
No pressure, no stress, just float like a dove.
The M6 stays gridlocked, but I'm flying high,
Dreaming and doodling, a pie in the sky.

Reality though, means jams every day,
Motorway madness, idling hours away.
So the image I saw still seems perfectly right,
The traffic moves slowly, in darkness and light.
My movements reflect it, slow as they are,
The roads are congested, both here and afar.
It's time to retire now, and switch off the key,
Just think of the old days, wide open and free.

MY MORTAL SIN

I prayed when I served on the altar
As a young Roman Catholic boy.
I pointed my hands to the Heavens,
It gave me a feeling of joy.

A time of great hopes for the future,
Just yearning to serve as a priest,
I prayed and responded devoutly,
On every Catholic feast.

Dressed up in my cassock and cotta,
Chanting Latin responses each day,
Holy times lay ahead without doubt then,
If things could have stayed the same way.
It all went so terribly wrong though,
One day after telling a lie,
I confessed that I'd gone out on Friday,
And eaten a Holland's meat pie!